Pádraig Óg Ó Ruairc

BLOOD
ON THE
BANNER

The Republican Struggle in Clare 1913–1923

MERCIER PRESS

WHAT YOU NEED TO READ

MERCIER PRESS

Cork

www.mercierpress.ie

Trade enquiries to CMD,
55A Spruce Avenue, Stillorgan Industrial Park,
Blackrock, County Dublin

© Pádraig Óg Ó Ruairc, 2009

ISBN: 978 1 85635 613 8

10 9 8 7 6 5 4 3 2 1

A CIP record for this title is available from the British Library

*Cover images courtesy of 1) The Imperial War Museum, London. Ref. Q107751,
2) Pat Greene, Spanish Point, County Clare, 3) the 'Soldiers of Oxfordshire trust',
4) Kilmainham Jail Museum.*

Mercier Press receives financial assistance from the Arts Council/
An Chomhairle Ealaíon

Printed and bound in the EU.

Contents

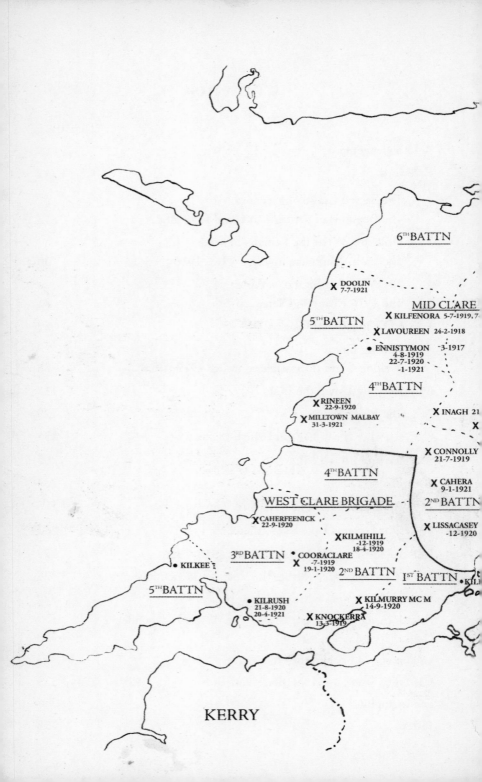

6ᵀᴴ BATTN

X DOOLIN
7-7-1921

MID CL'ARE

X KILFENORA 5-7-1919, 7-

5ᵀᴴ BATTN

X LAVOUREEN 24-2-1918

● ENNISTYMON -3-1917
4-8-1919
22-7-1920
-1-1921

4ᵀᴴ BATTN

X RINEEN
22-9-1920

X INAGH 21

X MILLTOWN MALBAY
31-3-1921

X

X CONNOLLY
21-7-1919

X CAHERA
9-1-1921

4ᵀᴴ BATTN

2ᴺᴰ BATTN

WEST CLARE BRIGADE

X CAHERFEENICK
22-9-1920

X LISSACASEY
-12-1920

X KILMIHILL
-12-1919
18-4-1920

3ᴿᴰ BATTN ● COORACLARE
X -7-1919
19-1-1920

2ᴺᴰ BATTN

1ˢᵀ BATTN ● KIL

● KILKEE

5ᵀᴴ BATTN

X KILMURRY MC M
14-9-1920

● KILRUSH
21-8-1920
20-4-1921

X KNOCKERRA
13-3-1919

KERRY

GALWAY

● BALLYVAUGHAN
✕ -10-1919
3-1-1920
20-5-1921
9-7-1921

✕ CARRAN
2-12-1919

BRIGADE
-12-1919

3ᴿᴰ BATTN

● COROFIN
✕ ELMVALE
-7-1921

✕ RUAN
17-10-1920
✕ MONREAL
18-12-1920

-7-1919
CROWES BRIDGE   1ˢᵀ BATTN
22-2-1920

■ ENNIS
24-4-1920
16-4-1921
24-6-1921
✕ DARRAGH   10-7-1921
CROSS
30-5-1921

✕ COOGA
✕ 26-3-1921

✕ DYSART

6ᵀᴴ BATTN

4ᵀᴴ BATTN
✕ BOHATCH
3-4-1921

✕ FEACKLE
2-7-1920
6-10-1920
● SCARIFF
2-7-1920
18-9-1920
19-9-1920

5ᵀᴴ BATTN
● TULLA
28-5-1921

3ᴿᴰ BATTN

EAST CLARE BRIGADE

1ˢᵀ BATTN
✕ CARRIGORAN NMF
24-6-1921
✕ NEWMARKET ON F.
5-8-1920

✕ BROADFORD
6-8-1919
✕ GLENWOOD
20-1-1921

● KILLALOE/BALLINA
24-9-1920

2ᴺᴰ BATTN

✕ CRATLOE
13-1-1921
✕ MEELICK AMBUSH
15-6-1921
✕ PUNCHES QUARRY
-11-1920

■ LIMERICK

TIPPERARY

LIMERICK

In memory of
bh–Fian Donnchadh Ó Séaghdha

The man who taught me that a good idea and a bit of luck are far more dangerous than any gun ... there are few of his make left in the world, and the world is a poorer place since he left it.

Acknowledgements

I wish to thank the following without whom this book could never have been written: my parents, Pat and Monica, to whom I never show enough gratitude for all the love and opportunities they have given me. Deirdre and Kevin, John White, Chris Coe, Dr Cyril Wall, Tom Toomey, Danny McCarthy, Daithí Ó Corráin, Thomas Mac Conmara, the late Miko Hayes, Pat Gunn, Mick Houlihan, Billy Mac gFhloinn, Andrew Clancy, Johnny White, Martin O'Dwyer, Donal O'Flynn, the late Colonel Seán Clancy, Niamh O'Sullivan, Seán O'Hehir, Chrissy Osbourne, Sinéad McCoole, Bill Peacock, Pat Greene, Derek Barron, Derek Jones, Pat Daly, Eoin Purcell, Neil Regan, Bailey Moore, Connor Farrell, Liam Hogan, Gavin O'Connell, Séamus Welsh, Patrick Fleckenstein, Mark Stephenson, Kevin O'Shaughnessy, John Nicholl, Win Scott, Ursula Walsh, Seán Donald, Brendan Griffin, Pat Mullane, Kevin and Julie Malone, Paddy Bassett, Dave Levins, Bertie McCurtin, Donnocadh Doyle, Liz Wier, Stanley C. Jenkins, Geoff Simmons; all the people of Cape Clear Island but especially Chuck Kruger, Fiona Mac Lachlan and Séamus Ó Drisceoil; the staff of Charles Fort, but especially Karen, Brendan and Claire; all the staff of the OPW Visitor Centre, Glendalough and in particular Joan, Fiona and Darragh; John Ratigan and the staff of the Clare Museum; the Limerick Civic Museum; the staff of the National Museum, especially Éamon P. Kelly; the staff of the Irish Military Archives; the staff of the National Archives; Peter at the Clare Local Studies Centre; all the staff of the Clare Library; the Khaki and Green War of Independence Re-enactors, especially Éamon Dunne and Ray Murphy; Seán O'Mahony and the 1916–1921 Club; Mercier Press; and to all those I owe so much to but haven't managed to name here – you know who you are.

Note: Dr Daithi Ó Corráin, of Trinity College Dublin, very generously provided me with information regarding casualties in Clare during the War of Independence from his book *The Dead Of The Irish Revolution 1916-1921* (Yale, forthcoming). Any errors regarding the dates and names of casualties are entirely my own.

Foreword

In the north-east corner of the old Bunratty graveyard stands the Commonwealth war grave memorial to Private R.W. Williams, 2nd battalion Royal Welch Fusiliers – the last British soldier killed in Clare during the War of Independence. The last line of its inscription reads in bold letters: 'Their glory shall not be blotted out.' Despite this epitaph, the story of Private Williams and the other British soldiers who enforced the occupation of Ireland has been carefully and deliberately blotted out. Official British history does not record the victories of natives' spears over machine guns nor does it wish to remember the triumphs of 'bog trotting Paddies' over the heroic British veterans of the Great War. You will not find the place names Rineen, Monreal or Crossbarry listed as battle honours on the flags of British regiments. Few British military museums or history books will even discuss the events in early twentieth-century Ireland – that first small crack that shattered an empire. If British imperialism was forced to face up to its past crimes then it might not be so quick to create new ones.

But this book is not about the history of foreign oppression, it is about the flame of freedom that once burned so bright in the hearts of the Irish people. This book is about us; who we are as a nation, and how we reached our current position. We live in the shabby afterglow of a generation who cherished the rights of the people so dearly that they were willing to endure any suffering to achieve freedom. We have gone from being that once proud people who craved liberty, equality and fraternity to being a nation corrupted by greed and a craving for celebrity. Today Irish politicians of all parties are clambering over each other to claim that they are the 'only true inheritors of the spirit of 1916'. Such protestations ring hollow – if we want to know exactly what the republicans of that generation stood for it is laid before us in black and white in the Proclamation of the Irish Republic and in the writings of Connolly and Pearse.

Fifty-three republicans from Clare gave their lives between 1918 and 1925 in the fight for freedom for the impoverished, downtrodden and oppressed. In the end what had it all been for? If they could see the Ireland of today, would they still make that sacrifice? Partition remains. Religious sectarianism, and the ignorance and divisions it breeds, still exist. The social order with all its inadequacies and inequalities remains intact and the exploitation of both native Irish and foreign immigrant workers continues. Political corruption, hypocrisy and public apathy are rife. Grasping politicians are always ready to sell Ireland's natural resources, privatise our public services or sell us into foreign military alliances. The Irish language, though not dead, seems at times moribund and its use has declined since the establishment of the state. Our rich heritage is continually destroyed in the name of so-called 'progress'. Irish culture and traditions are constantly under threat from both Anglicisation and Los Angeles-ation. The Ireland outlined in the Proclamation of 1916 and the Democratic Programme of 1919 that Irish republicans struggled and suffered for has never been realised. No finer monument could be built to their memory than the Ireland for which they fought and died; an Ireland where the all the people were united and free from the bigotry and sectarianism of the past.

Pádraig Óg Ó Ruairc

1

The Sacred Cause of Freedom:
The Republican Struggle in Clare 1798–1867

My lords and gentlemen, I will not attempt the mockery of a defence. You are about to condemn me for attempting to overthrow the oppressors of my country. You do not know nor neither can you appreciate my motives. I commit my sacred cause, which is that of freedom, to the vindication of prosperity. You may condemn me to immolation on the scaffold but you cannot degrade me. If I have appeared as a pioneer in the van of freedom's battles – If I have attempted to free my country from political degradation – My conscience tells me that I have done my duty. Your brief authority will soon cease, but the vindictive proceedings of this day shall be recorded in history. The principles for which I have contended are as immutable as the eternal laws of nature.

James Wilson, Scottish republican executed for his part in the Scottish
uprising of 1820

On 14 July 1789 a mob took to the streets of Paris to rally their fellow Parisians to defend the city. For months' anger at the corrupt regime of Louis XVI and the French nobility had resulted in mass protests and riots. Word circulated in Paris that the army units still loyal to Louis XVI were marching towards the city to suppress the protest using rifle and bayonet. The ordinary people of the city feared a massacre and began impromptu raids for arms all over the city. That morning a huge crowd raided *Les Invalides* for arms to protect themselves from the king's army, capturing 28,000 rifles but no powder or shot to use in them. As the crowd debated their next move to secure arms, the Bastille was suggested, and the crowd surged through the streets towards the prison. One of the first groups to force their way inside was led by a

Clareman, James Bartholomew Blackwell, a Protestant from Ennis who was a student at the Irish College in Paris.

The storming of the Bastille was the spark that set France and the world on fire. Republicanism was born – the corrupt nobilities, incompetent kings and all powerful monarchies of the world were to be toppled by ordinary people and replaced with democracy and the republican ideals of liberty, equality and fraternity. The shockwaves from the revolution quickly reached Ireland and broke the sectarian mould of Irish politics, which had pitted Catholics, Protestants and Presbyterians against each other. Inspired by the revolution in France, a new organisation of republican revolutionaries was founded in Belfast in 1791 – the Society of United Irishmen. The United Irishmen were founded with Wolfe Tone's stated aim: 'To subvert the tyranny of our execrable Government, to break the connection with England, the never ending source of all our political evils, and to assert the independence of my country – these were my objects. To unite the whole people of Ireland, to abolish all memory of all past dissentions and to substitute the common name of Irishmen in place of the denomination of Protestant, Catholic and Dissenter.' The society was declared illegal by the British authorities in Ireland and forced underground. The Irish republicans duly began plotting revolution against the British establishment in Ireland in an effort to set up an Irish Republic with the aid of the new French Republic's army. In 1798 the United Irishmen rose in open rebellion against Britain and her military forces in Ireland.

The rebellion was a staggered affair hindered by the mass arrests of rebel leaders and the activities of British spies. After battles in Dublin, Kildare and Meath during May, the insurrection enjoyed its greatest successes in Wexford, Carlow and Wicklow in June before the Leinster rebels were finally defeated at the battle of Vinegar Hill on 20 June. On the sixth of that month the United Irishmen rose up in Antrim, led by Henry Joy McCracken. The wealthy Catholic landlords who had promised to support him refused to join the rebellion, with the result that the United Irishmen's army in Ulster was a small force with little chance of success, made up almost entirely of Presbyterians. Dismayed by the wealthy Catholics' abandonment of the cause, McCracken, resigned to fight without any chance of military success, commented: 'The rich will always betray the poor'. McCracken's army fought in Counties Down and Antrim before being defeated by the British forces. A 1,100-strong military expedition force from republican France arrived in Mayo in August but despite initial successes it was surrounded by the British army and surrendered to them on 8 September.

James Bartholomew Blackwell, the Clareman who had led the crowd that stormed the Bastille, attempted to return to Ireland with Wolfe Tone on the French expedition to Bantry Bay in 1796 but bad weather had prevented the invasion force from landing. Blackwell returned to Ireland in 1798 with a French military force of 300 soldiers led by Napper Tandy, which landed on Rutland Island, Donegal. Upon discovering that General Humbert had already surrendered, they set sail for France. Finding a voyage south impossible because of the alertness of the British navy, they sailed north-eastwards instead, landing in Norway. Blackwell and Tandy attempted to return to Paris via Hamburg but their presence was discovered by the British, who ordered their arrest. Both men were handed over to the British government in September 1799, and transported to Dublin where they were interned in Kilmainham jail until after the signing of the Peace of Amiens in 1802. After his return to France, Blackwell was appointed *chef de battalion* of the Irish Legion in the French army and fought in the Prussian and Austrian campaigns. He died in Paris in 1812.

Although there was a strong United Irishman network in the county, Clare republicans did not rise up in rebellion in 1798. However, there was widespread unrest in north Clare and British soldiers stationed there were kept busy searching for weapons and known United Irishmen. When news of the French landing in Mayo finally reached Clare in late 1798 it spurred Hugh Kildea, a hedge-school master from Moy, and other United Irishmen in the north of the county into action. On 4 January 1799 a proclamation was posted on church doors in north Clare which read: 'No rent, tithe money, Church rates nor any County rates whatsoever should be paid, until further orders from the directory of the United Irishmen, who meant to plant the tree of liberty in a very short time, are received.' The proclamation was signed by Bryan Carrigg of Kilfenora and was said to contain 'several other treats of a treasonable nature'. Republican mobilisations, the swearing of oaths and raids for livestock and firearms were reported nightly by the loyalists in the north-west of the county. On Monday, 7 January a band of republicans assembled at Moy and marched on Ennistymon. The rebels captured the guardhouse and the small quantity of arms, before moving on to Lahinch where the home of James Thynne, a member of the Janesborough Cavalry, was raided for arms. On Friday, 11 January, Francis McNamara, his son and four yeomen travelling from Doolin with twenty muskets and bayonets were disarmed by a large group of armed republicans at Colouna. British troops were mobilised in Limerick and Galway on 12 January. Two hundred republicans marched to Ennistymon to challenge the British troops marching northwards. The republicans were disorganised, without strong leadership and armed with a motley assortment of weapons. They dispersed after the column of British troops did not enter the area. The rebellion failed to spread and was soon suppressed by the British military. For their part in the rebellion, Hugh Kildea and Michael Murphy were hanged in Ennistymon on 16 March 1799. Anthony Healy was hanged in Tulla on 23 March.

The United Irishmen enjoyed a revival with the short-lived rebellion of Robert Emmet in 1803 but with Emmet's execution the period of active rebellion was over. By the time the United Irish rebellions ended, over 30,000 people had died. The majority of these were ordinary Irish people killed in reprisal by the British, or United Irishmen killed in the field fighting for the rights of the Irish people. Though the republican rebellion ended in failure, the actions of the United Irishmen had created a revolutionary tradition which inspired later generations to act.

Fifty years later, in 1848, Irish republicans set about organising another revolution against British rule and the artificial famine it created, which caused the deaths of one and a half million Irish people at a time when tons of food were exported. The Young Irelanders, led by a Clare

Protestant, William Smith O'Brien, sparked a rebellion at Ballingarry, Tipperary on 29 July 1848 but it was suppressed within a few hours and its leaders arrested within a few days. The emblem of the Young Irelanders was a tricolour flag of green, white and orange presented to them as a gift from the republican government in France – green symbolising Irish Catholics, orange Irish Protestants and white for peace and unity between them in the common cause of a free Ireland.

Ten years later the veterans of the Young Irelanders rebellion founded the secret Irish Republican Brotherhood (IRB) with the aim of freeing Ireland from British rule, by armed force if necessary. The organisation became known as the Fenian Brotherhood and its members Fenians. The IRB was organised on a cell structure of 'circles' organised in parish areas around a senior IRB man known as a 'centre', who in turn was part of a larger county 'circle', the county circle reporting to one of the eight provincial circles in Ireland. Each of these circles elected a member to the IRB's supreme council. The theory behind this system was that it would limit the damage if British spies penetrated the organisation. The IRB believed that British rule in Ireland was a usurpation of the Irish people's right to freedom; its supreme council declared itself the legitimate government of Ireland and that the head of the brotherhood was president of the 'Irish Republic'. The supreme council also claimed the right to levy taxes, raise loans and declare war on behalf of the Irish Republic.

The IRB quickly began arming and training in preparation for military action. The activity of British informers, arrests of Fenians and splits within the organisation, however, disrupted plans for action in 1865. A hardcore group of IRB men, determined to organise a rising against British rule, took military action on 5 March 1867. In Dublin the 'Fenians' captured two Irish Constabulary (RIC) barracks before their defeat at the Battle of Tallaght. Uncoordinated actions by the Fenians in Munster formed the main campaign of the 1867 rising; police barracks were attacked in Cork, Limerick, Waterford and Tipperary. Lieutenant Colonel Healy, an Irish veteran of the American Civil War, was placed in command of the IRB's military network in

Clare. However, an informer alerted the British authorities to Healy's involvement, and Healy was arrested at Limerick railway station on 11 February, throwing the Fenian network in Clare into chaos. Harsh weather made communications between the different IRB circles in Clare difficult. On Shrove Tuesday night the Fenians in Ennis raided several houses for horses and firearms before assembling at 'The Fenians' Grove', a wooded area overlooking Ballyalla lake, two-and-a-half miles from Ennis. Jack Maguire mobilised the republicans for military action but received no orders. The Fenians eventually disbanded in confusion. In Kilbaha, on the West Clare coast, a small band of Fenians attacked the coastguard station in an unsuccessful attempt to capture arms. Like the United Irishmen and Young Irelanders, the Fenians' efforts to establish an Irish Republic was suppressed by superior numbers of better organised, trained and equipped British forces. However, the IRB survived the British suppression of the rebellion and kept the ideals of Irish republicanism alive.

By the turn of the century Ireland was a poverty-stricken country due to inequalities in the distribution of wealth under British rule. In the midst of the unbelievable poverty suffered by the people, the Catholic Church had magnificent churches built and paid for by their congregations. Wealthy landlords living on huge estates evicted their tenants and turned the lands they had farmed into hunting grounds, spending their days shooting and fishing. In the cities wealthy merchants, members of the 'gombeen' class (wealthy self-serving sham patriots) supported the Irish Parliamentary Party (IPP) and British rule, in the hope of political favours and appointments. They had their rent books always at the ready waiting to evict working-men's families when they could not afford regular rent increases. The high standard of living enjoyed by the Catholic bishops, the landlords and gombeen men showed that despite the widespread poverty, or more likely because of it, Ireland was a country rich in wealth, closely guarded by the pro-British establishment.

There was no unemployment assistance and the Poor Law boards, controlled by the large ratepayers, gave little heed to the needs of the poor. The British government was taking over £18 million out of Ireland annually in taxation, and about 25,000 men per year enlisted in the British army. Up to 550,000 members of the army were being supported and trained in Ireland, where three-quarters of wage earners were paid less than £1 per week. The employees of the public bodies in Ireland were compelled by their middle-class town councillors, their compatriots, to accept wages of between 4/- and 8/- per week less than their fellow workers in English councils received for the same work. Urban male workers were paid just 14/- for a seventy-hour week, while women got 5/- for a ninety-hour working week. No wonder then that the gombeen class, of all the political and religious persuasions who benefited from this, united against any attempt to grant women the vote or equal rights. The Catholic Church warned that 'allowing women the right of suffrage is incompatible with the Catholic ideal of the unity of domestic life', and the IPP claimed that 'women's suffrage would be the ruin of western civilisation'. Tuberculosis was rife in the Dublin slums and spread rapidly, so that the infant mortality rate there was worse than in Moscow.

Some 21,000 families in Dublin lived in single rooms, while emigration bled the youth of Ireland dry. Although the poverty of the countryside was as extreme as in Irish cities, the generosity of neighbours who shared their meagre supplies helped fend off starvation. As the new century began, the nobility of the countryside were the landlords, their representatives, the retired officers of the British forces, the doctors, clergy and the RIC officers.

The Royal Irish Constabulary were the mainstay of British rule throughout Ireland. They were garrisoned in barracks in every village and town over which flew the British union flag. The RIC was not a normal police force; it was a huge paramilitary and political force unnecessary to police the small Irish population and low level of crime. They were armed with rifles and revolvers, the eyes and ears of the British intelligence network, filing reports, spying on republican and labour organisations and anyone else who dared step outside their appointed station under British rule. They were effectively the private army of the pro-British establishment, were frequently used to evict impoverished farmers at the behest of Irish landlords and acted as the first line of defence against rebellion.

While the RIC represented the armed force of British oppression in Ireland, the Catholic Church served as the moral force of British rule in the country. The Church was opposed to the non-sectarian politics of republicanism and steadfastly condemned every rebellion, ever since the British government bribed the Catholic bishops by paying for the building of the Catholic seminary at Maynooth in 1795. In return for this, and a large annual contribution to the running of the seminary, the British won the unwavering loyalty of the Catholic Church towards British rule. Occasionally independent-minded priests rebelled against the bishops and support the Irish cause, but these were always in a minority. The bishop of Kerry, Dr Moriarty, condemned the Fenians as criminals who deserved God's heaviest curse: 'His withering, blasting, blighting curse on them and for whose punishment eternity is not long enough, nor hell hot enough.' Not a single Catholic bishop ever spoke out in support of the right of the Irish people to use armed force to win their freedom. When the spending of such large sums of money on the Catholic Church in Ireland was condemned in the House of Commons the British government responded by outlining the reason for its actions: 'Are not lecturers in Maynooth cheaper than state prosecutors? Are not professors less costly than Crown prosecutors? Is not a large standing army and a great constabulary force more expensive than the moral police with which the priesthood of Ireland you can be thriftily and efficaciously supplied.' Catholic parish priests, the local dictators of faith, morals and political opinion, ruled their parishes with an iron fist. They lived in luxury paid for by their poor parishioners. Each family in the parish had a set levy to pay for the priest's support; the contributions were announced in public to shame those who held back their donation. Parish priests enjoyed the hospitality of the local landlords and feared any challenge to the status quo that kept them in comfort. They were, with few exceptions, exploiters of their flocks and the enemy of any progressive political movement.

The majority of schools throughout Ireland were managed by the Catholic Church in conjunction with the British authorities. The Catholic clergy guarded this position jealously and worked hard to engrain their students with their own conservative political outlook to ensure they would grow up to be practising Catholics who supported the existing political and social establishment.

The aim of the British education system in Ireland was to Anglicise each pupil and give them a sense of their 'Britishness'. Not only did this education system deny that Ireland had its own language, culture and history; it also denied Ireland the very existence of a country, instead stressing that Ireland was merely a district of Britain. The Board of National Education ensured that every Irish child had to sing a song in school that ran:

> I thank the goodness and the grace
> That on my birth have smiled,
> And made me in those Christian days
> A happy English child.

The Catholic religious orders running Irish schools participated fully in this system. Irish was not taught, though Latin and other languages were. Lessons were given in English history and culture, but Irish history and traditions were largely ignored. Where religious orders did teach Irish history it was a carefully sanitised right-wing Catholic version, which whitewashed over the republican rebellions of the previous hundred years and the Catholic Church's role in suppressing them. Todd Andrews was educated at a Christian Brothers school in Dublin at the time:

> Contrary to an assertion often made, the Brothers did not deliberately indoctrinate their pupils with Irish Nationalism or hostility to Britain ... The persecution of the Catholics rather than the persecution of the Irish as such was the burden of the brothers' history teaching. Most of the heroes held up for our edification were post reformation ... We were taught much about the saints and scholars and the wonderful *Book of Kells*, but we also began to hear of Dermot McMurragh and the perfidies of Strongbow. He was the first innocuous Englishman

we encountered. We met many more cases of English treachery, from
Silken Thomas to the earls who took flight, to Sarsfield, Emmet and
O'Connell. We heard rather less about Tone and not much about the
Fenians ... It was a very simplistic history ... Fr Murphy had become
a symbol of faith and fatherland. The fact that he was a rare, almost
unique example of clerical participation in the [1798] rebellion was
never referred to; the general opposition of the Church to the rebellion
was forgotten.

Where Tone and Emmet were mentioned, the fact that they were
Protestants was not. More often they were completely ignored in favour
of Fr Murphy, the hero of the sectarian Catholic version of the 1798
rebellion. Any references to Fr Murphy as one of the only Catholic
priests who took part in the rebellion and the fact that the Catholic
hierarchy supported British rule were censored. Fr Murphy had become
famous for leading the United Irishmen at the Battle of Oulart Hill; but
the three other rebel leaders at the battle – Byrnes, Roche and Sparks
– were not mentioned because they were Protestants. The fact that the
North Cork Militia, defeated in the battle, were mostly Catholic was not
mentioned either; neither was Fr Murphy's excommunication from the
Church. Irish children were taught that rebellion was something in the
past tied up with the Catholic religion and led by the Church; now that
the Catholic Church was free to operate in Ireland the lesson was that
rebellion was no longer necessary and the pupils should accept British
rule and their place within the British empire. The bishop of Killaloe,
Bishop Fogarty, who regularly denounced republicans and their efforts
to win the most basic rights and freedoms for the Irish people, proudly
told his congregation the blatant lie that: 'Down through the years your
kith and kin have stood side by side with your Bishops in the struggle for
faith and fatherland.' This hypocrisy prompted the Protestant historian
W.P. Ryan to write: 'The most brilliant thing ever done by Irish priests
was the invention of the legend that they had always been on the side
of the people.'

There were few higher elementary schools, except those run by the
various religious orders, many of whom came in the mid-nineteenth

century to educate the poor and now laboured in great comfort to educate the offspring of the rich. They trained their pupils for careers in the service of the British crown and thus anything relating to Ireland was excluded. Madam Czira had attended Alexandra School, one of the more prestigious girls' schools in Dublin, and remembered the system of British political indoctrination that took place there:

> There the children were not educated at all – they were just processed so as to manufacture English children of the upper classes. You were trained to look down upon the people of Ireland and of all other countries as 'natives', you were taught to regard every language but English as a jargon, and so you spoke all foreign languages with a Mayfair accent to show how much you held them in contempt. Your geography was chiefly an inventory of leading manufacturers and raw materials produced in various parts of England and her colonies, and provided you could name them glibly, it didn't matter if you hadn't the faintest idea what these raw materials were. English history was taught as if it were a rubber stamp, to be pressed on to your brain and give you a British trade mark. You learnt the dates when English kings reigned, fought battles and died.

The Catholic Church, the British government and their supporters in Ireland all combined forces against the Irish language, condemning 'the waste of time and money on the teaching of a useless and obsolete language'. The Church willingly supported this British effort at cultural genocide by objecting to Irish being taught in the new National University.

The Irish Parliamentary Party, under John Redmond, was a religiously sectarian assembly of conservative politicians and opportunists. John Dillon described Ireland as the most Catholic country in the world and claimed the IPP was the right arm of the Catholic Church. The IPP wished to break the connection with England by constitutional means, but they had no plans to change the system or alleviate the conditions of the majority of the population.

Nevertheless, behind this sad façade there was an awakening of consciousness. Traces of organised revolutionary Ireland still existed through the IRB. After the failure of the 1867 uprising the IRB in Clare had disintegrated into a series of 'unofficial circles', the remnants of the original Fenian organisation kept alive by veterans and republican families. Because of this, Clare republicans were uncoordinated and isolated from each other. They didn't follow any common policy or definite political strategy; the activities of each circle depended on the personality and ability of their centre. An IRB circle survived in West Clare led by the O'Donnells of Tullycrine. Thomas O'Loughlin, a Fenian veteran, had organised another IRB circle in the Ennistymon district. IRB circles also existed in Ennis, Crusheen, Carrigaholt, Newmarket on Fergus and Killaloe.

In 1873 the IRB adopted a new constitution which committed it not to attempt armed insurrection until such a move had the support of the majority of the Irish people. This was intended to avoid a disastrous repeat of the Fenian rising of 1867. In the meantime the organisation decided to support any movement which would advance the cause of Irish freedom as long as it did not interfere with the IRB's revolutionary aims. This involved a reluctant recognition that armed revolution was not realistic in the immediate future, and the Fenians were either being dragged into the wake of the home rule movement by the IPP or else completely marginalised. By the 1880s the IRB had abandoned its plans for rebellion and had linked its fortunes to Parnell and the home rule movement. By now the IRB in Clare restricted its activities to attacks on landlords and agrarian violence as part of the land war.

By the 1890s the prospect of another rebellion seemed so remote to the British establishment that James Dougherty, the British assistant under-secretary in Ireland concluded that: 'There is no evidence that the IRB is anything but a shadow of a once terrifying name.' By the turn of the century in Clare some IRB circles had become more like debating societies than secret societies. Seán McNamara remembered that the IRB as he knew it in 1897 '... was nothing more than a political organisation ... I attended a number of IRB meetings in the year 1897 and in the following few years, but there was never anything discussed at them but matters affecting current political questions.'

At this time a persuasionist element was prominent in the IRB who advocated supporting home rule as the only practical strategy for advancing the Irish cause as long as there was no realistic prospect of military action. The IRB infiltrated the cultural nationalist and Gaelic revival movements; the United Irish League, Conradh na Gaeilge and the GAA were all infiltrated in an attempt to recruit members and promote republicanism within different cultural groups. Sydney Brooks, an English journalist visiting Ireland during this period, wrote about the separatist Irish spirit fostered by the Gaelic revival: 'It seems to me that wherever the Gaelic League spreads it leaves behind a broader and more genuine spirit of nationality and that on the heels of this new spirit of nationality comes a vivid sense of separation, a more pungent consciousness of the eternal gulf that parts the English from the Irish.'

The foundation of Sinn Féin by Arthur Griffith provided the IRB with a new, more useful political outlet than the IPP. Many IRB men had grown disillusioned with the IPP, who looked to Westminster for positions and wages for everything except genuine freedom. In February 1905 Arthur Griffith published a series of articles entitled 'The Resurrection of Hungary', in which he examined the Hungarian campaign for independence from Austria led by Franz Deak. Deak had organised Hungarian parliamentarians to abstain from sitting at Vienna and form their own independent Hungarian parliament which remained within the Austrian empire. Griffith believed Hungary's experience with Austria proved that no empire in the world had any effective weapon against a nation which refused to acknowledge its rule. Griffith planned to use strictly constitutional methods to achieve this end.

In November 1905 Griffith proposed his 'Sinn Féin' policy to the National Council, a forum of Irish separatists formed in 1903. Griffith credited a Clarewoman, Máire Ní Buitléar, with proposing the name Sinn Féin (We Ourselves) for Griffith's new political movement. Ní Buitléar was a leading member of the Gaelic League and a cousin of Sir Edward Carson. In April 1907 Cumann na nGaedheal merged with the Dungannon Clubs, an IRB political front, to form the Sinn Féin League, which later simply became known as Sinn Féin.

Griffith's Sinn Féin party was a right of centre nationalist party but it was not a republican party. In May 1907 Griffith wrote:

> The Sinn Féin platform is and is intended to be broad enough to hold all Irishmen who believe in Irish independence, whether they be republicans or whether they be not. Republicanism as republicanism has no necessary connection with Irish nationalism, but numbers of Irishmen during the last 116 years have regarded it as the best form for an independent Irish Government.

Griffith proposed that the IPP MPs should abstain from the British parliament at Westminster and re-establish Grattan's Irish parliament of 1782 in Dublin. Though this parliament would be completely independent from Britain, the king would remain the head of the Irish state. Griffith claimed that the Irish could achieve this goal through boycott, abstentionism and pacifism. While Sinn Féin was a monarchist party, its advanced nationalist position was far more radical than the IPP's simple demand for home rule. Sinn Féin's only real radicalism lay in its abstentionist policy; its social policy was as conservative as that of the IPP. IRB leaders were concerned at the IPP's compromising position on the Irish people's right to complete independence. Republican efforts to manipulate the IPP had been unsuccessful, and at a grassroots level IRB members in Clare began to support Griffith's party.

Griffith's newspapers (e.g. *Nationality* and *Sinn Féin*) were available in Clare and popular in IRB circles. The first branch of Sinn Féin in Clare was established in the north of the county by the IRB centre for the area, Thomas O'Loughlin, in 1907. A second branch was started in Crusheen by Tadhg McNamara, an Irish teacher and member of the IRB, while a third Sinn Féin club in Clare was based in Cranny. Under O'Loughlin's guidance the politics of the fledgling Sinn Féin party in the county went beyond Griffith's intended political methods; instead of Irish MPs merely abstaining from Westminster, the Clare Sinn Féin clubs decided to abstain completely from participating in parliamentary elections in line with the views of the IRB's newly emerging leaders such as Tom Clarke.

At the same time that Arthur Griffith was launching the Sinn Féin party, a younger, impatient, more radical element of the IRB led by Denis McCullough and Bulmer Hobson came to the fore. They had the support of some older hard-line physical force men including John Daly and Thomas Clarke. This alliance of older physical force men and young revolutionaries successfully challenged the elderly, placid and often corrupt IRB leaders for control and staged a coup within the organisation. The reorganisation process of the Clare IRB began in 1907 when prominent members of the more radical IRB faction began to visit the county. In 1908 Con Colbert visited his cousins the O'Donnells in Tullycrine and swore Art O'Donnell into the organisation. Seán Mac Diarmada, a leading IRB member and full-time Sinn Féin organiser, visited Clare in September 1908 and addressed a Sinn Féin meeting at Kilkee. Cathal Brugha subsequently accompanied him on an organising visit to Kilrush in 1910 where they formed an IRB circle. By this time republican activity and agrarian violence in Clare had troubled the British authorities so much that the county was classified as being 'in a state of disturbance'. RIC garrisons throughout the county were strengthened until there were 487 members of the force serving there. Only Galway had a larger garrison of RIC and only Cork had a higher concentration of barracks.

In 1910 Thomas Clarke founded the radical newspaper, *Irish Freedom* in Dublin. The paper was distributed through IRB circles in Clare and eventually gained a nationwide circulation of 6,000 copies a month, giving the reorganised IRB a united policy and definite voice. The established media at the time were biased either towards British imperialism or the parliamentarianism of the IPP. Republican and separatist ideas were not found in the national press, and papers such as the *Irish Times*, *Irish Independent* or *Daily Mail* omitted all references to the Gaelic revival and republicanism, except to ridicule them.

The IRB nationally became increasingly militant in outlook and this was reflected in its activities in Clare. According to Michael Brennan, the new leadership completely shook up the organisation in the county: 'In Clare they were the conspirator type and didn't want to fight at all.

Our fellows wanted to get out into the open and fight. They just pushed the old IRB men aside.' Thomas O'Loughlin successfully recruited a number of young men into the IRB in the Ennistymon and Kilfenora areas, including Martin Devitt and John Joe Neylon, Séamus Connelly and Andy O'Donoghue. O'Loughlin, a native of Carrow in North Clare, was in contact with the supreme council of the IRB and knew Thomas Clarke well. He held meetings of the IRB circle in Miss McCormack's hotel in Ennistymon and Markham's house in Kilfenora. After his introduction to the north Clare circle of the IRB Martin Devitt founded another circle at Cloonagh, outside Ennistymon and became its centre. Séamus Conealy recalled that 'The principal business transacted at these meetings was to listen to Thomas O'Loughlin's appeals to make ready for the fight against British rule and to endeavour to collect arms wherever the opportunity presented itself.' From 1911 to 1913 the circle collected a number of guns. At the time there were no restrictions on the sale of firearms and Neylon worked in a hardware shop that sold guns and ammunition. He managed to 'pinch' six revolvers and a large amount of ammunition and trained the other members of his IRB circle in their use. 'I would say that by the end of 1913, when the first Volunteer company was formed in Ennistymon the members of the Cloonagh IRB centre were all familiar with the use of the revolver and could fire fairly accurately with it.'

The IRB circle in Crusheen was reorganised by Séamus Mór Ó Griofa in 1910. Ó Griofa, who worked as a post office linesman in Crusheen, swore Seán McNamara and Seán O'Keefe into the circle. Fourteen other members in the Crusheen circle met regularly in McNamara's home:

> At the meetings we spent most of the time discussing military training, using for this purpose hand books issued by the army authorities. It was our great ambition to learn as much as possible about this subject as we were certain that another rising against English rule would occur in our time and we wanted to be as efficient as possible as soldiers of Ireland.

In 1911 Michael Brennan from Meelick joined Na Fianna Éireann, the Irish Republican boy scout movement which had been established to counter the pro-British cultural influence of the British Baden Powell scout movement. He was also a member of the Wolfe Tone Club, a cover organisation for the IRB in Limerick: 'For the next two years we mustered and paraded in the Fianna, while in the Wolfe Tone Club and the IRB we met regularly and discussed ways of infiltrating local organisations and public bodies. Occasionally a new member appeared but progress was very slow and we didn't appear to be getting anywhere.'

By 1913 the IRB was reorganised throughout Ireland and engaged in recruitment, military training and procuring arms. Bulmer Hobson claimed that the new leadership of the IRB was waiting until 'some new situation should arrive of which they could take advantage to emerge as a decisive force'. The Ulster unionists were about to present the IRB leadership with that opportunity.

2

Finishing What the Fenians Started: The Irish Volunteers in Clare 1913–1916

> We are getting ready to fight against the foreigner and finish the job the Fenians set out to do.
>
> *Martin Devitt*

In April 1912 the third Home Rule Bill passed the House of Commons. It proposed to establish an Irish parliament that would have limited powers dealing with internal affairs. The implementation of the bill was delayed for two years after it was rejected by the House of Lords. Immense opposition to the bill among the unionist minority in Ireland, led by Edward Carson, resulted in the formation of the Ulster Volunteer Force (UVF) in 1913. For forty years the Irish people had placed their faith in the IPP and believed that constitutional pressure would win them home rule, and within a few months the militant action of a fanatical minority had swept forty years of constitutional progress aside.

The emergence of the Ulster Volunteer Force destabilised Ireland to the advantage of Bulmer Hobson and his IRB colleagues by introducing the gun into mainstream Irish politics:

> In the IRB we knew Carsonism had opened a door that could not easily be closed again. In an Ireland doped into an unlimited patience and credulity, an unlimited confidence in its Party Leaders and the British Liberal government and a confident expectation of Home Rule, came Sir Edward Carson to save the situation for the physical force party. He defied law, appealed to force; he preached the doctrines that led to the founding of the Irish Volunteers – and the amazed Irish people with their pathetic faith in the infallibility of their party leaders, and

the honesty of the British Government, saw that Government recoil before the bluff of the 'Ulster Volunteers'. They found threats of physical resistance by a minority accepted as successful argument against justice to a majority ... Here was the opportunity of the IRB.

Irish republicans were quick to imitate the actions of the UVF and in response to a newspaper article by Eoin McNeill a public meeting was held in Dublin on 25 November to establish an Irish Volunteer Force. Three thousand men enrolled in the Irish Volunteers that night and a number of women who were refused admission founded Cumann na mBan. Even though the moderate nationalist McNeill was elected president of the Irish Volunteers, twelve members of the provisional committee were IRB men and McNeill became the respectable public front behind which the IRB controlled the organisation and led it down a revolutionary path.

Clare republicans were swift to respond to events in Ulster and Dublin. A week after the Dublin meeting a company of Volunteers was established in Killone, at the bidding of Joe Barrett and other local republicans: 'The members of the IRB started the Volunteers on their own, without assistance from any outside body or person, that is to say they had no instructions from the supreme council of the IRB on the one hand or the newly formed Volunteer executive on the other.' By early 1914 Irish Volunteer companies had been established in Bunratty, Crusheen, Carrigaholt, Ennistymon, Kilkee, Kilrush, Kilfenora, Kildysart, Newmarket and Tullycrine. On 26 April over a thousand paraded at Killaloe. Though the IRB maintained a strong influence on the new movement all shades of Irish opinion joined the new force. These Volunteer units were initially unarmed and drilled by ex-British soldiers using broom handles, timber rifles or hurleys.

A public meeting in Ennistymon on 11 April established a strong Volunteer company in that area and a committee was set up to control the new body. The IRB chief Thomas O'Loughlin did not join the movement and only one IRB man, Séamus Connelly, was appointed to the committee, but local republicans like John Joe Neylon were manipulating the situation:

Myself and a dozen others, mostly IRB men, met a week or so earlier in a carpenters workshop [*sic*] in the town and discussed the idea of following the lead given to the country by the people of Dublin who had launched the Irish Volunteer movement. At the meeting it was agreed to call a public meeting in the town hall and invite the most prominent persons in the town to come on the platform. The public meeting was a great success and about 150 members were enrolled that night.

Volunteer companies at Donaha and Carrigaholt were progressing well, being drilled and trained by British naval reservists. These sections were also well equipped, with most of the Volunteers able to borrow shotguns for drilling. Éamonn Fennell's unit also used .22 rifles for target practice but, tragically, carelessness with the weapons led to the first casualty of the Volunteer movement when a young lad named Keane from Kilbaha was shot dead by accident during rifle practice.

The size of the new movement became a concern to the IRB, who worried that it was growing too quickly for them to control. The growth of the Irish Volunteers also began to unnerve John Redmond, the leader of the IPP, who would not allow the organisation to threaten his position. Some 75,000 men had enlisted in the Volunteers by May 1914. Initially Redmond and the IPP opposed the formation of the organisation and publicly discouraged men from joining, but when they realised the strength of the new movement Redmond demanded that McNeill include twenty-five nominees from the IPP on the provisional committee of the Volunteers; if not, Redmond threatened to establish a rival movement. An angry debate emerged at the meeting of the Irish Volunteers provisional committee with McNeill and Hobson reluctantly proposing Redmond's nominees with the hope of preventing a split. The IRB were opposed to allowing Redmond erode their supremacy within the Volunteers, but lost the debate and Redmond's demands were agreed to. The IRB leadership, bitter at Hobson's actions in supporting Redmond's demands, forced him to resign from the supreme council.

On Monday, 27 June word reached the IRB in Clare of dramatic events in Dublin. Art O'Donnell had been shown a telegram from Dublin which contained news of hundreds of rifles being landed at

Howth by the Volunteers and an attack on them by British troops. Members of the Volunteers, Na Fianna Éireann and the IRB had landed a cargo of 900 rifles and 29,000 rounds of ammunition at Howth. There was no law against the Volunteers arming in this manner but as the Irish Volunteers and Fianna members marched back to Dublin they were confronted by members of the RIC and British army, who failed to disarm them. That evening members of the King's Own Scottish Borderers opened fire on a crowd who were jeering them, killing four and wounding thirty-eight. The British military's excuse for the killings was that the order 'prepare to fire' was mistaken for the order 'fire'.

A few days earlier Captain E. Gerrard, a British officer stationed at Wicklow, had been riding horseback with Major Haig, who had commanded the company of the King's Own Scottish Borderers that would commit the massacre. Captain Gerrard commented on what a beautiful country Ireland was and that he hoped the major would enjoy himself there. Major Haig replied: 'I hate the fucking place! I hate the fucking people!' Major Haig's anti-Irish bigotry took on a new importance in the mind of Captain Gerrard after the Howth gun-running: 'I often wondered was there any connection between what he said to me and his action. He was always known in the British army afterwards as "the man who made the war".'

The victims of the Bachelor's Walk massacre were given public funerals by the Volunteers and huge crowds turned out to mourn. The British forces were confined to barracks on the day of the funerals and the only British soldier seen in Dublin that day was Private Duffy, who appeared as a mourner. His mother had been shot dead by his comrades in the British army on Bachelor's Walk.

The political situation within Ireland was reaching boiling point; the Home Rule Bill was due to become law, while nationalist and unionist Ireland were arming and training for war. However, conflict in Ireland was averted by events in Europe. On 1 August 1914 war was declared between Austria-Hungary and Serbia. Two days later Britain entered the war. The European war brought a sudden reprieve to the Irish crisis because the Home Rule Bill would not become law until peace was declared.

On 20 September John Redmond made a speech at Woodenbridge, County Wicklow urging the Irish Volunteers to enlist in the British army to 'resist German aggression in Europe'. As well as promising Irish nationalists that their service in the army would ensure home rule, the British government promised Irish unionists that their service would prevent home rule. In addition British propaganda carefully fanned the flames of sectarian hatred. In predominantly Protestant areas people were told of the atrocities of the 'Papist Bavarian regiments' in the German army, while people living in mainly Catholic areas were regaled with propaganda of Belgian nuns being bayoneted against the convent doors. The army's own, very real, atrocity at Bachelor's Walk was already forgotten. In the rural areas the vast majority of Volunteers, duped by their clergy, marched with Redmond to their doom in the trenches of Europe, believing they were fighting to stop German atrocities in 'poor Catholic Belgium'. In fact 'poor Catholic Belgium' was one of the most savage imperial powers, whose atrocities in the Congo had been exposed by Roger Casement. The Belgians had been regularly mutilating Congolese natives who couldn't keep to set levels of production by chopping off hands and feet. These were the 'poor Catholics' that the Church encouraged so many deluded young Irishmen to die for in Britain's war.

Redmond's speech caused an immediate split in the Irish Volunteers, with his nominees on the Volunteer executive supporting the British war effort and the IRB faction, including McNeill, opposing Irish involvement in the war. The vast majority of the Volunteers supported Redmond, with over 150,000 Volunteers forming the pro-war Irish National Volunteers. Ten thousand Volunteers supported the republican position and retained the title 'Irish Volunteers'. The Irish Volunteers were supported in their anti-war stance by Griffith's Sinn Féin party, with the result that the Irish Volunteers were often incorrectly referred to as 'Sinn Féin Volunteers' by the public and the British authorities, even though there was no formal connection between the two.

By August 1914 the Irish Volunteers in Clare had a membership of 5,000 divided into over sixty companies. There was no real split in

Clare as whole companies transferred their loyalties to Redmond's Irish National Volunteers. The Clare county inspector of Redmond's Irish National Volunteers, Edward Lysaght, reported in October that 'The men are falling away and whole companies have lapsed rather than disbanded.' In Liam Haugh's company at Kilkee there was no major difference of opinion:

> It may be safely said that 90 per cent of the able-bodied population joined the Redmond Volunteers. Leadership of the various units was accepted by the professional and influential classes and drilling with dummy arms etc. was intensively carried on ... The classes who accepted his leadership accepted Redmond's suggestion but on endeavouring to impose their views on the rank and file were simply deserted en masse. A minimum enlisted into Britain's army, but the Volunteers as such disintegrated.

Art O'Donnell saw Redmond's activities destroy the Volunteers in Kildysart: 'A notable feature of those that called themselves the National Volunteers was that after the first month in which all were exhorted to join the Volunteers and parade in defence of their country against German aggression, their activities actively ceased.' The Irish National Volunteers quickly disintegrated nationwide as 25,000 of their members enlisted in the army. Their officers and drill instructors who were mostly ex-soldiers were called up for service.

Diarmuid Coffey, a leading member of the Irish National Volunteers in Dublin cited more sinister reasons for the decline of the movement:

> A good deal of money was spent on buying a house as headquarters, 44 Parnell Square, and a weekly newspaper, *The National Volunteer*, was started with a man called Gaynor, from the staff of the *Freeman's Journal*, as editor. This paper was run nominally as a Volunteer paper but Gaynor was really only a party hack and the whole effort of those running the paper was to abuse the Sinn Féiners and boost the Parliamentary Party. Those of us who had, though Redmondite in politics, joined the Volunteers because it seemed to be a fine national movement were disgusted with 'The National Volunteers' ... It was gradually borne in on

us that the intention of the majority of the committee was to get rid of the money and let the Volunteers fade away.

A review of the remaining Irish National Volunteers was held in the Phoenix Park in 1915. Special trains were arranged from many different parts of the country and there was an attendance of several thousand Volunteers, but the review marked the end of the Irish National Volunteers. The movement was sidelined within the IPP as the focus turned to recruitment for the army. Within two years the Irish National Volunteers had almost disappeared completely.

The Ennistymon company of the Volunteers voted overwhelmingly to support John Redmond, and the dozen or more Volunteers who continued to support McNeill's authority were expelled and formed a company of the Irish Volunteers at Cloonagh, under the direction of Martin Devitt's IRB circle. Austin Rynne, who had been a section commander in the Ennistymon unit, was elected O/C of the company with Martin Devitt and Séamus Connelly as his lieutenants. The Kilfenora Volunteers, who had initially decided to remain neutral, held a meeting two weeks after the split, decided in favour of McNeill's policy and joined the Cloonagh company. The group had kept two of the Winchester rifles belonging to the Ennistymon Volunteers for rifle drill and instruction. Thomas O'Loughlin supplied the company with two revolvers and two .22 rifles that he had obtained in Dublin. Ammunition was readily available from Volunteers working in hardware shops, and target practice took place on Sundays. Targets were set up in a remote area of Ardmore where there was an unoccupied farmhouse which became known as 'Liberty Hall'. At practice every Volunteer had an opportunity to fire the .22 rifles or the revolver and the company soon achieved a high level of marksmanship. The IRB's control over the Cloonagh company was evident in the militancy remembered by Martin Devine's younger brother, Patrick:

> There was something more sincere, more determined and more active about the Cloonagh company than the Unit in Ennistymon. Though it was much smaller in numbers and had not any of the prominent or business people associated with it, yet it was soon convinced that the

men in charge had a definite military objective in mind; less attention
was paid to the spectacular side such as uniforms and public parades
and more instruction was given on extended order drill, skirmishing
and shooting exercises.

At the end of 1915 a number of men from the Ennistymon Volunteers,
who had declared in favour of Redmond, joined the Cloonagh company,
which now contained about fifty members, and it was decided to form a
separate company in Kilfenora. Peadar O'Loughlin, a relative of Thomas
O'Loughlin, was elected their O/C. An almost unanimous rejection of
Redmond's policy by the Crusheen company of the Irish Volunteers
meant that they were unaffected by any split except in losing their
ex-British army drill instructor. The company had neither arms nor
ammunition until 1915 when the company captain, Seán McNamara,
a member of the IRB, purchased six Martini Henry rifles and some
.22 rifles from IRB sources in Dublin. The movement spread and
within the year Volunteer companies were formed in Barefield, Corofin,
Knockjames, Kilkeady and Ruan.

In May 1915 Ernest Blythe was appointed as an organiser for
the Irish Volunteers and was sent to Clare to train the Cloonagh and
Kilfenora members. The authorities were well informed about Blythe's
activities in Clare; hotels and guesthouses were warned not to give him
accommodation and he was kept under constant RIC surveillance. Blythe
was well aware of his RIC 'escort' and deliberately led the Volunteers
on challenging route marches over rough terrain to tire and frustrate
their pursuers. Blythe established Irish Volunteer companies at Doolin
and Liscannor and supplied the Crusheen company with seven rifles.
Because of his success in organising and arming the Clare Volunteers,
Blythe was arrested and deported a few weeks later under the Defence
of the Realm Act.

Michael Brennan had moved to the capital to study wireless
telegraphy in the hope of getting a job as a radio operator. Brennan
continued his republican activities by training members of Na Fianna
Éireann in signalling classes until Seán Mac Diarmada advised him

when war broke out that all radio operators would be conscripted into the British military. The IRB directed Brennan to return to Clare and renew his involvement with the Volunteers and Na Fianna there. From Meelick he trained the signals section of the Limerick Volunteers and helped organise Volunteer companies in Meelick, Oatfield, Clonlara, Cratloe and Sixmilebridge. It was not long before the RIC began to take an interest in Brennan's activities. At Sixmilebridge a group of Redmond supporters took a Volunteer's shotgun by force and Brennan intervened by producing a revolver. He was arrested by the RIC for 'causing alarm to His Majesty's subjects' and sentenced to keep the peace for several months. The Feakle Volunteers came into more direct conflict with the police at the same time. On one occasion their captain, Tadhg Kelly, was addressing them under the watchful eye of RIC Constable Lawless when the constable decided that Kelly's speech was of a 'seditious' nature and attempted to stop proceedings and take Kelly's papers. The Volunteers subdued Constable Lawless and made off with his rifle. Tadhg Kelly was arrested, fined £5 and bound to the peace for two years.

The IRB were also reorganising after the collapse of the Volunteer movement in West Clare. The Carrigaholt company of the Volunteers survived the split and were beginning to arm with the support of a local IRB member, Tim Hehir, who secured five rifles and a small quantity of ammunition. Art O'Donnell swore Martin Griffin, Seán McNamara and Frank McMahon into the IRB after the Redmondite split and with their help formed Volunteer companies in Kildysart and Tullycrine. O'Donnell resigned his job as a teacher to become an unpaid full time organiser in the area. The Volunteers organised dances and concerts to raise funds but local support was minimal and progress was slow. A dozen rifles were landed in Carrigaholt from America towards the end of 1915, concealed in a coffin.

By 1916 that there were over 400 Irish Volunteers in Clare. To coordinate the activities of the different companies, a meeting was held in the Fianna Hall in Limerick two weeks before Easter. Clare was divided into four different battalions for organisational purposes. The area from Meelick north-east to Killaloe formed the East Clare battalion, under

Michael Brennan; the Crusheen, Inagh and Ennis districts became the Mid Clare battalion, commanded by Seán McNamara; the North Clare battalion contained Corofin and Ennistymon, with H.J. Hunt in command; while Éamonn Fennell was placed in charge of the West Clare battalion.

There was a police presence at every Irish Volunteer meeting or route march recording the names and details of those attending and taking notes on any speeches made. Rumours were rife that the British authorities were about to disarm the Volunteers, arrest their leaders and declare the organisation illegal. A general mobilisation of the Irish Volunteers was held on St Patrick's Day and Michael Brennan addressed the issue in a speech to the Meelick company:

> I want to say a few words for your own information about the seizure of arms. My advice to you is, if such an attempt is made to use them, and not the butts of them, but the other ends and what's in them. Some of you will not like to commit murder, but it is not murder it is self defence! You know well if your arms are taken the next thing will be conscription.

Brennan was arrested and charged with incitement to rebellion and was sentenced to three months' hard labour in Limerick prison.

Despite British propaganda claims in 1914 that the troops would be 'home by Christmas', the war in Europe was still raging. The IRB and the Volunteers were engaged in an anti-recruitment campaign, though this had little effect within the county as British military recruitment remained steady. As long as conscription was not enforced, the public remained indifferent. Irish Volunteer companies continued arming in resistance to the threat of military conscription but there was also a sense that something else was happening; a feeling that a more serious confrontation with the authorities was imminent. Patrick Devitt and the Cloonagh company were under no illusion that conflict was inevitable: 'Almost from the start it was made clear to every man that at the first suitable moment the Irish Volunteers would go into armed insurrection against British rule. Practically every Sunday my brother, Martin, would lay stress on this particular subject – we are getting ready to fight against the foreigner and finish the job the Fenians set out to do.'

3

No Word, nor Sign of a Word:
The 1916 Rising in Clare

Colm: And no word from Galway yet?
Diarmaid: No word, nor sign of a word.
Colm: They told us to wait for the word. We've waited too long.

From 'The Singer' by Patrick H. Pearse

A month after the British declaration of war on Germany, the IRB supreme council met in Dublin. At the meeting it was decided that the British military commitments to the war provided a new opportunity to challenge British rule in Ireland. A military committee was formed to plan a rebellion and contact was established with the German military. Military action was to begin if any of four things happened:

1. If the German military invaded Ireland
2. If the British government imposed conscription
3. If the Irish Volunteers were about to be disarmed
4. If the war appeared to be ending

Since the 1870s the hard-line element in the IRB had believed that a republic would only be won through open rebellion and that the ideal time to launch this was when Britain was involved in a major imperial war. Charles Kickham, president of the IRB in 1873, had summed up this philosophy with the phrase 'England's difficulty is Ireland's opportunity.' The republicans estimated that the British army in Ireland would be reduced to a quarter of its usual strength for the duration of the war and that there were only about 25,000 British troops in Ireland, most of whom were raw recruits. The establishment of the Volunteers had provided the IRB with a weapon to renew the republican struggle. All previous republican rebellions had relied on the membership of secret societies to provide troops and to train and equip them. Now for the first time republicans had at their command a public, armed and well-trained body of men who could be used to launch a rebellion. It was also obvious to the IRB that the Irish Volunteers could not be kept together indefinitely and would either be suppressed by the British government or else membership would dwindle because of inaction.

It was a common belief in August 1914 that the war would be short and victorious for Britain. There was a fear among the republicans that the war might end before the opportunity to establish an Irish Republic was seized. Many of the physical force men also felt a sense of shame that there had not been an insurrection asserting the Irish people's rights since 1867. The younger members of the IRB were concerned that they would be the first generation to break the continuity of the republican struggle and deal their cause a fatal blow. Even if their rebellion was unsuccessful, the IRB felt they would at least pass a legacy of struggle and resistance to a future generation.

The IRB also thought that if a provisional government could be established during the rebellion that it would be entitled to belligerent rights in negotiations following the war. Irish nationalists had already submitted Ireland's case for independence at the Conference of Small Nationalities in Berne, Switzerland at the instigation of Seán Mac Diarmada.

The IRB's military committee was replaced by a military council in 1915 comprising Thomas Clarke, Patrick Pearse, Éamonn Ceannt, Joseph Plunkett and Seán Mac Diarmada. James Connolly, the socialist republican commander of the militant labour group, the Irish Citizen Army, was making it increasingly difficult for the IRB to delay. Connolly kept calling for military action and threatened that if no one else would act he would lead the Citizen Army in rebellion. He stood in the same republican tradition as the IRB and felt the same urgency and sense of duty in calling for military action. He was also bitterly disappointed by the failure of European socialist movements to prevent the First World War, which he denounced as a quarrel between profit-seeking capitalists. The IRB paid close attention to Connolly's actions and when he published yet another editorial calling for immediate action on 19 January, the IRB co-opted Connolly onto the military council and informed him of the IRB plans for a rebellion. He joined them in the conspiracy and offered them the services of the Citizen Army.

The plans for a rising were already in motion. Joseph Mary Plunkett had originally hoped for a large German invasion force to assist the republicans and envisaged that 12,000 German troops would land at Limerick with 40,000 rifles to arm the Irish Volunteers. The German aid given was on a much smaller scale, however; the German military authorities promised diplomatic recognition of the Irish Republic, and to supply the Volunteers with arms and a limited number of German officers to command them. Roger Casement and Robert Montieth were in Germany trying to recruit an Irish brigade among Irish soldiers in German prisoner-of-war camps. These reinforcements were to rendezvous with the Irish Volunteers along the north Kerry coast and land the arms shipment at Fenit between Friday 21 and Sunday 23 April. The arrival of German aid was to be the signal for the rising.

The Irish Volunteers and the Irish Citizen Army were to seize a number of key buildings which formed a defensive ring around Dublin city. The bridges leading into the city centre were to be defended by snipers who would slow any British advances. Volunteer companies in Wicklow, north Dublin and Meath were to carry out actions against the RIC and army in their own counties before retiring to Dublin. Volunteers in the midlands and the south were to attack local RIC barracks and sabotage railway and telegraph lines to disrupt communications between the British forces. The Irish Volunteers in Ulster were to assemble in Coalisland, County Tyrone and march towards Galway to alleviate pressure on Liam Mellows' command there.

The western counties had the largest numbers of unarmed Volunteers and the plan was to use the German shipment to arm the Volunteers in Kerry, Clare, Limerick and Galway, and for them to mount attacks on the RIC. The Irish Volunteers from the West Clare battalion, under

Patrick Brennan, were to cross the Shannon at Carrigaholt and march to Listowel. They would capture the town and await the arrival of Volunteers from Kerry with rifles from the German shipment. Then they would return to Clare and begin attacks on barracks. A group of Volunteers who worked as railway men in Kerry would hijack a train to transport the majority of the arms shipment by train to Limerick.

With 1,000 British soldiers stationed in Limerick, the city was to be bypassed using the Ballysimon railway loop. The Limerick Volunteers, under the command of Michael Colviet, were to proceed to Killonan where they would cut telegraph cables and sabotage the railway connection to Limerick Junction. Colviet was to receive rifles from the arms shipment at Abbeyfeale and use these against the British military in the east of the city. Volunteers from the East Clare battalion under Michael Brennan would await another shipment of arms at Bunratty. Armed with these rifles they were to march to the western suburbs of Limerick where they would hold the bridges on the Shannon and the roads leading into Clare. In cooperation with Colviet's command at the opposite side of Limerick, Brennan's group would attempt to confine the British army within the city.

The arms shipment would continue by rail through Ennis to Crusheen where Seán McNamara and the local Volunteers would guard it on the last part of its journey to Gort. Here Liam Mellows was to take control of the arms and issue the Clare Volunteers with a supply of rifles and new orders. Mellows' own orders from the IRB were to transport the arms to Athenry and attack the British forces there while the Clare Volunteers would attack barracks along the line of the Shannon and cause enough trouble there to draw the British troops westwards away from Dublin. Some of the Limerick Volunteers were ordered to join them in this objective and take action along the Shannon from Limerick to Killaloe.

While these plans were being formulated by the IRB military council in Dublin, the Irish Volunteers continued to train and drill in Clare. Most Volunteers in the county were unaware of the formation of the plans for a rebellion, but there was an expectant atmosphere among them that armed conflict with the British forces would begin as a result of attempts to suppress the movement. These fears were not without foundation; there had been over 500 prosecutions nationally under the Defence of the Realm Act since the outbreak of war. A number of republican papers were suppressed because of their opposition to the war and there was increased political surveillance by the RIC. The IRB in Clare were preparing the Volunteers for a rebellion even though they had not yet received definite orders as to when it might take place. The IRB centre in Newmarket on Fergus, Seán Murnane, was equally uninformed but like other Volunteers he guessed it was imminent: 'As Easter 1916 approached it became clear to me that military action against British rule was being contemplated by the Irish Volunteer leaders. This was apparent from the speeches made by those leaders throughout the country and also from weekly papers which we received from Dublin.'

The military council's concern for secrecy meant that many senior IRB members were not told about the plans for a rising until the last moment. Diarmuid Lynch, the Munster representative on the IRB supreme council, was not informed of the military council's plans until Holy Thursday. Among the first Claremen to learn of the IRB's plans for the rebellion were the Brennan brothers. Patrick Brennan had retired from his civil service job in London as the threat of conscription loomed. He returned to Clare and took up residence at McNamara's bar in Ennis. He learned about the plans for a rebellion in spring 1916 after he was appointed a Volunteer organiser for Limerick and Clare. His brother Michael was still in Limerick prison for making a seditious speech in Meelick. He was in jail for a week when he received a message that Seán Mac Diarmada wanted him to lodge an appeal at once. Dr Charles McDonnell, who brought the message, was a justice of the peace and was able to have Brennan released, pending appeal. Brennan reported to the IRB centre for Limerick, George Clancy, who told him that a rebellion was planned for Easter Sunday and that he was to take command of the Volunteers in East Clare. Brennan set off cycling through East Clare issuing orders to Volunteer companies for

Sundays 'general mobilisation' and giving IRB centres instructions for the rebellion.

Patrick Brennan visited Murray, the captain of the Newmarket on Fergus Volunteers at the start of Easter week and told him that the company was to mobilise on Sunday at Bunratty Bridge with whatever guns they could gather. Next Brennan called to Seán Murnane, the IRB centre for the area, and revealed to him the real purpose of that Sunday's mobilisation. The Volunteers called on local farmers and collected a dozen shotguns and ammunition. On Holy Thursday Brennan travelled to Carrigaholt and informed Éamonn Fennell that he had been sent to take charge of the battalion. He added that arms were due to arrive in Kerry and a rebellion would begin on Sunday. Fennell was to select twenty-five trusted and well-trained Volunteers to parade in Carrigaholt on Sunday morning. These Volunteers would cross the Shannon by boat to Beale, attack the barracks at Listowel, capture the town and wait until the Kerry Volunteers arrived with arms for them. The Clare Volunteers would then return to Carrigaholt and begin attacks on barracks there. The rest of the battalion were to move out of the Carrigaholt peninsula and attack barracks further east. After receiving these orders Fennell circulated a story for the benefit of the RIC that the Volunteers were crossing the Shannon that Sunday to compete in a shooting competition.

Seán McNamara, leader of the Crusheen Volunteers, was visited by Michael Brennan on Good Friday. McNamara had met Éamonn Corbett of Galway the previous evening and knew of the planned rebellion. Brennan gave McNamara detailed verbal instructions that his battalion were to hold the railway line between Ennis and Gort and that arms for the battalion would arrive from Kerry. McNamara issued orders for the other companies to mobilise on Easter Saturday night and gave them instructions listing the positions they were to secure along the railway line.

Thomas O'Loughlin was already actively informing the IRB centres in north Clare that a rebellion was planned. Martin Devine was to take charge of the Cloonagh company at their usual parade on Sunday morning at 'Liberty Hall' and await arms and further instructions. Plans for the rebellion were proceeding well in the county; security was tight, with only a few IRB men being aware of the importance of the manoeuvres. The Newmarket on Fergus Volunteers continued collecting shotguns, while the Crusheen company spent Good Friday at Seán McNamara's house charging shotgun cartridges with heavier shot.

Everything was in place for the transfer of arms to Liam Mellows' command at Gort and the distribution of the German arms when Éamonn Fennell's brother, the lighthouse keeper at Loop Head, returned to Carrigaholt on Good Friday evening. He told Éamonn that he had received reports of a strange ship anchored off the Kerry coast, apparently waiting for something, before it was escorted out to sea by the British navy. Fennell reported this to Patrick Brennan, who dismissed the idea that the arms shipment had been captured. However, Fennell's instincts were correct – the boat that his brother had received reports about was the *Cairo*. It had been disguised as a neutral Norwegian vessel and renamed the *Aud* and loaded with 20,000 rifles, ten machine guns and millions of rounds of ammunition. The original plan for the vessel to rendezvous with the Kerry Volunteers between Thursday night and Easter Monday morning was changed to prevent the arms arriving too early. The German military were notified of this change after the *Aud* had set sail and could not contact her. U-boat 19 was sailing for the same destination with Roger Casement and Robert Montieth aboard.

Unaware that the *Aud* was uncontactable, the IRB sent three Volunteer radio operators to Valentia in Kerry to raid a radio station and transmit a message to the boat. The car the three were travelling in took a wrong turn and plunged off Ballykissane pier; Volunteers Con Keating and Alf Vonohan were drowned. The driver, Tommy McInerny, swam ashore and was arrested by the RIC. The *Aud* was intercepted by two British warships and escorted to Cobh, where the German crew scuttled the ship rather than surrender it. Casement landed on Banna strand, Fenit on Good Friday but was captured shortly afterwards.

The Clare Volunteers remained ignorant of the events in Kerry and continued their preparations for the rebellion. On Saturday morning Art O'Donnell was travelling to Limerick to collect a Volunteer uniform and was about to take the train when he met Patrick Brennan. Shocked that O'Donnell was going to Limerick, Brennan ordered him to return to Carrigaholt and mobilise the Volunteers there for action. O'Donnell insisted on keeping his appointment in Limerick but promised to return to Carrigaholt immediately afterwards. Upon arrival in Limerick, O'Donnell met an equally surprised Michael Brennan who told him that he was required at the Fianna Hall in Brunswick Street. O'Donnell collected his uniform and went to the hall with Brennan where they discovered Commandant Colviet, Seán O'Dea and other Volunteer officers in heated debate. They had just received news of events in Kerry, including Casement's arrest and reports of the arms shipment. The plans for rebellion in Limerick and Clare relied completely on the arms shipment and the Volunteers were divided on whether to take action. Commandant Colviet, the senior officer, instructed O'Donnell, Brennan and O'Dea to remain at the Fianna Hall until contact could be made with Volunteer headquarters in Dublin. Just before 8 p.m., Colviet returned to the hall and stated he hadn't received any news from Dublin and was cancelling all operations but that Volunteer companies were still to mobilise for action and await orders.

Seán O'Dea set out to inform the County Limerick Volunteers of the cancellation. Brennan and O'Donnell rushed to catch the last train to Ennis. O'Donnell collected his bike in Ennis and called to McNamara's pub in the hope of meeting Patrick Brennan, but discovered that he had already left for Carrigaholt.

News of events in Kerry had also reached Dublin. The Irish Volunteers' director of arms, Michael O'Rahilly, brought two Volunteer officers from Kerry to meet Eoin McNeill. The pair gave McNeill detailed accounts of the loss of the *Aud* and Casement's capture. McNeill had only discovered the IRB's plans for rebellion on Good Friday and threatened to do everything he could to prevent a rebellion until Mac Diarmada pointed out that with German assistance due to arrive the rebellion was inevitable. Realising Mac Diarmada was right, McNeill reluctantly agreed to the join the conspiracy. On hearing that the arms shipment was lost, McNeill despatched O'Rahilly by car to Munster with a countermanding order on Holy Saturday night. McNeill then placed a countermanding order in the *Sunday Independent* cancelling the orders for a general mobilisation. On learning of McNeill's actions the IRB postponed the rebellion until Easter Monday, hoping that if the republicans went into action in Dublin the Irish Volunteer companies in the country would follow suit.

Back in Clare Michael Brennan had called to Frank Shinnors in Ennis and proceeded to Crusheen to try and contact Seán McNamara. Fifteen members of Crusheen company had already mobilised and were about to occupy the railway line when Michael Brennan called to McNamara's house. McNamara had returned home to rest having mobilised his troops and was not long in bed when Brennan and Shinnors arrived. They told him his orders were cancelled as the arms shipment had failed, but that the Volunteers were to remain mobilised for action. McNamara recalled the mobilised Volunteers and despatched messengers to Gort, Doora and Ruan.

Fifty members of the Feakle company had mobilised in Kelly's field on Easter Saturday night. Tadhg Kelly ordered them to return to their own districts and seize whatever arms they could. The company returned with enough weapons to equip thirty men. Kelly read a despatch he had just received ordering Volunteers to be ready to participate in a rebellion and stating that further instructions would be issued giving details of when and where to strike. The whole company remained mobilised and slept in farm buildings attached to Kelly's farm expecting that orders would come to attack the local barracks.

That night, on reaching his home in Tullycrine, Art O'Donnell woke his brothers and sent Willie and Frank to mobilise the Tullycrine and Cranny companies. Jack O'Donnell was sent to Ennis to await news there, while Art went to Carrigaholt and contacted Éamonn Fennell on Easter Sunday morning. Patrick Brennan was contacted at Behan's hotel; he was furious at the loss of the arms shipment but decided to go ahead with that morning's parade. The Volunteers were inspected and carried out training manoeuvres before disbanding.

After mass Michael Brennan marched the Meelick and Oatfield companies to Bunratty Bridge, hoping to receive new orders from the IRB. He was joined by the Cratloe and Newmarket on Fergus Volunteers. They waited all day in ceaseless rain, watched from a distance by two RIC men. No messenger came and that afternoon the different companies were dismissed with orders to be ready to mobilise for action at a moment's notice. Brennan marched his company back to Meelick and held them together for the rest of the evening.

Fifty members of the Garraunaboy company, Killaloe, who had not received any cancellation orders from Limerick marched to Castleconnell expecting the arrival of the German arms. In north Clare the Kilfenora and Cloonagh companies held their usual Sunday parade at 'Liberty Hall' in Ardmore before being dismissed as a result of McNeill's countermanding order. Martin Devitt, who had been expecting further orders to arrive from the IRB, instructed the Volunteers to report again at Ardmore the following day. The Feakle Volunteers received a despatch telling them that all previous instructions were cancelled and the Volunteers should disband. Tadhg Kelly decided that it would be safer for the Volunteers to remain in Kelly's field until that night and then go home without receiving any attention from the RIC. At about 10 p.m. the company was dismissed.

The entire plan for rebellion in Clare and Limerick had depended on the arrival of the arms shipment – with its failure the IRB's plans throughout Clare lay in ruins. Colviet's cancellation order on Saturday night prevented any premature action and kept the Volunteers mobilised, but McNeill's countermand made the situation critical. The IRB in Clare had not received new orders from either the military council or Liam Mellows in Galway. They remained mobilised without any idea what action to take, or even whether the rebellion was called off or postponed.

At noon on Easter Monday the Irish Volunteers, Citizen Army, Hibernian Rifles, Cumann na mBan and Na Fianna Éireann mobilised in Dublin. The GPO in Sackville Street, the Four Courts and other large buildings in the city were seized and barricaded. The Magazine Fort in Phoenix Park was blown up and Dublin Castle was attacked.

At 2 p.m. a message from Dublin reached the Limerick Volunteers. It read: 'The Dublin Brigade goes into action at noon to-day (Monday). Carry out your orders. P.H. Pearse.' Michael Brennan attended a meeting of the committee of the Limerick Volunteers that evening where a debated raged for hours on whether the order should be obeyed, and if so what action should be taken. Michael Brennan and six others voted to take action, the other twenty-five voted against. The committee agreed to meet again the next day and reconsider this decision.

Thirty members of the Cloonagh company mobilised again at Liberty Hall in Ardmore. Martin Devitt instructed them to split up and gather whatever firearms they could find in Cloonagh, Kilfenora and Corofin. They returned at dawn with forty shotguns and two rifles which were divided among the assembled Volunteers, with the remainder hidden in an outhouse at Whitemount. Orders had still not arrived and after a conference they decided to return to their homes with their arms and mobilise for action again that night in the hope that orders would arrive.

The debate between the Volunteer officers in Limerick continued and became more heated, but the votes in favour of, and against, action remained the same. The Carrigaholt Volunteers remained mobilised since hearing news that morning of the fighting in Dublin, expecting orders to arrive from Limerick. Art O'Donnell sent word to Seán O'Dea requesting orders, and O'Dea advised O'Donnell not to take action. Michael Brennan realised that a decision to fight would not be taken by the Limerick Volunteer officers, and decided to go to Galway where it was reported that the local Volunteers were in action against the British forces. Brennan intended to return to Limerick if the reports of fighting in Galway were true, rally the Limerick and Claremen willing to fight and march them towards Galway. He cycled northwards and spent Wednesday trying to reach Galway, but continually found his route blocked by armed RIC patrols. Brennan decided that it would be impossible to reach Galway and was arrested upon his return to Limerick.

Meanwhile, Thomas O'Loughlin and Séamus Murrihy were busy in north Clare hoping to aid the rebellion in Galway by sabotaging communications. The pair felled telegraph poles and cut telegraph wires between Ennistymon and Ennis. They arrived at Andrew O'Donoghue's home on Easter Tuesday evening bringing with them several hundred yards of telecommunications wire.

The Cloonagh Volunteers were still ready for action when the first apparent military orders, allegedly issued by Thomas O'Loughlin, reached Andrew O'Donoghue. A schoolteacher came to O'Donoghue claiming he had received a written order from O'Loughlin to the Volunteers to mount an attack on the Ennistymon RIC barracks. The Cloonagh company of the Volunteers believed that if O'Loughlin had really issued the order he would have delivered it in person, or at least issued it through a more reliable source, and they decided to ignore the teacher's message. A number of Volunteers believed the teacher was a spy and should be executed. But this man had a large family and it was decided that no action should be taken. O'Loughlin later confirmed that he had never issued the teacher with any orders, though it is likely that the teacher acted out of misguided enthusiasm rather than from British orders.

On Saturday the rebellion ended in Dublin when Patrick Pearse surrendered to Brigadier General Lowe of the British army. The rebellion ended, without the Volunteers in Clare receiving any definite orders. The whole effort appeared to be a disastrous re-run of the 1867 rising but it should be remembered that a force of 2,000 poorly armed and trained republicans, had challenged the superior numbers and military might of the world's largest empire, and defied them without reinforcements for a week.

A number of Claremen took part in the rebellion in Dublin. Martin Lynch, from Coolmeen, was one of the group of rebels who raided and destroyed the British army's magazine fort in the Phoenix Park before taking up duty in the GPO where two other Claremen, Dan Canny and his younger brother, were part of the garrison also stationed in the GPO. Jim Slattery, a member of the IRB from Feakle, fought in Jacob's mills during the Easter Rising. Peadar Clancy, from Cranny, was promoted to lieutenant during the rebellion and was in charge of the republican positions at Church Street as part of the Four Courts garrison. He personally burned out a British army sniper's post on Bridge Street and successfully directed his men in repelling a British army attack near Church Street Bridge. Clancy was sentenced to death by a British military court-martial but this was commuted to ten years' imprisonment.

The Volunteers in Clare began preparing for the backlash from the British authorities in response to the rebellion. The Crusheen Volunteer company's arms were gathered together and hidden under the floor of Seán McNamara's brother's house. Volunteer companies disbanded temporarily and their members maintained a low profile to avoid arrest. The British administration, which had been taken by surprise by the rebellion, acted swiftly in interning those it thought responsible. In the days after the Rising 3,149 men and 77 women were arrested throughout Ireland. Twenty republicans were arrested and interned by the British forces in Clare. These were: Michael and Patrick Brennan – Meelick; Art O'Donnell – Kilrush; Thomas O'Loughlin and Éamonn Waldron – Ennistymon; Tadhg Kelly, Joe Tuohy, Tom Grady, Jack Malone and Mitchell Dynan – Feakle; Michael Murray and Seán Murnane – Newmarket on Fergus; Denis Healy – Bodyke; C. O'Halloran – Tulla; Martin Crowe – Ruan; Brian O'Higgins – Carrigaholt; Thomas Kierse – Killeen; Hubert and William Hunt – Corofin; and Patrick O'Connor – Killaloe. Fearing more trouble, the British government increased their garrison in Ireland by commandeering large buildings as temporary barracks. In Clare British soldiers took over the Lakeside Hotel in Killaloe as a barracks, while at Tulla the workhouse and the courthouse were occupied.

Claremen Martin Lynch and Jim Slattery, who had taken part in the fighting in Dublin, were also interned. Dan Canny, who had fought in the GPO, was jailed in Knutsford prison but his younger brother was released by the British because of his age. Peadar Clancy was held in both Portland and Lewes prisons after the Easter Rising.

General Maxwell had issued a proclamation requiring all Volunteer companies to surrender their arms to the RIC, an order that was ignored by the Irish Volunteers in Clare. The shotguns seized by the Volunteers were returned to their owners in Ennistymon to prevent ill feeling between them and the local people. The revolvers, rifles and ammunition belonging to the Cloonagh and Kilfenora companies were hidden away safely, in case of raids by the RIC. The Carrigaholt Volunteers were approached by the local Catholic canon and told to turn over all their arms to him. He was presented with the company's rifles, which he later surrendered to the RIC. Carrigaholt was the only place in Clare where Volunteer arms were surrendered to the British forces.

The canon's collaboration with the British authorities is not surprising because, with few exceptions, the hierarchy of the Catholic Church condemned the Easter Rising outright. The Vatican praised the Irish clergy for the zeal with which they supported the efforts of the British government to restore order. Bishop Edward Thomas O'Dwyer of Limerick stood alone against the senior Irish Catholic clergy and condemned the executions. By this time the *Manchester Guardian* was calling the executions an atrocity and campaigning for them to end. Edward Carson, the Unionist leader, called on the British government to be more moderate and yet the executions of Mac Diarmada and Connolly were cheered by members of the IPP in the British House of Commons. William Martin Murphy, who had a personal grievance against James Connolly since the 1913 lockout, was afraid that Connolly might escape execution because he was seriously wounded and Murphy called for his execution. Murphy's newspaper, the *Irish Independent*, published a photograph of James Connolly with an editorial demanding: 'Let the worst of the ringleaders be singled out and dealt with as they deserve.'

At least one of the republican leaders, Thomas Clarke, was refused absolution the night before his execution by the Catholic priest sent to give him the last rights, because Clarke would not say his participation in the Easter Rising was a sin. At the British crown enquiry into the causes of the rebellion, the RIC's county inspector for Clare, Inspector

Gelstone, testified that in Clare: 'Any of the priests who had Sinn Féin tendencies were of a younger variety. The older men as a rule – the parish priests in a number of cases – have spoken against the Sinn Féin movement.'

The Clare internees were imprisoned in Limerick until 9 May when they were taken to Richmond barracks, Dublin by train. It was during the train journey that Art O'Donnell learned of the execution of his cousin, Con Colbert, in Kilmainham jail the previous day. Over the next two weeks the interned men were marched in small batches to the North Wall for deportation to prisons in Britain. Most groups of prisoners were abused and spat at by angry crowds as they were marched along the quays to their deportation.

But the executions of rebel leaders, and in particular the execution of the wounded James Connolly, had shocked the Irish people. Journalist F.A. McKenzie also noted that the ordinary working-class people of Dublin who had been beaten back into their slums during the 1913 lockout had a deep sympathy for the rebel cause:

> I have read many accounts of public feeling in Dublin in these days. They are all agreed that the open and strong sympathy with the mass of the population was with the British troops. That was so in the better parts of the city, I have no doubt, but certainly what I myself saw in the poorer districts did not confirm this. It rather indicated that there was a vast amount of sympathy with the rebels, particularly after the rebels were defeated. The sentences of the courts martial deepened this sympathy.

On 9 June the British authorities started transferring the Irish prisoners to Frongoch prison in Wales. An old whiskey distillery, Frongoch was converted into a prison camp for German prisoners-of-war. The internment of almost 2,000 republicans in one concentration camp was a grave mistake by the British authorities. Eleven Claremen were interned in Frongoch which the Irish republicans quickly converted into a political university and military academy. Within the camp the IRB began to reorganise under Michael Collins and Henry Dixon.

Republicans from every county in Ireland drilled, trained, debated and organised.

Not all of the republican combatants had surrendered after the rebellion. Despite the loss of the German arms shipment, fighting had taken place in Galway under the command of Liam Mellows. Almost 1,000 Volunteers had mobilised throughout the county having received Pearse's orders for the rebellion on Easter Monday evening. They captured the barracks in Oranmore and occupied the town of Athenry, for a time successfully defending the area from RIC assaults. On Thursday night of Easter week word reached Mellows' headquarters at Moyode Castle that the British army were advancing on their position. On Friday morning Mellows demobilised the majority of his men and led a column of 500 republicans southwards in a retreat towards Clare. With the British military in pursuit, the column was disbanded on Saturday 29 April when the Volunteers in Dublin surrendered. Mellows, a wanted fugitive, continued southwards towards Clare with Frank Hynes and Alfie Monaghan.

Michael Moloney, a member of the Irish Volunteers and the IRB from Crusheen, was searching the Knockjames hills for a stray horse when he spotted the three crouching on the ground trying to hide from him. He approached, and when he was close enough hailed them. Liam Mellows was sleeping while Hynes was kneeling beside him trying to remain hidden from the approaching stranger. The three republicans came into the open and returned Moloney's greetings. Moloney approached, waving a white handkerchief as a flag of truce. Mellows and his comrades told Moloney they were cattle drivers on their way from the Scariff fair, but this did not impress Moloney: 'You're Sinn Féiners. But they're not bad fellows at all. Indeed I'm one myself.' The three fugitives remained sceptical of their good luck and quizzed Moloney on his knowledge of internal IRB politics. When they were satisfied that he was a genuine republican they admitted that they were republican rebels who had escaped from the fighting in Galway. He led them to an abandoned building on his land. It was the perfect hideout, overgrown with heather and blackthorn trees. The building was hardly visible ten yards away but its doorway commanded a wide view of Tulla and Sliabh Bernagh. Moloney assured the men that they would be safe there and he would return with food and help later.

Moloney contacted Con Fogarty and Seán McNamara with news of Mellows' arrival. McNamara began to collect funds to support the three men, among trusted Volunteers and local IRB men. Con Fogarty visited the shelter every few days after dark, bringing the men food and supplies. Moloney later travelled to Galway to see Hynes' wife, who lived at Athenry. He was carrying a message that Mellows was trying to get to the Dublin republicans, when he was stopped and searched by the RIC. Moloney had hidden the message in his pipe and while the police were searching his shoes Moloney casually lit his pipe, destroying the message.

Mellows, Monaghan and Hynes had spent almost five months hiding in the Knockjames hills near Crusheen with the help of the local republicans until word came from Irish Volunteer headquarters in Dublin in October 1916 that Mellows should go to America. Mellows travelled to Cork where he met with Captain Robert Montieth, who had come ashore from the German U-boat with Roger Casement on Good Friday. Both men travelled to Birmingham together and then onto New York.

The public shock caused by the executions of the republican leaders led to a swing in support, from John Redmond's IPP and its demands for home rule, towards the republican ideal and unlimited independence for the Irish people. This shift was a gradual one. Clare republicans like Seán McNamara still had to be careful about their political activities: 'I continued as a member of the Irish Volunteers after the 1916 Rising but in my locality, though the organisation did not disintegrate, we had to lie low. There was a good deal of condemnation of the rising to be heard among the people in general and it took some time before the motives of the executed leaders were fully appreciated.' The Irish Volunteer organisation had survived the arrests that followed the rising but remained inactive for a short period afterwards to avoid attention from the authorities and further arrests. The Volunteer companies that continued meeting and drilling through May and June did so in remote areas beyond the eyes of the RIC.

If executing the republican leaders was the British administration's first mistake, the internment of almost 2,000 republicans in Frongoch was its second. On 21 December 1916 Henry Dukes, the British chief secretary for Ireland, announced: 'The time has come when the risk of liberating the internees would be less than the risk which might follow detaining them longer.' The releases were greeted with parades and other celebrations in Clare. In Feakle the local Volunteer company paraded to welcome home Tadhg Kelly. Within hours of his return Kelly was in contact with Thomas Tuohy arranging the mobilisation of the local company and their continued reorganisation. In West Clare Art O'Donnell followed suit and immediately started training and drilling the local Volunteers. Seán Ó Muirtheille, a member of the IRB and Gaelic League organiser in Clare, met O'Donnell in Limerick and asked him to attend a conference in Kilrush with Éamonn Fennell and a number of other Volunteers. The meeting was informal but it began the reorganisation of the Volunteers in West Clare. The Volunteer organisers still had no contact with the republican leadership but resumed communications with their battalion headquarters in Limerick. O'Donnell also encountered the change of public opinion in favour of the republicans: 'The people in general were a lot more friendly toward us, and where previous to the insurrection we ran up against open hostility we now encountered friendliness.'

4

I Die in a Good Cause

They have branded me a criminal.
Even though I die, I die in a good cause.

Thomas Ashe

While radical events in Ireland were changing the political landscape, hundreds of thousands of Irishmen continued to fight for Britain in the First World War. The death of William Redmond, MP, at Messines brought political matters in Ireland to a head by causing a by-election for East Clare. The IPP had held the seat without contest since 1892 but were now facing a serious challenge from the new Sinn Féin party, who had already defeated the IPP in two by-elections.

At the time of the Easter Rising the IRB had no substantial political wing. In the absence of a republican party of their own the IRB had attempted to manipulate the moderates of the IPP and Griffith's Sinn Féin party into supporting their aims. The republicans had far more influence within Griffith's Sinn Féin party than the IPP but by 1910 the *Irish Nation* accurately described Sinn Féin as being 'in the last stages of an inglorious existence'. The IRB attempts to influence both parties were effectively abandoned after the outbreak of the European war when the republicans and supporters of Irish neutrality were collectively dubbed 'Sinn Féiners' by the British establishment in Ireland. Other than trying to exploit Griffith's Sinn Féin party for their own purposes the IRB had little interest in its politics. The only real connection between Griffith's Sinn Féin party and the republicans was their common policies of Irish neutrality and opposition to military conscription. The pro-British press in their ignorance failed to distinguish between the positions of the

IRB leaders and Griffith and on 28 April *The Irish Times* claimed the rebellion in Dublin was a Sinn Féin insurrection. The name Sinn Féin stuck in the minds of the Irish people and forced an unlikely union between Griffith's monarchist Sinn Féin party and the republicans. Frustrated by the British government's failure to grant home rule and appalled at the executions that followed the Easter Rising, the Irish people expressed increasing support for the republicans and developed a keen interest in 'the Sinn Féiners'. The takeover of Griffith's party by the republicans was inevitable.

The first two elected Sinn Féin MP's were not followers of Griffith's Sinn Féin policy and were elected on the strength of their connections with the Sinn Féin rising. The first man elected on a Sinn Féin ticket, Count Plunkett, had no definite political policy and was elected because of his son's execution after the rising. It was only after his election that Plunkett gave his public support for abstentionism. The only consistent part of Plunkett's policy throughout his campaign was his promise that he would represent Ireland's claim to independence at the international peace conference after the war.

The second man elected for Sinn Féin was Joe McGuinness, a member of the IRB interned in Lewes jail after the Easter Rising. McGuinness was opposed to his selection as a candidate because he believed constitutional politics was a compromise of traditional republican policies. In an effort to strengthen the IRB's hold over Sinn Féin, Michael Collins ignored McGuinness' wishes and established a successful campaign on his behalf. The campaign to elect McGuinness used posters featuring a man in prison uniform with the slogan 'Put him in to get him out. Vote for McGuinness, the man in jail for Ireland.' The campaign was based almost entirely on the fact that he was interned after the Easter Rising.

In March 1917 Count Plunkett organised a conference between the different groups of Irish separatists in Dublin. IRB members dominated the meeting and over the next few months the republicans succeeded in completely taking over the Sinn Féin leadership; the selection of candidates was controlled by the IRB. Throughout Ireland, branches of nationalist and separatist organisations applied to affiliate to Sinn Féin, transforming the ailing political party into a national movement. Sinn Féin was still the 'broad platform' Griffith has described in 1907 but now the IRB and their supporters were in a clear majority. The new Sinn Féin executive contained a wide range of different political views, home rulers and right-wing nationalists led by Arthur Griffith and Eoin McNeill, who found themselves in a coalition with hardline republicans like Rory O'Connor and socialist republicans such as Countess Markievicz. The republicans gradually succeeded in converting Sinn Féin policy from Griffith's ideal of dual monarchy to support for an Irish Republic.

At the Sinn Féin ard fheis in October 1917 the delegates adopted a new constitution, and Éamon de Valera was elected president of the organisation. Despite the misgivings of many republicans, Eoin McNeill was brought back into the fold by de Valera and became a leading member of the new Sinn Féin party, despite protests from Kathleen Clarke and Countess Markievicz. With McNeill's arrival the 'respectable' class again had a foot in the revolutionary movement.

The East Clare by-election presented the reformed Sinn Féin party with another opportunity to exploit the shift away from conservative nationalism towards republicanism. The Sinn Féin clubs in Clare began to search for a republican candidate who could successfully contest the election. Thomas Ashe, a Kerry republican and a veteran of the Easter Rising who had succeeded Patrick Pearse as president of the IRB, was widely proposed as a candidate. Ashe was assured by his cousin Pádraig Ashe, an Irish teacher in West Clare, that he could easily head the poll in the county. However, Ashe refused the nomination. Instead Peadar Clancy, a native of West Clare who was sentenced to death for involvement in the 1916 Rising in Dublin, was selected as the republican candidate for Clare by the existing Sinn Féin clubs in the county but this decision was not accepted by the central executive. A convention was held in the Old Ground Hotel in Ennis on 14 June to decide on a final candidate for the elections and de Valera was selected as the republican candidate.

De Valera was an unknown figure in Clare at the time, although he had a reputation as 'the hero of Boland's mills' for his role in the rising. De Valera was still in prison at the time of his nomination and many local republicans were puzzled by his selection over better known personalities like Peadar Clancy. Seán Murnane of the Newmarket Volunteers said: 'I might as well be candid and say that, to me, the name of the candidate was unknown, and when I came back home our local supporters were all surprised to hear we were going to back up a person bearing such a strange name.' The reservations about de Valera's selection were not limited to Newmarket on Fergus and de Valera was commonly known in Clare as 'the Spaniard' or 'the man with the strange name'. The newspapers of the day were not filled with photos of political figures and few of the electorate would ever have seen the candidate; instead they encountered dozens of young republican members of Sinn Féin, Cumann na mBan and the Irish Volunteers campaigning on his behalf. De Valera's low personal profile was irrelevant; the poll was presented to the electorate as a straightforward choice between home rule and an independent Irish Republic. As with the two previously elected Sinn Féin MPs, all that mattered was that de Valera had a strong association with the Easter Rising and supported an Irish Republic.

The people of Clare caught their first glimpses of 'the man with the strange name' when de Valera arrived at Ennis railway station on 23 June. He was received by a large crowd of Sinn Féin supporters and a display of force by over 1,000 members of both Cumann na mBan and the Irish Volunteers. He was then taken by car to O'Connell Square, where he addressed the first in a series of highly charged political meetings, before retiring to the Sinn Féin election headquarters at the Old Ground Hotel. The Sinn Féin campaign in the East Clare by-election was built on de Valera's support for an Irish Republic but principally on his involvement in the Easter Rising. Because of this, other leading figures who had fought in Dublin were brought to Clare to support the campaign, including Countess Markievicz, who had fought for the Citizen Army, Thomas Ashe, who commanded the Irish Volunteers at the battle of Ashbourne, and Peadar Clancy.

The election campaign became increasingly bitter as the IPP realised it was fighting to maintain its political existence. Sinn Féin did not want to lose the momentum of their previous victories in Roscommon and Longford. Patrick Brennan was appointed commander of the Irish Volunteers, who were to act as a republican police during the East Clare campaign, keeping order during political meetings, protecting Sinn Féin speakers from assault, canvassing for Sinn Féin, whitewashing republican slogans on walls and guarding ballot boxes and polling stations.

Republican supporters and Sinn Féin speakers came under frequent attack during the campaign and members of the Irish Volunteers, including William McNamara, accused ex-British army soldiers and members of the Irish National Volunteers of sparking the violence:

> They attacked anywhere they saw a Sinn Féin supporter, particularly if he happened to be wearing the Sinn Féin colours or if they happened to be alone. They were supplied with free drink by many of the publicans, the majority of whom were hostile to Sinn Féin. At times they were like lunatics attacking with knives and heavy sticks. The Volunteers in Ennis were on duty night and day during the whole election … On a few occasions violent clashes occurred between themselves and the supporters of the Irish Party candidate.

During the first few days of campaigning a group of Sinn Féin supporters from Limerick who were travelling with de Valera between Broadford and Tuamgraney were stopped in their journey by a barricade of stones built across the road. When they attempted to clear the barricade a volley of rifle fire rang out from a nearby hedge, with one bullet piercing the petrol tank of their car. A week later when de Valera was again due to use the same road Patrick Brennan and eight of the Ennis Volunteers lay in ambush along the stretch of road hoping to engage de Valera's attackers, but the assault on the republicans was not repeated. On this occasion de Valera and the other Sinn Féin speakers travelled to O'Callaghan's Mills unhindered, and succeeded in addressing an election rally. While the speeches were being made, the attention of the RIC was drawn to a tricolour that had been raised opposite the police barracks. While most local people were a good distance away attending the Sinn Féin rally, the RIC tied a rag soaked in paraffin to a long wooden staff in an attempt to burn the republican flag. The police succeeded it setting fire to the flag but the flames were fanned by a strong wind and set fire to the roof of a thatched house, burning it to the ground.

During the campaign people were arrested by the RIC for singing 'disloyal' songs, speaking in Irish, flying tricolours or wearing Sinn Féin badges; in short, they were arrested for any trivial reason the RIC could find which could be interpreted as an expression of political feeling. A young man was given a month in prison for carrying a Sinn Féin banner; another man was given five months for being in the company of a group of youths carrying a republican flag; a sentence of a month in prison was also imposed on a man who 'whistled derisively at the police'.

The Catholic Church could sense the rising support for the republicans and they realised that if Sinn Féin replaced the IPP as the dominant force in Irish politics their iron grip on Irish society could be broken. However, if Sinn Féin's successes were only temporary and the Church supported the wrong party, then the IPP would punish them for it. In the end the bishops played a careful waiting game. The most senior Church figures – bishops, canons and parish priests – continued to support the IPP as long as they held political power, but they hedged their bets by allowing some priests to come out publicly in support of Sinn Féin. They intended to sit firmly on the fence until it was clear who was going to hold power in Ireland and then come down on their side.

Only five Catholic priests in Clare had spoken publicly against the IPP and their policies before the 1916 Rising, but now whenever de Valera mounted a platform to give a speech he was immediately surrounded by Catholic priests eager to show their supposed conversion to republicanism. These were the same men who had condemned the rising only a year earlier, called for the execution of Pearse and Connolly and had never spoken out against any aspect of British rule in Ireland. There were some priests, such as Fr O'Flanagan, a Sinn Féin national organiser, who were genuine republicans but these clerics were always in a minority and rarely held positions of any power in the Church.

Fr Hayes from Feakle denounced Sinn Féin as having a policy of 'socialism, bloodshed and anarchy which struck at the root of authority' and appealed to his congregation 'to save our country and our religion from a great danger by returning Mr Lynch and not a foreigner by an overwhelming majority at the head of the poll'. The result was declared on Wednesday, 11 July. De Valera had polled 5,010 votes against Lynch's 2,035. This was a huge victory for Sinn Féin and the Irish Republic.

Since early 1917 Clare republicans had become increasingly aggressive in gathering rifles and ammunition for the Irish Volunteers. At the time Irishmen home on leave from the British army routinely carried their rifles, ammunition and equipment with them. With a fresh air of defiance against the British authorities, the Irish Volunteers in Clare regularly held up soldiers at gunpoint and relieved them of their burden. Some British soldiers, such as Joseph Clancy, a native of Kilkishen, were in sympathy with the republicans and arranged to be 'robbed' of their rifles and equipment while home on leave.

Three British soldiers, Private John Bolger of the Australia and New Zealand corps, and Privates Patrick Keane and Michael Keane of the Royal Munster Fusiliers, were returning from leave on the Kilrush to Ennis train when they met Countess Markievicz, who was doing electoral work for Sinn Féin. Markievicz engaged them in political debate and managed to convince the three that they were fighting the wrong war. So strong were her arguments that having arrived in Ennis the three soldiers made contact with members of the local company of the Irish Volunteers and handed their rifles and ammunition over to the republicans. When the soldiers reported to the barracks without their rifles an investigation discovered what had happened and all three were court-martialled. Private Bolger was given a stern reprimand but no other punishment. Michael Keane was sentenced to six months' continuous service at the front. Private Patrick Keane was sentenced to death, but this was commuted to continuous service at the front; later he won a reprieve after he saved the life of a British officer.

De Valera's electoral victory had given a fresh impetus to the republicans and scared the British authorities, so much so that the county inspector of the RIC applied for an extra 150 soldiers to be sent to Clare immediately, with the additional promise that another 150 would be trained at the Curragh for duty in Clare. New Sinn Féin clubs and Irish Volunteer companies were established throughout the county where there had never been any republican organisations before. The ranks of the established Irish Volunteer and Cumann na mBan companies were swelled with new recruits. Though public drilling and training had been declared illegal in Ireland after the Easter Rising, as part of de Valera's election campaign Patrick Brennan had continued to organise, train and publicly drill the Irish Volunteers in Ennis. The RIC were always present at Volunteer mobilisations, monitoring proceedings and noting the names of the participants.

Patrick Brennan received information through a sympathetic RIC man that the police planned to arrest him. Brennan discussed the situation with a number of other senior Volunteer officers in Clare including his brother Michael:

> We were all well aware of how quickly men would tire of the monotony of repetitive drill movements and the necessity of emotional stimulants. We knew we would have to go forward or in spite of our efforts we would be dragged back. Public drilling would stimulate interest as the British would have to treat it as a challenge and take action against us … We felt the people were right for a defensive attitude and that we might give them a lead.

The Clare Volunteers continued to defy the ban on public drilling and to exploit the arrests of Volunteer leaders for political reasons in an attempt to embarrass the British authorities. The agreed strategy was simple: Volunteer units were to hold public parades, preferably in the presence of the RIC. When they were inevitably arrested and charged before a British court the Volunteers were to refuse to recognise the right and authority of a British court to try them in Ireland and not offer any defence. If they were sentenced to imprisonment, the Volunteers were to go on hunger strike until they were granted prisoner-of-war status.

Hunger striking, called 'cealacha' in old Irish, was an ancient tradition dating back to the pre-Christian era – if a person had been unjustly treated by a chieftain and had no other recourse, they would sit on the doorstep of their offender and begin a hunger strike, until death if necessary, and bring to public attention the injustice of their plight, shaming the offender into compromise. Hunger striking re-emerged as a political tool in the early twentieth century when it was used by imprisoned suffragettes fighting for women's right to vote. By 1913 the brutal and painful method of force-feeding used against suffragettes had become so controversial that the British government introduced the Prisoners Temporary Discharge Act, better known as the 'Cat and Mouse Act'. This act allowed hunger strikers to be unconditionally released for short periods and re-arrested when they had regained sufficient health. Inspired by the suffragettes' successes in fighting for women's rights, the Clare republicans adopted the hunger strike as a weapon in their struggle against British rule in Ireland.

Orders to commence public drilling were issued to all Volunteer company captains in Clare in an attempt to force the arm of the British authorities, who took the bait when Patrick, Michael and Austin Brennan became the first Volunteer leaders arrested in Clare for illegal drilling. Patrick Brennan had already selected ten trustworthy Volunteers to take charge of the Ennis Volunteer companies and continue public drilling in defiance of British rule. As soon as Patrick Brennan was arrested, James Madigan stepped from the ranks and began to drill the assembled Volunteers, and was in turn arrested. After Madigan's arrest James Griffey took command and was also arrested. Each time the police arrested the Volunteer drill instructor another man would immediately step forward and continue instructing the Volunteers, making a mockery of the proceedings. Public drilling by the Volunteers and arrests of their leaders followed throughout the county.

The RIC men monitoring one group of Volunteers drilling were shocked to hear their drill instructor announce: 'Don't be afraid of the Peelers. All you have to do if you are sent to Mountjoy is go on hunger strike.' Their report read: 'The law is openly defied, and everything points to a time in the near future when it will be set aside in favour of laws made by the Sinn Féin Convention in Dublin ... Sinn Féin is the law of the land.'

In early August the three Brennan brothers were court-martialled with Peadar O'Loughlin from Liscannor. The four refused to recognise the right of a British court to try Irishmen in Ireland and took no further part in the proceedings. All four were sentenced to two years' hard labour and removed to Cork prison. Michael Brennan and the Claremen began their hunger strike. By this time Irish Volunteer headquarters had adopted the Clare Volunteers' method of protest and issued it as a general order. While the four hunger strikers were being transferred to Dublin by an RIC escort, Michael Brennan received an message from Michael Collins ordering him and his comrades to end their hunger strike:

> At Limerick junction we were given a message from Michael Collins to the effect that large numbers of men had just been arrested and we were to call off our hunger strike until they joined us, as four of us was too small a number to make a resounding fight. We were told that all these men would follow our lead at their trials and Collins had information that they would all be collected into Mountjoy so we would have a strong party.

The four Clare Volunteers ended their protest after receiving this message.

When they arrived in Mountjoy jail they were joined by the other Clare Volunteer leaders who had been arrested for public drilling. Other republican prisoners were transferred to Mountjoy at this time; among them was Thomas Ashe, who commanded the republicans at the battle of Ashbourne in 1916. The republican prisoners in Mountjoy began their protests for prisoner-of-war status by refusing to wear prison uniform. While interned awaiting trial, the republicans were allowed to wear civilian clothes and still wore these when they arrived in Mountjoy. If the jailed republicans wore prison clothes they would be conforming to the British authorities' view that they were criminals rather than prisoners-of-war. The protesting republicans were placed in solitary confinement and given a number of mailbags, which they were expected to sew in their cells. Sewing mailbags was prison work traditionally carried out by criminals and the republicans refused to comply. The prison authorities reacted by confiscating the bedding of the protesting prisoners and in turn the republicans began to break the silence imposed during exercise in the prison yard.

Galway Volunteers, who had been in Mountjoy before the protest began, had been adhering to the prison regulations and worked throughout the prison. They were able to pass messages between the republicans who were held in solitary confinement and republicans held in other areas of the prison. Patrick Brennan had been selected as leader of the republican prisoners from Clare and managed to circulate a message ordering all the protesting prisoners to request a meeting with the prison governor the following Saturday morning, 11 September, to demand treatment as prisoners-of-war. That Saturday every republican prisoner in Mountjoy arrived in the governor's office making the same demand; this sent the governor into a rage and he ordered all the prisoners to be returned to their cells.

A few days afterwards the republicans were given work chopping timber in the wood yard, with each prisoner confined in a separate cubicle. While this work segregated the republicans from criminal prisoners and gave them limited association, it did not give them free association or the right to congregate and talk freely. The prisoners threw off all restraint and began openly flouting the rules, moving about, talking freely and abandoning their work. They were taken back to their cells and the governor cancelled their association in the wood yard. The next day when the republican prisoners were taken for exercise they were brought to the yard with the criminal prisoners. Prisoners were supposed to exercise spaced out, three or four yards apart, without talking. The republicans ignored the rules and walked around in groups talking freely while the infuriated prison warders could only watch and threaten them with even harsher conditions.

The prison governor cancelled all exercise for the republican prisoners, and ordered them to be confined to their cells. William McNamara and the other republicans were quick to respond:

> Then the fun started. We broke the cell windows, furniture and everything we could lay our hands on. The first move in reply by the prison authorities was that all prisoners detained for political offences were transferred to one wing, C.I.18, and all convicts removed to other wings. This was really to our advantage and it was then easier to arrange for concerted action. The smashing of furniture was followed by the breaking of our cell windows, which in my case at any rate was later to cause me considerable discomfort when there was nothing to seal off the cold draughts when I was lying in my cell on hunger strike. Several warders who were rushed into our wing made an attempt to put us in irons but failed as they were resisted; we fought with legs of tables and stools.

Word spread quickly among the republican prisoners that a hunger strike had been called and that evening thirty-eight of the republicans refused dinner. The hunger strike began on 20 September 1917. Seventeen of the thirty-eight republican prisoners on hunger strike were Clare Volunteers, imprisoned for illegal drilling.

For the first two days of the hunger strike the republicans were without any bedding, sleeping on the bare floor of each cell. At meal times each day food was placed outside the republican prisoners' doors but none of them touched it. On Saturday 23 September the prison authorities began the force-feeding of the republican prisoners. The methods that had been used against suffragettes who fought for women's freedom in British prisons were now being used against Irishmen fighting for the freedom of their people.

Prisoners were brought to the prison doctor's rooms and put into a high wooden chair with their legs and arms strapped down. The prisoner's mouth was forced open with a wooden spoon and a rubber tube attached to a pump was forced down the nose or the mouth of the hunger striker and down their throat. A liquid mixture of one pint of milk and two beaten eggs was then pumped into the prisoner's stomach. The whole process usually took ten minutes. Art O'Donnell was one of the first prisoners who experienced the trauma of being force fed:

> Forcible feeding was commenced and the hunger strikers were fed for the first time with milk and eggs pumped through rubber tubing into the stomach. The operation was repeated on Sunday, twice on Monday and once on Tuesday morning. I was taken to be forcibly fed on this Tuesday morning. A new doctor named Dr Lowe was in the cell where the food was forcibly administered and he proceeded to insert the tube, which I thought hurt more than usual, and on the first stroke of the pump I coughed violently. Dr Lowe withdrew the tube, re-inserted it after the fit of coughing had ceased and then completed the operation. I was on the ground floor and after I was taken back to the cell I saw Thomas Ashe going to be forcibly fed. After a short while I saw a warder go to his cell, which was placed on the floor over mine and opposite to me, and I then saw the warder return with his overcoat ... On that day we were forcibly fed once only, but on the next day we were forcibly fed twice, twice again on Thursday, on Friday and on Saturday.

O'Donnell had witnessed Thomas Ashe being led away to his fifth and final force-feeding at 11:15 a.m. It seems he physically resisted being force fed and the doctor had trouble in putting the tube down his throat into his stomach. As soon as the tube was inserted Ashe started coughing violently, the tube was removed and Ashe told Dr Lowe the tube had been pushed down the wrong passage. Dr Lowe dismissed Ashe's claim and again inserted the tube after Ashe stopped coughing. The liquid food mixture was then pumped into Ashe's body. When the tube was withdrawn Ashe vomited up a small amount of the mixture and collapsed in the chair. Dr Lowe ordered the warders to take Ashe back to his cell and let him lie down. At noon Ashe was removed to the Mater hospital where he died two days later of heart failure and congestion of the lungs caused by the attempt to force feed him.

The effect of Thomas Ashe's death on the prisoners was to harden their attitude against any compromise. The hunger strike and force-feeding continued for another five days until 30 September when the prison authorities relented and agreed to grant the republicans prisoner-of-war status. The republicans began taking nourishment again and received medical treatment until they were restored to full health.

The next day, Thomas Ashe's funeral took place. The republicans executed in 1916 had been buried privately by the British in quick-lime graves and as a result neither their families nor the Irish people were able to mark their deaths. In contrast Ashe's funeral became a massive political demonstration in solidarity with the republican struggle. Tens of thousands of people queued to pay their respects as Ashe lay in state in Dublin's city hall. Over 20,000 people attended the funeral, led by a guard of Irish Volunteers and members of the Irish Citizen Army marching in uniform, fully armed in public defiance of the law. The British became embarrassed by the concessions made to the republican prisoners in Mountjoy, yet they had abandoned force-feeding in case the process might create another republican martyr.

After the hunger strike ended, the republican prisoners were transferred to Dundalk jail. There they found that the prison regulations were infringing the prisoner-of-war status they had secured from the British authorities. They were served the same poor quality food as the criminal prisoners and their cell doors were being locked much earlier than the times conceded to the republican prisoners in Mountjoy. It was clear the British authorities were intent on dismantling the republicans' prisoner-of-war status bit by bit. The prisoners began another hunger strike, which lasted fourteen days. The hunger strikers were examined regularly during the protest and weak prisoners were released under the 'Cat and Mouse Act' in large groups over three or four days.

The seventeen Clare Volunteers who had been involved in the Mountjoy hunger strike marched with the other released prisoners and their new MP, Éamon de Valera, to Glasnevin cemetery where they placed a wreath on Thomas Ashe's grave. After the brief ceremony the Clare Volunteers returned to Ennis by train. The political effect of Ashe's death was immediately obvious to William McNamara: 'In Ennis to meet the train that night was a huge crowd to greet us and in that crowd I noticed several people who were our bitter opponents before we were arrested. In my opinion, Thomas Ashe's death on hunger strike did more to help the Sinn Féin cause than anything that had previously happened.' In the year after the Easter Rising republicans had struck two decisive and very public blows against British rule – through their struggle in their prison cells and at the ballot box. While the Irish public eagerly followed these political events in the newspapers, the IRB and the Irish Volunteers were continuing the fight for the Irish Republic far from the gaze of the media, in the by-roads and hills of Clare.

The Brennans continued their work in the East Clare battalion and the Barretts set about building a stronger Volunteer organisation in the Ennis area. Peadar Clancy was sent from Dublin to his native West Clare to reorganise the Irish Volunteers. Volunteer companies that had not met since the Redmondite split in 1914 were reformed and completely new companies were formed throughout the county. The Clare Volunteers had been part of the Limerick brigade until early in 1917 when the organisation in the county had become so large that a separate Clare brigade had been created. While the public followed the fortunes of the Sinn Féin politicians and republican prisoners in their newspapers, the Irish Volunteers continued training and drilling in preparation for the conflict with the British forces that had become unavoidable.

In March the Clare Volunteers had made their first attack on a member of the British forces when the Cloonagh company shot and wounded RIC Constable Johns who was carrying out intelligence work in the Ennistymon area. Martin Devitt, Jack Walsh and John Joe Neylon attacked Constable Johns with a shotgun as he was returning from the barracks at night. Although the Volunteers only succeeded in wounding Constable Johns, he was relieved from duty for a long period while he was recovering from his wounds. Johns took the assassination attempt very seriously and lost his enthusiasm for intelligence work.

The most pressing problem for the Irish Volunteers in Clare remained the lack of arms and ammunition. To remedy this the Volunteers began raids to capture private weapons, starting in the Tubber district on 2 January where the republicans told one man when relieving him of his rifle: 'We will give it back when the war is over.' The same night members of the Ennis company broke into Mulligans' gun shop on Church Street taking a number of rifles, shotgun cartridges and revolver ammunition. The Ennis Volunteers found that the soldiers of the Southern Irish Horse regiment stationed at Edenvale House, outside Ennis, could easily be persuaded to part with their rifles after a few drinks and some bribery. Joseph Barrett and the Ennis Volunteers succeeded in getting twelve Lee Enfield rifles and ammunition from the regiment, before the British army discovered their losses and transferred the Southern Irish Horse out of the area. As soon as the British army realised how many of its soldiers were selling arms and equipment to the republicans they stopped the practice of Irish soldiers taking their rifles home on leave.

New British army regulations had temporarily dried up the supply of rifles but James Madigan, the leader of the Ennis Volunteers, had noticed that the police stationed at the Inch RIC hut usually sent out a patrol every night between 10 and 11 p.m. While this patrol was on their rounds only a sergeant and one other RIC man would be inside the hut. Madigan planned to raid the hut for arms and ambush the foot patrol. He selected eight Volunteers for the ambush, while Madigan himself and William McNamara would lead three more men to raid the hut. Their plan was to knock at the door of the hut and claim that there was a fire in the area; when the door was opened Madigan and McNamara would rush the two policemen inside and hold them up with their revolvers. While the first party captured the RIC hut the second group of eight Volunteers would ambush the patrol as it returned. Only Madigan and McNamara would be armed and the success of the plan relied completely on the element of surprise.

The attempted raid took place on 8 January 1918. McNamara described the attack:

> We knocked on the door of the hut which was partly opened by one of the men inside. However, the door was secured to the jamb inside by a strong chain and this prevented us from getting inside. The policeman inside the door, by putting his back to an interior wall, managed to force the door against us, catching my hand in the jamb. We tried to fire but at first the revolvers refused to work. Eventually we succeeded in letting off two shots, which caused the policeman to release some of his weight

against the door, which then opened enough to enable us to free ourselves. We had no sooner managed to do so when the door was slammed against us and then locked and bolted. The police then opened fire and we were obliged to retreat. The patrol heard the shooting in the distance, as also did the party of Volunteers who were detailed to disarm them. Knowing that the element of surprise, on which they entirely depended, had been lost, they did not wait for the patrol to come along but vacated their positions and moved back to Ennis where we all arrived safely without incurring any suspicion.

When the Clare brigade's headquarters heard about the failed attack at Inch they forbade all arms raids and attacks on the RIC until the Volunteers were better armed and trained.

The continuing war in Europe spread fears of food shortages in the west of Ireland. Following their recent successes in publicly confronting the British forces and capturing arms from them, the Irish Volunteers followed in the Fenian tradition of the Land War. In late 1917 the Clare Volunteers received orders to begin driving cattle off large estates and claiming the land for the Irish people in the name of the Irish Republic. The seized land was then divided among landless men and local farmers with small holdings before being tilled for growing food. As well as gaining the support of the local farming population, republicans like Thomas McNamara, from Mountshannon, felt that they were putting right the land seizures, plantations and evictions that had taken place under British rule:

In many districts large tracts of land had been cleared of tenants in order to make ranches for people of the landlord class, who were mostly absentees and who used the land solely for grazing purposes. The descendents and friends of the evicted tenants never gave up the idea of recovering the farms from which they had been ejected and a continuous agitation was carried out to get the ranches divided. The British government sided with the ranch owners and used the RIC to suppress the popular demand.

The Cloonagh and Kilfenora companies seized three large estates in

Kilfenora and succeeded in ploughing up and redistributing thirty acres of land to local farmers. In the Ennis area cattle were driven from the lands of Dr Howard at Drumcliff and Tom Crewe at Loughivilla; both men were accused of being absentee landlords and were strongly opposed to republicanism. Volunteers from the Bodyke, Feakle and O'Callaghan's Mills companies armed with sticks and hurleys seized cattle belonging to Dr Samson at Moyone and General Gore at Bodyke. The cattle drives began early in the morning and the captured beasts were driven along the road to Scariff with placards affixed to their horns reading: 'The land for the people – the road for the bullocks.' At Scariff bridge the leading section of the Volunteers received word that three armed RIC men were on duty outside the National Bank about a hundred yards away on the road to Mountshannon. Thomas McNamara and the leading Volunteers from the Mountshannon company decided to disarm the police and capture their carbine rifles:

> As soon as the bank was reached we rushed the police. One of them tried to make off on his bike and as he did so I grabbed his carbine and pulled it from him, at the same time knocking him to the ground. I gave this gun to Joe Tuohy of Feakle. Other Volunteers disarmed a second policeman but the third man got away with his gun. He managed to get his back to the wall and fired a number of shots, which caused the crowd to scatter.

On the morning of 24 February 1918 the Ennistymon Volunteers planned to ambush and disarm an RIC patrol at Lavoreen, three miles outside the town. The RIC had been providing a protective escort to the Marrinan family who were involved in a local land dispute. On the morning of the attack two RIC men, Constables Sullivan and Dennehy, were escorting three of the family home from mass in Ennistymon when they were ambushed by six Volunteers – Martin Devitt, Mick and Jack Maguire, Tom and Mickey Kelliher and John Joe Neylon. Devitt and Neylon were armed with revolvers while the other four carried cobblers' knives to cut the straps of the two RIC men's rifles if they tried to resist. Neylon describes the attack:

We took up position on the side of the road, actually sitting on the fence. As soon as the police came along Devitt gave the order 'Hands Up!' They did not comply, but instead threw down their bikes, which at that stage they were pushing beside them, and attempted to un-sling their carbines. We opened fire and knocked out both of them ... We took the carbines and left one of them in the Lavoreen area and hid the other in Devitt's place in Cahersherkin until we got a chance later to take it away to my dump in Ennistymon. We were not masked on that occasion, and though we may have been known to the Marrinan family, the RIC must not have got any information from them as to the identity of the attackers as none of us was arrested.

That evening the Newmarket on Fergus Volunteers carried out a cattle raid at Manus, about five miles outside Ennis. The cattle had been commandeered from the McInerneys' land and were being driven towards Ballygireen when the Volunteers encountered a force of RIC men at Castlefergus, a mile south of the McInerneys' lands. The police opened fire on the Volunteers, wounding three of them. Volunteer John Ryan from Crossna had been shot in the back by the RIC and was taken to the Ennis infirmary where he died of his wound on 1 March. The RIC claimed to have given repeated warnings to the republicans and fired over their heads as a final warning before opening fire. Ryan was given a military funeral by the local company of the Irish Volunteers but due to a large British army presence they were unable to fire a volley over Ryan's grave until the mourners and British soldiers departed.

By the end of February raids for arms, intimidation of landlords and their agents, shootings, cattle driving, trespassing and illegal ploughing were widespread throughout Clare and the attack on the RIC at Ennistymon made it clear to the British government that they were losing control. In an effort to enforce British rule, Clare was declared a 'special military area'. Extra British soldiers were transferred to the county and British army garrisons were established in almost every town and village. The RIC's strength in Clare was also greatly reinforced. A curfew was imposed in Ennis with military checkpoints established and soldiers patrolling the town's streets. Fairs, markets, GAA matches and all public occasions were prohibited. Drinking hours in pubs were restricted and the use of cameras in public was banned. The *Clare Champion* was temporarily banned and the British authorities censored telegrams and letters. Entry into Clare and travel through the county was restricted and motor cars were frequently stopped and searched. An RIC permit was needed to travel from one RIC sub-district to another, while the main roads were frequently barricaded and guarded by British soldiers. Political meetings were banned and all printed matter was censored.

Clare's designation as a 'special military area' did not stop the Irish Volunteers from drilling and training; they simply carried on in secret. At the same time orders arrived from Irish Volunteer headquarters in Dublin forbidding Volunteer participation in cattle drives and land disputes. Cattle drives has earlier been supported by the IRB element trying to control the Irish Volunteers but had only received a cautious welcome from the more conservative members of Sinn Féin, who conceded that cattle drives were 'justifiable' but warned against 'foolish or indiscrete action'.

On 28 March the Carrigaholt Sinn Féin club was holding its weekly meeting in the town hall. The night before, a group of Royal Welch Fusiliers stationed in Kilrush had travelled to Carrigaholt by boat and camped in Burtons' wood, a quarter of a mile outside the town. The presence of these soldiers was not detected until they marched into Carrigaholt shortly after the Sinn Féin meeting began and raided the hall. Éamonn Fennell was chairman of the meeting:

About noon, a knock came to the door, which I opened. A British military officer was outside along with some soldiers carrying fixed bayonets. He inquired if I was in charge and I said 'Yes'. He then inquired if Michael Keane was inside. I again said 'Yes'. He then asked for Keane who went out to him. The officer then said to me: 'You must clear this hall.' I asked what he meant by this action and said this was a meeting of the Sinn Féin club which we had a perfect right to hold, that we had been holding meetings every Sunday without interference. He thereupon shouted an order to his men to charge and, simultaneously, soldiers with fixed bayonets burst in through the door and formed up into a square in the centre of the room. A military sergeant gave orders to clear the room. Some of the members got out by the back door. I was still at the front door trying to keep it open as the soldiers had begun to lunge with their bayonets and our people began to stampede. I next felt a bayonet stab in the back which caused me to let go of the door, and in a rush out of the building the crowd swept me out into the street. Outside I heard that Doctor Studdert was in Behans' hotel and I went up to see him. I found him attending Thomas Russell, a Kerryman who was employed by the Gaelic League as an Irish teacher. Russell had been severely wounded by a bayonet thrust while at the Sinn Féin meeting. Dr Studdert treated my wound and also those of two others who had been bayoneted. Russell was removed to Kilrush hospital the following morning but died that night.

A dozen members of the Sinn Féin club received serious bayonet wounds during the British military's raid on the meeting. Thomas Russell's body was returned to his native Dingle for burial.

However, German advances on the western front quickly over-shadowed these dramatic events in Clare. As the war dragged on and Irish newspapers printed long weekly lists of casualties, British recruiting advertisements became even more desperate – without result – in their search for cannon fodder. The German army's March offensive was a disaster for the British army in France as the Germans had almost completely encircled Reims and were now within striking distance of Paris. The British army's need for fresh recruits became the British government's top priority. In Britain the age limits for con-scription were expanded and the British cabinet now proposed that conscription should be enforced in Ireland. The decision to extend conscription to Ireland was publicly announced on 9 April. To soften the blow of enforced conscription Lloyd George offered the Irish people a simultaneous Home Rule Bill, which included the partition of part of Ulster. So thousands more young Irish men and boys would have to die in a foreign war before Britain would finally grant them a meagre measure of independence. One thing was clear: the British war effort still needed thousands more Irishmen to secure a British victory, but British politicians were not prepared to grant these same Irishmen any further measure of independence in return. Some employers and supporters of the IPP had already done their part for the war effort by firing large numbers of their employees. This served two ends: men were forced through unemployment to join the British army while women workers, exploited as cheap labour, took their places. In spring 1917, a British government decree institutionalised this practice by barring employers from filling vacant positions with men between the ages of 16 and 62 which the Irish dubbed 'hunger conscription'.

The effect of the conscription threat was to force a temporary alliance between Sinn Féin and the IPP which blurred the anti-conscription and nationalist movements into Sinn Féin's image. This was something that the Sinn Féin leadership had been attempting to achieve for over nine months. The conscription crisis was a major boost for the Sinn Féin party as it effectively destroyed the IPP's stranglehold on Irish politics. When the conscription bill passed through the British parliament on 16 April, the IPP withdrew from the House of Commons in protest. This was seen by the Irish public as an admission by Redmond's followers that Sinn Féin's policy of abstentionism had been right all along. The British government's actions had shown that Sinn Féin's three MPs who refused to take their seats in Westminster had more influence than the seventy members of the IPP who sat in the British parliament. Sinn Féin had always been consistent in opposing Ireland's participation in England's war using the slogan 'If you have to fight for the freedom of small nations, fight for the freedom of Ireland first', but the IPP had encouraged the Irish National Volunteers and thousands of other Irishmen to fight in the British army and its members were still appearing on British army recruiting platforms while supporting the anti-conscription campaign. The IPP's support for the British war effort and British army recruitment, while opposing conscription, was seen as deeply hypocritical and cynical. To the ordinary Irish people it seemed that Sinn Féin alone was blocking conscription, and as a result Sinn Féin quickly gained control of the anti-conscription movement.

On 18 April an anti-conscription conference took place in the Mansion House in Dublin. Representatives from Sinn Féin, the Irish Transport and General Workers Union, the IPP, the All for Ireland League (a smaller home rule party that had split from the IPP) and various Church leaders met to coordinate their efforts against conscription. An anti-conscription pledge was drawn up and signed throughout Ireland. The ITGWU issued a call for a one-day general strike against conscription on 24 April which closed shops and industries everywhere, except the most hard-line unionist areas.

The ranks of Irish Volunteer companies in Clare swelled as young men, in whose interest it was to prevent conscription, joined up. For them there was no way to avoid a fight – they could either be forced into the British army and fight for them in France or they could resist this by force and join with the Irish Volunteers to fight against Britain. The republican anti-conscription campaign had changed the public's perception of those opposed to conscription from a self-serving movement by men who simply did not want to fight into a patriotic and principled stand against a foreign government's tyranny. Republicans began arming and training to resist the enforcement of conscription. Irish Volunteer leaders like Andrew O'Donoghue noted the great effect the resistance to conscription made to the movement in his area:

> The development of the Irish conscription threat during the winter of 1917 and spring of 1918 caused the Volunteer movement to grow stronger in north Clare. By February of 1918 companies had been established in Ballyvaughan, Ennistymon, Kilshanny, Kilfenora and Toomevara, and the companies which had lapsed in Ballinalacken, Doolin and Liscannor were revived. Protest meetings were held outside every chapel gate on Sunday after mass, and collections were made to which practically every householder in Clare contributed. Within the ranks of the Volunteers the men became more enthusiastic and the determination to resist conscription by every means increased in intensity.

Volunteer parades and mobilisations achieved 100 per cent attendance rates and public drilling and the number of arms raids increased, but most

Volunteers still remained unarmed. Orders were received from Volunteer headquarters in Dublin that these men should be armed with pikes if guns were not available. Pikes were cheap and easy to manufacture and held a strong symbolic value because they had been used in every Irish revolution since 1798. These 'conscription pikes' would almost certainly have been useless if a serious conflict arose with the British forces; however, any weapon was better than none, and as long as the Volunteers were armed in some fashion to resist conscription, it could not be enforced. The armed republican opposition to conscription made it obvious that conscription could not be extended to Ireland without sending thousands of British troops to Ireland to suppress the Irish Volunteers and Sinn Féin. Since the aim of conscription was to provide more troops for the British army, this situation would have been very counter-productive in both military and political terms. The republicans had outmanoeuvred Lloyd George and he had to abandon his plans for conscription in Ireland, but rather than admit defeat the British government kept threatening to enforce conscription until autumn 1918.

However, the British government found another excuse to suppress Sinn Féin in May 1918. On 12 April Joseph Dowling had landed from a German submarine at Crab Island, off the coast of Doolin. Dowling was a British soldier who had been taken prisoner by the German army and joined Roger Casement's German brigade, formed to invade Ireland and fight for the Irish Republic during the Easter Rising. However, Casement's efforts only raised a small force of Irishmen, most of whom, like Dowling, were not sent to Ireland in 1916. By summer 1918 the German military realised that they were losing the war and were searching for a way to open a new military campaign. The German military leadership had been impressed by how long the republicans had held out against the British forces during the Easter Rising and the growth in republican militancy since. The German army recruited Dowling to return to Ireland on a mission to establish contact with the IRB leadership and the new Sinn Féin movement, in the hope that they could use another republican rebellion as a second front against the British army.

After Dowling landed on Crab Island from the German submarine, he swam ashore and travelled to Ennistymon to try and contact the local Irish Volunteer company. He eventually found his way to Roughans' garage where Volunteer Tom McDonough worked:

> A strange looking, rather peculiarly dressed man came into the garage and told me he was anxious to get in touch with Irish Volunteer officers. As he was a complete stranger I gave him no information. He hung around the vicinity of the garage for an hour or so, during which time I learned that he had only just arrived in the town, having got a lift in a car from Lisdoonvarna. I went to the shop where [John Joe] Neylon, the company captain, was employed, and told him about the stranger and his enquiries. Neylon came with me but before we got back to the man or had any chance to talk to him, RIC men came out of the barracks and took him in with them.

Dowling was arrested for his suspicious behaviour and the RIC men searching him found documents from the German military intended for the republican leadership requesting that they re-establish contact, and seeking information on the prospects for a second republican rising. Dowling was tried by the British and sentenced to life imprisonment. Neither the IRB, the Irish Volunteers nor the leadership of Sinn Féin had any prior knowledge of Dowling's mission. This did not stop the British government from inventing a 'German plot' led by Sinn Féin.

Lord French, the new British viceroy in Ireland, was only five days in office when he issued a proclamation announcing the discovery of the German plot and Sinn Féin's fictitious involvement in the conspiracy. The British government used the announcement of the plot to arrest a large number of leading Sinn Féin activists in the hope of destroying the party and breaking the anti-conscription movement. A Dublin Metropolitan Police detective named Kavanagh managed to send notice of the imminent arrests to Michael Collins. Collins informed the Sinn Féin leadership of the British authorities' plans at a meeting that night at Sinn Féin headquarters. De Valera and most of the Sinn Féin leaders, who saw the republican struggle in terms of politics only, decided to accept arrest, knowing that the public outcry at continued British government suppression of Sinn Féin would ultimately be turned into support for the party. Seventy-three leading members of Sinn Féin including de Valera and Griffith were arrested that night and imprisoned without trial. However, the IRB leadership including Michael Collins and Harry Boland, men motivated by military rather than political concerns, escaped arrest along with Cathal Brugha and went on the run. The imprisonment of the political leadership left the IRB and physical-force republicans in control. Under their leadership Sinn Féin became increasingly militant in its tactics and outspokenly republican in its politics.

In September 1918 the Clare IRB lost its most senior member with the death of Thomas O'Loughlin. O'Loughlin was the living link connecting the generation of new republicans with the earlier Fenian movement and had kept militant republicanism alive, armed and trained in north Clare when the other IRB circles throughout the county had been reduced to small groups which talked politics in hushed tones but never contemplated armed action against British rule. O'Loughlin's funeral was an impressive military affair in defiance of the British authorities, with hundreds of Volunteers taking part. Among them was Thomas Shalloo, a member of the Cloonagh company of the Irish Volunteers:

> It was probably the most impressive ceremony that had ever been held in the district. Peadar O'Loughlin ... was in charge of the parade, and the firing party was in the charge of Pat Powell, alias Cahill. Two RIC men from a nearby police hut in Ballydoura came into the graveyard to watch and report on the proceedings. Before the firing party fired the last volleys or produced their guns Cahill called aside myself, Paddy Devitt, Joe Moloney, Ballyagh, Ennistymon, and a fourth man whose name I can't remember and asked us to hold up the police and make them face the graveyard wall while the firing party were discharging their volleys. We got close to the police without arousing their suspicion and then, feigning to be armed by sticking our hands through our coat pockets, we gave them the order 'About Turn'. The firing party then did their job. Though the occasion was a solemn one everyone who

witnessed the hold-up of the police could not help laughing at their plight, and it became the subject of 'song and story' far and wide. The RIC were never popular in Clare but had the reputation of being almost invincible. They were more feared than respected. It was astonishing the effect that small incident had in helping to lessen the people's fear of them in north Clare at least.

The armistice of 11 November 1918 ended the war in Europe and the conscription crisis in Ireland. Some 300,000 Irishmen had fought for Britain; many had enlisted in an attempt to secure Ireland's right to home rule from the British government. Of that number, some 49,000 had been left dead on the battlefields of Europe. Around 4,000 Claremen had enlisted in the British army during the war and at least 500 of these were killed. The ending of the war was celebrated by crowds of loyalists in Dublin who attacked Sinn Féin headquarters at No. 6 Harcourt Street. The frustrated loyalist crowd destroyed the new republican party's headquarters but they had not destroyed the movement itself.

Twelve days later the British government announced the 'khaki election' that would decide the post-war government. Sinn Féin had already been conducting their campaign before the announcement and had decided to act as if the election was a straightforward referendum on the issue of Irish independence. Sinn Féin portrayed itself as the party that had kept Ireland out of the war and had defeated conscription. The party now called upon the Irish people to give it a mandate to represent Ireland's claim to independence at the peace conference which would follow the end of the war and was supposed to be about the rights of small nations. This idea had formed a major part of the republican strategy of the IRB leaders to be implemented after the Easter Rising. Sinn Féin declared that they stood for complete independence and an Irish Republic.

It was obvious that de Valera would stand as the main republican candidate in East Clare but it was uncertain who else would stand for Sinn Féin in the county. Peadar Clancy was proposed as a candidate but the Sinn Féin leadership in Clare were unable to contact him before the deadline for nominations and selected Brian O'Higgins, imprisoned in Birmingham jail, as their candidate. The British authorities in Ireland did their best to disrupt the republican campaign and intimidate Sinn Féin supporters. The British censor deleted one quarter of the Sinn Féin election manifesto. Sinn Féin posters were torn down by the RIC and Sinn Féin papers were suppressed. In Clare and the other counties which had been declared special military areas, the British authorities could simply ban or proclaim Sinn Féin meetings. Outside these areas the RIC broke up Sinn Féin meetings, raided republican clubs and confiscated Sinn Féin election literature. Individual members of Sinn Féin were harassed and intimidated by the police. Robert Brennan, the Sinn Féin director of elections, was arrested and deported to England. In some areas aeroplanes were used to distribute leaflets warning people of the dangers of voting for Sinn Féin. This campaign reinforced the Irish people's belief that the party represented the only real challenge to British rule in Ireland and served to build more support for the republicans.

For the first time the right to vote had been given to all men over twenty-one and to all women over thirty. Seventy-three per cent of the electorate turned out to vote and the large number of young and working-class people voting for the first time resulted in a landslide victory for the republicans. Sinn Féin stood seventy-seven candidates in the election and won seventy-three seats out of a total of 105. De Valera and Brian O'Higgins won their seats unopposed in East Clare. The IPP was reduced to six seats. In the twenty-six constituencies the IPP was so weak that it was not able to stand a candidate to compete with the new republican opposition. The wealthy supporters of the IPP were horrified by the victory of Sinn Féin because it meant that all their inherited political appointments and business contracts were at risk. Without any warning the right of distribution of local appointments and the granting of contracts to family members and cronies had been torn from their hands. They were confronted by a militantly republican populace who had up until then shown interest only in local parish-pump politics. They lay low and were soon spouting patriotically acceptable slogans to the electorate.

Irish unionists had won twenty-six seats in the election. In the province of Ulster the unionists had won the popular vote in only four of the nine counties – Antrim, Armagh, Derry and Down. The people of Tyrone, Fermanagh, Donegal, Cavan and Monaghan had voted for either Sinn Féin or IPP candidates who supported differing measures of Irish independence. It would now take the most twisted view of democracy for the British government to give special treatment to the six of the nine Ulster counties that had been selected for partition.

Sinn Féin's election victory gave them the popular mandate to agitate for an independent Irish Republic, the right to represent the Irish people's claim to independence at the peace conference and the ability to put abstentionism into practice. The republicans were about to move from simply campaigning for the Irish Republic back to fighting for it.

5

Hitting First:
Making Clare Impossible to Police 1919–1920

When you go to war,
hit first, hit hard,
and hit anywhere.

Michael Brennan

Now that Sinn Féin had secured a republican victory in the general election, it began to implement its programme for setting up an abstentionist republican government as an alternative to British rule in Ireland. Harry Boland, the secretary of Sinn Féin, called a meeting of elected Irish MPs for 7 January which decided to fully implement Sinn Féin's policy by convening a public meeting of Dáil Éireann, the parliament of the Irish Republic, on 21 January which would 'accept nothing less than complete separation from England in settlement of Ireland's claims'.

The first meeting of the Dáil took place in the Mansion House; all 105 Irish MPs were invited to attend, including members of the IPP and Unionist Party. Only the Sinn Féin MPs chose to attend, and only twenty-seven were free to do so with the remaining forty-six still imprisoned for their alleged part in the 'German plot'. As the register of Irish MPs' names was read aloud the reply frequently came: 'Fé ghlas ag gallaibh' ('imprisoned by foreigners'). In de Valera's absence Cathal Brugha was elected chair of the proceedings, which were conducted entirely in Irish. Fr Michael O'Flanagan, a Catholic priest and member of Sinn Féin, said a brief prayer. Fr O'Flanagan had been banned from his priestly duties by his bishop for supporting the republican campaign in Cavan East.

The Irish declaration of independence was read aloud and un-animously adopted. As the elected Sinn Féin members stood up to pledge themselves to implementing this declaration Cathal Brugha declared: 'We are now done with England.' Dáil Éireann then ratified the election of de Valera, Count Plunkett and Arthur Griffith as the Irish delegates to the international peace conference. The 'Democratic Programme of the Irish Republic', outlining the rights of the Irish people, was ratified and the proceedings came to an end. The British reacted by introducing censorship of the press and banning publication of the Declaration of Independence, Democratic Programme and speeches made by republican TDs.

At the same time that the elected Sinn Féin TDs asserted the Irish people's right to independence in Dáil Éireann, members of the Irish Volunteers in Tipperary asserted that same right by armed force. Dan Breen, Seán Treacy, Séamus Robinson and six other members of the 3rd Tipperary brigade ambushed two RIC men who were guarding a quantity of explosives being transported to a quarry at Soloheadbeg. The policemen were called upon to surrender as they reached the gates of the quarry. Taken by complete surprise, they raised their rifles to fire and were shot dead.

Though a number of barracks and policemen had been attacked in other parts of Ireland, the fact that the Soloheadbeg ambush took place the same day that the Dáil met and declared independence meant that it received widespread attention in the media. The attack was widely condemned in the press and by the Catholic Church. The ambush was denounced as criminal the following Sunday by the bishop of Cashel. Monsignor Ryan, speaking at St Michael's church in Tipperary, said: 'God help poor Ireland if she follows this deed of blood. But let us give her the lead in our indignant denunciation of this crime against our Catholic civilisation, against Ireland, against Tipperary.' Another priest in Tipperary declared: 'No good cause would be served by such crimes, which would bring on their country disgrace and on themselves the curse of God.'

Alarmed at this backlash, some moderate members of Sinn Féin condemned the attack, but the strong IRB and hard-line republican element at Irish Volunteer headquarters led by Cathal Brugha, the Minister for Defence, issued a statement challenging the Church's position, supporting the action taken by the 3rd Tipperary brigade, and stating that Dáil Éireann was the legitimate government of Ireland and held the right to inflict death on enemies of the state.

With the establishment of the Dáil as the seat of government of the Irish Republic the Irish Volunteers became increasingly known as the Irish Republican Army or IRA. In Clare companies of the IRA came under increasing pressure from the RIC and British army as the British government sought to suppress the growing support for the Irish Republic. While the conscription threat had swelled the ranks of Volunteer companies throughout 1918, the end of the war meant that young men who had joined the Volunteers out of fear rather than for genuine patriotic reasons, abandoned the force. This situation greeted Michael Brennan after he returned from prison to take control of the movement in East Clare: 'I found that the end of the war and the removal of the anti-conscription simultaneously had taken much of the 'kick' out of the Volunteers, and it was difficult to hold them together. On paper we had large numbers, but it was unusual if more than 25 per cent of these reported for any parade. In many places no organised unit remained and all I could contact were two or three individuals.'

In December 1918 Patrick Brennan was issuing reports to IRA head-quarters on the military situation in Clare. Brennan suggested dividing Clare into three areas which would still form part of the one Clare division under the control of a single divisional staff. Brennan and Art O'Donnell met with Richard Mulcahy, assistant chief of staff of the IRA, in December 1918. Mulcahy informed Brennan of the IRA leadership's decision to divide the Clare brigade and its four battalions into three separate brigades in East, Mid and West Clare. Each brigade would be completely independent and responsible only to IRA headquarters in Dublin. Control and discipline among IRA companies throughout Clare was regarded as uneven, and active IRA companies were often isolated with little cooperation between them. It was thought that a more localised leadership would make them more effective. It might also remove the rivalry and tension between the Barretts in Ennis and the Brennans in East Clare. Patrick Brennan opposed headquarters' interference in local brigade politics and resigned his position in protest. Mulcahy travelled to Clare in January 1919 to preside over the creation of brigade areas and the election of brigade officers. Following this the IRA in Clare divided into the three brigades. A border running north from Latoon Bridge outside Ennis towards Killanea and the county border with Galway separated the East and Mid Clare brigade areas. The border between the Mid Clare and West Clare brigade areas ran from Kildysart north-west to Spanish Point outside Miltown Malbay. Each brigade was then divided into six battalion areas labelled A to F, which was further divided into local IRA companies.

The East Clare brigade area contained Feakle, Killaloe, Newmarket on Fergus, O'Brien's Bridge, Quin, Scariff, Sixmilebridge and Tulla. Michael Brennan was commandant of the brigade, while Seán Murnane was brigade quartermaster. The Mid Clare brigade area contained Bally-vaughan, Corofin, Crusheen, Ennis, Ennistymon, Lisdoonvarna and Miltown Malbay. Frank Barrett was commandant of the brigade, Martin Devitt was vice-commandant, Joseph Barrett was brigade adjutant and Éamonn Waldron was brigade quartermaster. The West Clare brigade area contained Carrigaholt, Cooraclare, Kildysart, Kilkee and Kilrush. Art O'Donnell was commandant, Jack O'Donnell was vice-commandant, James Lorrigan was brigade adjutant and Seán Breen was brigade quartermaster.

This reorganisation of Clare into three brigade areas brought a number of rivalries and petty disputes in the Mid Clare brigade area into the open, with some IRA Volunteers opposed to Frank Barrett's selection as commandant. A number of IRA Volunteers of the 1st, 2nd and 3rd battalions and officers in the East Clare brigade split from the IRA to form their own 'independent brigade', an unofficial grouping not recognised by IRA headquarters in Dublin. Over the following months a few Volunteers who had joined the splinter group returned to the Mid Clare brigade, but the 'independent brigade' survived until the following year and their continued existence was a thorn in the side of the Mid Clare Brigade.

Ernie O'Malley, a veteran of the 1916 Rising, was sent to Clare to organise the three new Clare brigades and keep IRA headquarters in Dublin informed of the situation. O'Malley arrived in the Mid Clare brigade early in March and began by contacting Martin Devitt and Peadar O'Loughlin, who were organising the IRA in the Ennistymon area. O'Malley travelled through the area with Devitt and O'Loughlin acting as his guides; all three were wanted by the RIC. The training the Mid Clare brigade received under O'Malley's direction was basic, but it gave the Volunteers experience which proved useful in the coming struggle. The British authorities were aware of O'Malley's presence in Clare and followed his movements closely. One night as he was travelling with his two guides O'Malley was surprised by an RIC patrol:

Peadar O'Loughlin, Maurteen Devitt and I were cycling from Ennis to Kilfenora. At a crossroads we saw police with carbines; at the same time came a command 'Halt There!' We drew our revolvers and fired running for cover. The police used their carbines. It was near sunset. We had carried our bicycles over the ditch. When twilight came Peadar carried our bicycles across the next field while we replied slowly to the ragged police firing. Then we crawled away, reached our bicycles and cycled into the welcome friendly darkness.

The main problem still affecting all three brigades was the lack of arms and ammunition needed for carrying out attacks on the British patrols and barracks. As the IRA in Clare became more active the British authorities increased the number of British soldiers in the county in response. The IRA in Ennis quickly realised this was a blessing in disguise. As William McNamara put it: 'It became apparent to the local Volunteers that some of these new troops had not much faith in the efforts of their government to crush the movement for Irish independence and that they might provide the means to acquire arms and ammunition.' Volunteers approached off-duty soldiers drinking in Ennis enquiring whether they would be willing to sell their rifles and equipment. Many

were, and word of how to earn extra money soon spread among the
British troops. William McNamara was approached by a young Welsh
soldier who said he wanted to sell his rifle because he planned to desert
from the British army. The soldier agreed to meet McNamara the next
morning behind the back wall of his barracks where he handed over
his Lee Enfield rifle and was paid £4 for it by McNamara; the soldier
deserted shortly afterwards and returned to Wales.

About the same time Peadar O'Loughlin met a Scottish soldier named
Donal Campbell from whom he purchased ammunition:

> He was a Devil-may-care type, fond of drink and a good time. I met
> him in much the same way as I had met the other soldier except that
> he came directly into my workshop and straightaway began talking in a
> frank and friendly manner. I sized him up as a man who would be useful
> and safe, and when he had done a good deal of talking in condemnation
> of a soldier's life in this country and of the poor pay he had, I put the
> proposition up to him that he could supplement the pay by selling me
> .303 ammunition which was badly wanted then by the Volunteers, and
> he said it was a bargain.

Over the course of a year Campbell sold O'Loughlin about 1,500 rounds
of .303 ammunition. One night when O'Loughlin was moving a few
hundred rounds he was stopped and searched by a British army patrol:
'One soldier covered me with his rifle while another searched me. The
soldier conducting the search put his hand on my pockets containing
the ammunition and pretended nothing, but on completing the job,
shouted, "OK sergeant" and I was let off. The man who conducted the
search was my confederate, Donal Campbell.'

The Scottish soldiers based in Ennis became particularly useful
as a source of arms for the IRA in the area as they kept approaching
republicans with offers to sell them rifles. One of the local Fianna
Éireann scouts called to William McNamara's home to report that he
had met two Scottish soldiers who wanted to sell their rifles and were
waiting in a field near St Flannan's college. McNamara met the soldiers
and bought their rifles and 100 rounds of ammunition for £8. The two

soldiers said they planned to desert and go back to Scotland. McNamara gave them civilian clothes and in turn the two soldiers traded him their boots, leggings and equipment. The IRA made transport arrangements for the pair but shortly afterwards they reappeared in Ennis looking for McNamara: 'A few days later I was in the bar having a drink with Michael Kennedy. The two of them came in accompanied by four or five other soldiers. They at once recognised us and introduced us to their pals who, they said, were also anxious to desert.' McNamara remembered that many of them had a genuine sympathy for the Irish people's cause: 'They were a decent body of men and the vast majority of them did not relish the particular class of soldiering at which they were employed in Ireland. On pay nights, when a good number of them got a bit tipsy, they could be heard in the pubs in Ennis singing Irish rebel and Sinn Féin songs.'

In the Mid Clare brigade area, information reached Ernie O'Malley and the local IRA officers that a large quantity of arms and ammunition were being stored at the British army outpost in the Golf Links hotel, Lahinch. On Sunday 13 March O'Malley planned to lead a group of twenty local Volunteers to raid the hotel and capture the arms. The attack was due to take place on Sunday night, but that morning the IRA company in Lahinch told O'Malley that the British soldiers there knew of the planned raid and O'Malley was forced to cancel the action. O'Malley then moved to Knockerra in the West Clare brigade area to review the local IRA company at its weekly Sunday parade after 11 a.m. mass. A police sergeant and two constables from the Kilrush barracks had cycled to Knockerra to monitor the parade and gather information on the local republicans. The RIC sergeant was armed with a revolver and the two constables had carbine rifles clipped onto their bicycles.

John Flanagan, the commander of the local IRA battalion, approached Art O'Donnell and O'Malley suggesting that the RIC men be disarmed. Flanagan proposed that the IRA should march past the RIC men on parade, and as they approached, he and Mick Ryan would rush the constables and disarm them while O'Malley would hold up the sergeant. O'Malley agreed to this and went to Miss Nolan's house to collect his .38 revolver. He returned a few minutes later with one hand behind his back concealing the gun. Flanagan, who was drilling the local Volunteer company, took this as the signal that O'Malley was armed and ready. As he began to march the Volunteers off the three RIC men approached Flanagan to arrest him. Flanagan turned to Ryan and gave him the order 'Now Mick!' Flanagan and Ryan had already knocked the two RIC men to the ground when the police sergeant drew his revolver and started shooting at the Volunteers:

> The sergeant at once began to fire from behind, causing the Volunteers to stampede and in their rush forward they knocked Ryan and myself on top of the police on the ground. However, we wrenched the carbines and handed them to a couple of Volunteers to take away. As soon as the sergeant began to fire he was promptly engaged by O'Malley at a range of about fifty yards. He grazed the crown of the sergeant's head with one bullet, knocking off the sergeant's uniform cap. The latter took to his heals and ran towards the main Ennis–Kilrush road. He was followed by the two constables. The Volunteers had scattered in different directions and O'Malley, Ryan and myself were left. We went off to the top of a hill overlooking the church and we were there for some time when a Volunteer came to tell us that the three policemen had returned and gone into Nolans' house. We decided to go down towards Nolans' to watch what was happening but before we got that far we learned that the police had gone off with Art O'Donnell, Michael Mahony and Tom Howard as prisoners. To our intense disgust and amazement we also heard that the two carbines had been recovered by the police. It appears that the Volunteers to whom we had given the carbines took them into Nolans' and hid them under a piece of sacking, and that O'Donnell remained in the house after the police had retreated where he was joined by the other two men. As the only gun we had at our disposal was O'Malley's revolver, the question of pursuing the police and prisoners was considered to be suicidal.

Art O'Donnell was sentenced to two years' imprisonment, while Michael Mahony and Tom Howard were sentenced to one year. John Flanagan and Mick Ryan were now wanted by the police and immediately left for Dublin. When Ernie O'Malley returned to IRA headquarters in Dublin that May Michael Collins had heard about the RIC sergeant's close shave at Knockerra and issued O'Malley with a Webley .45 revolver to replace his .38. Collins used the occasion to tease O'Malley about his poor aim. 'Now get the rifles, and for Christ's sake, Earnan, learn to shoot straight or I'll lose you one of these days.'

As a new initiative to try and break British rule in Ireland, the Dáil sent out a directive to Sinn Féin clubs telling them to form republican courts to replace the British courts. These were to be supported by an unarmed republican police force made up of Volunteers. These two bodies working in conjunction offered a real alternative to the British legal system in Ireland, rendering it completely redundant. Three parish courts and a district court were immediately set up in the West Clare brigade area following this directive and quickly gained jurisdiction over their local area. The courts were presided over by Brian O'Higgins and three other justices who drew up rules of court, rates for costs and scales of fines. The republican police were unpaid and without uniform; they carried out regular policing duties, arresting thieves, breaking up fights and in many cases enforcing drinking hours in pubs much to the despair of local drinkers. Those convicted were usually imprisoned in isolated farm houses and for a time Mutton Island was used as a prison. The republican courts and police became so effective that the British legal system was made redundant in many areas. Soon they had replaced British-controlled courts in twenty-seven counties.

In Clare the IRA continued their attacks against the RIC with the dual purpose of capturing arms and attempting to spark a full-scale military campaign against the British army and the RIC. The Cooraclare barracks was attacked but not captured by the local IRA company. The British responded by building a military post to reinforce the police in the town.

Information gathered by the IRA in the Kilfenora area noted that a police patrol of four RIC men left their barracks at Kilshanny to visit the home of a man named Dwyer each night because of his involvement in a local land dispute. Andrew O'Donoghue, the commander of the local IRA, selected six Volunteers to ambush the patrol at Cahermore Cross, one and a half miles from Kilfenora. The attack took place on

5 July. O'Donoghue posted scouts in the area to keep watch for other police patrols while he positioned the ambushing party. Two of the Volunteers were late in arriving and the RIC patrol arrived earlier than expected. Three members of the IRA were hidden behind a fence facing the Wingfield Road under the command of Thomas Shalloo, while O'Donoghue and Peter Considine were in the corner of a field on the Kilfenora side of the cross. O'Donoghue had a rifle and the other Volunteers were armed with .38 revolvers and shotguns.

The police patrol arrived at 10.30 but was half the expected size with only two RIC men instead of four, one was armed with a .45 revolver the other with a rifle. As the patrol approached, O'Donoghue shouted the order 'Hands Up!' The two RIC men refused, raised their weapons to fire on the Volunteers, but were shot by O'Donoghue and Considine. The policeman carrying the rifle was shot through the wrist and dropped his rifle on the roadside. The pair then fled back towards their barracks. The second policeman armed with the .45 revolver also dropped his weapon after being wounded in the arm, but the gun was attached to his shoulder by a lanyard and the revolver was dangling from him as he ran in retreat. The republicans pursued the two wounded RIC men in the hope of capturing the second policeman's revolver but he arrived back at his barracks safely.

Encouraged by the RIC's withdrawal from Cooraclare the brigade staff of the IRA's Mid Clare brigade decided to attack RIC posts at Connolly, Inch and Lissycasey. Joseph Barrett explains the strength of the RIC in north Clare:

Due to the prevalence of land trouble in Clare for generations before our time, the British government erected all over the county a number of special stations which became known as 'RIC huts'. These stations were additional to the ordinary RIC barracks of which Clare had its quota, like every other county in Ireland. The result was that, by the commencement of the Black and Tan struggle our county had perhaps twice as high an 'RIC population' and twice as many 'RIC centres' to contend with, in proportion to its size, than the rest of the counties. From these very numerous police centres, the authorities were able to keep a close watch on the movements and activities of the Volunteers. The Mid Clare brigade council keenly appreciated these facts and felt that, in order to secure greater freedom of action and more security, it was essential that the RIC should, if possible, be cleared at least out of the smaller stations or huts ... At that particular stage of the struggle, our brigade was poorly equipped with the necessary means for capturing any kind of stone or brick building. We had only about two dozen serviceable rifles, with a small quantity of suitable ammunition. Shotguns were not much use for anything other than preventing the police from coming out, or making a good deal of noise. We had, however, a large number of homemade bombs which I thought might be an effective means of getting the police to surrender and my plan was to open the attacks by getting men to crawl up to the barracks and throw in the bombs through the windows. I hoped that, by doing this, the police would be taken by surprise and they would then yield to our demands to surrender.

The Mid Clare brigade decided to attack the three RIC huts on the same night, 21 July 1919. Joseph Barrett was in command of the attack at Inagh and Martin Devitt led the attack at Connolly. The attack on the RIC post at Lissycasey was cancelled by the local IRA company captain on moral grounds when he heard that the sergeant's wife who lived in the hut was ill.

The attack at Inch lasted several hours. The IRA's homemade hand grenades succeeded in blowing away the rear of the RIC hut but the RIC men inside continued to resist. One of the Volunteers under O'Donoghue's command, Seán Griffey, was trying to force a bomb with its fuse lit through the iron bars guarding the window when it exploded in his hand and the attack had to be abandoned.

The Volunteers also failed to capture the RIC hut at Connolly. The barracks there was a single-storey stone building in an open area guarded by a sergeant and four RIC constables. John Joe Neylon, the captain of the Ennistymon company of the IRA, was transporting the homemade grenades for the ambushing party from Ennistymon to Cloonagh when he fell off his bicycle and was badly injured. Martin Devitt decided to attempt to capture the RIC hut without the grenades when Neylon failed to arrive. Ignatius O'Neill, captain of the Miltown Malbay company, and his cousin, Frank McKenna, a deserter from the British army, had rifles but the other members of the attacking party were armed with shotguns. Devitt began the attack by calling on the sergeant to surrender the barracks while a Volunteer attempted to force the door in with a sledgehammer. When this failed O'Neill and McKenna opened fire with their rifles but the police returned fire from the safety of well-prepared rifle loops. The attack was called off after half an hour because the explosives still had not arrived and Devitt considered that they were simply wasting ammunition.

The Mid Clare brigade kept up the pressure on the RIC by planning to ambush another foot patrol at Derrymore, outside Ennistymon. The IRA in Ennistymon noted that foot patrols left an RIC hut at Derrymore regularly. Andrew O'Donoghue led four Volunteers to disarm the patrol but no patrol came. A week later on 4 August 1919 Martin Devitt was in Ennistymon with John Joe 'Tosser' Neylon when they noticed the two RIC men, Sergeant John Riordan and Constable Michael Murphy, cycle through the town. Both policemen were armed with revolvers and Devitt decided to ambush and disarm them that evening. Sergeant Riordan had been heard boasting in the local area about what he would do to 'any bloody Sinn Féiners' who tried to disarm him. Devitt and Neylon cycled to Séamus Coneally's house and he agreed to accompany them. Devitt selected the same ambush site used a week earlier, a crossroads at Islandbawn, known locally as '81 Cross'. Coneally and Neylon were armed with revolvers but only had six bullets each, Devitt was armed with a revolver to threaten the RIC but had no ammunition. The three republicans did not expect the police to resist when they were confronted, and it was agreed Coneally would tackle one policeman with Devitt, while Neylon disarmed the other. Neylon was crouching behind a bush with the two other IRA men when the RIC approached:

> It was approaching dusk when the two policemen came along. They were cycling abreast and when they were a few yards from the cross

Devitt gave the order 'Hands up!' At this stage we were facing the police in the middle of the road. Instead of putting up their hands the police pulled their guns and opened fire. The sergeant, Riordan, hit Devitt in the first few shots, wounding him through the breast. Devitt disappeared over the fence. Coneally fired one shot and then dropped his rifle and made off. I began firing as soon as the police did and shot the two of them – the constable died almost immediately while the sergeant lived for a few hours. In all seventeen shots were fired in this engagement; the police fired eleven and we fired six. There was only one round in the two revolvers we collected from the police after I shot the two of them. Seeing none of my comrades around I cycled back to Coneally's house. There I found Séamus Coneally in a bad way. He was most depressed, particularly since he thought Devitt was killed. We were talking outside his house … when we heard a good deal of clattering. The next thing we found Devitt along with his own bike, the two policemen's bikes and the rifle which Coneally had thrown away.

Devitt was moved to Con Kearney's house, where his wound was tended to by Dr McDonough of Quin. Constable Murphy had died instantly, but Sergeant Riordan survived long enough to write a short note in a prayer book he had with him. It read: 'Shot by three assassins, wounded them. A repeater did us.' The RIC carried out widespread raids in the area following the ambush but no arrests were made. Although several local people had seen the three Volunteers near the ambush site the RIC received no information.

On 6 August the IRA's East Clare brigade carried out a sniping attack on the barracks at Broadford. The republicans made no serious attempt to capture the barracks and were content with keeping up the pressure on the RIC. Despite the failure of the IRA to capture either the Inagh or Connolly barracks, the RIC decided to evacuate a number of the weaker barracks in the area a few weeks later. The vacated RIC huts at Lissycasey, Inagh and Quilty and the abandoned barracks at Doonbeg were burned by the IRA shortly afterwards. The RIC were withdrawn to larger barracks in towns alongside British army barracks. Piaras Béaslaí later wrote that he considered the attacks a turning point in the history of the struggle: 'It was really in Co. Clare that guerrilla warfare may be said to have started'.

On 14 August, fifteen-year-old Francis Murphy, a member of Na Fianna Éireann from Glann near Ennistymon, was shot dead. Rumours were spread that Murphy's home was attacked because his father had been working for a relative who received RIC protection because of his involvement in a local land dispute, or that young Murphy spoke too freely about republican activities and was shot by the IRA. But the inquest into Murphy's killing ruled that he was killed after a British army patrol fired shots into his home.

With large districts throughout the county having no police or military presence the IRA were able to move freely, train their Volunteers and plan further attacks in relative security. Dáil Éireann and Sinn Féin were also able to take advantage of the situation by setting up units of the republican police and republican courts in these areas. However, the removal of the smaller barracks meant that the IRA needed to find new sources of arms and ammunition. The remaining barracks were too well defended to be raided by the republicans, and RIC foot and cycle patrols were becoming less frequent and larger in size.

In October 1919 the IRA in Clare made their first arms raid on the British coastguard. The coastguard were a British police force stationed along the coast, and concerned mainly with maritime duties. They were armed, but unlike the RIC and British army, they did not concern themselves with political issues or take any action against local republicans. The Ballyvaughan company of the IRA received information that the coastguard station in the village had just been equipped with Lee Enfield rifles and it was decided to raid the station. A group of twenty Volunteers from Kilfenora, including Commandant Andrew O'Donoghue of the Mid Clare brigade, carried out the night-time raid:

> Seán McNamara and Ignatius O'Neill surprised the night-watchman, who made no effort to resist, and after that the remaining seven or eight of his colleagues were made prisoners. The booty was not as big

as expected – only one service rifle, a couple of telescopes and some ammunition. The poor old coastguards were a rather harmless crowd, who generally were on good terms with the people. They were mostly Englishmen whose duties consisted principally of keeping a look-out for smuggling by sea and offering a lifeboat service. After the station had been captured, all the coastguards were assembled in one room where we joined with them in a sing-song and in friendly conversation. Being strangers we tried to give the coastguards the impression we were from Dublin, and we parted with them on the best of terms.

In the same month the IRA began raiding the homes of known unionists. In December the Mid Clare brigade were given another chance to improve their firepower. A herdsman named Genessy reported that H.V. McNamara, a local landlord, had invited local unionists and British army officers for a day's hunting at his game reserves in Carron. On 2 December the IRA set up an ambush to disarm the hunting party. At daybreak O'Loughlin and seven Volunteers built a barricade across their route at the crossroads near Genessy's house. About 9 a.m. the shooting party approached in two cars. McNamara and five British army officers were joined for the day's sport by one of McNamara's gamekeepers named Osbourne and Lady Beatrice O'Brien.

When the first car reached the barricade it stopped and O'Loughlin called on McNamara and his friends to put their hands up and surrender their guns. The shooting party responded by opening fire on the republicans. The IRA returned fire and the shooting lasted about twenty minutes. McNamara's party retreated to Genessy's house where they continued their resistance and wounded O'Loughlin and two other Volunteers. O'Loughlin called off the attack and the IRA disabled the shooting party's two cars and withdrew. All eight members of H.V. McNamara's shooting party had been wounded in the ambush, including Lady O'Brien. She had taken an active part in the fighting and the IRA laid the sexism and chivalry of the day aside and had to regard her as a dangerous combatant equal to the men. The ambush received widespread attention in the British and Irish newspapers and for weeks afterwards the Carron area was the focus of military searches.

As a result of this ambush the remaining barracks in the district were reinforced. It was noticed that two young RIC men stationed at Kilfenora often left their barracks to meet local girls and were regularly out late at night. Andrew O'Donoghue and the 5th battalion of the Mid Clare brigade decided to attack them in the hope of drawing more of the RIC out of their barracks. The attack was planned for 7 December. At 7 p.m. four Volunteers armed with revolvers were waiting at Howley's Corner, thirty yards from the barracks. Eight IRA riflemen were stationed nearby to deal with the expected RIC reinforcements. As the two RIC men approached from the village, some women crossed between them and the ambushing party and the IRA held their fire until the policemen were within a few yards of the barracks door. The Volunteers fired about twelve shots, wounding one of the policemen before they reached safety inside the barrack door. The rest of the RIC garrison did not move out of the barracks and the IRA withdrew.

The IRA's West Clare brigade planned to assassinate an RIC sergeant stationed at Kilmihil who was particularly aggressive in pursuing local republicans. Ten Volunteers took up ambush positions one night an the Cahercanivan Road, a mile from the village on the route that an RIC foot patrol, led by the sergeant, was due to travel. When the RIC patrol was about fifty yards from the ambush site an excited Volunteer fired a shot at the RIC, giving away the element of surprise. The RIC patrol opened fire, shooting Lieutenant Michael Honan of the IRA through the chest. The IRA retreated under fire, taking Honan with them.

In East Clare Michael Brennan had appealed to IRA headquarters for arms to continue the struggle, but none were forthcoming. Jack Coughlan, a post office worker, told Brennan that a large amount of pension money paid by the British government would be sorted at the GPO in Limerick and sent out to the sub-post offices on New Year's Day. Brennan decided to rob the post office and use the money to purchase arms. The robbery raised £1,500 for the East Clare brigade's arms fund, but a response from the British authorities was not long in coming. Joseph Clancy was arrested by the RIC and imprisoned in Ennis jail. Brennan, who was already wanted by the RIC, travelled to Dublin to buy weapons and was ordered to appear at IRA headquarters:

> GHQ completely disapproved of my raid on Limerick GPO. They paraded me and announced that I was being removed from my position as O/C East Clare brigade. To make this decision even more extraordinary, I was informed we could retain the money for the purchase of arms. It was of course obvious to me even then that the post office raid was only one of the causes for my removal. The various instances in which we had acted first and sought approval afterwards (or not at all) had apparently created in their minds a feeling that we were 'forcing the pace' and might let them in for a situation they were not prepared to meet.

Michael Brennan was replaced as brigade O/C for East Clare by his brother Austin. This decision by IRA headquarters was unpopular; there were rumblings about refusing to recognise headquarters and setting up a second 'independent brigade', but ultimately this came to nothing.

As the new year began the Mid Clare brigade kept up the pressure on the RIC by attacking a foot patrol at Ballyvaughan. A patrol of four RIC men usually left Ballyvaughan barracks each evening to protect the home of a man called Davoren, at Ballyaliban, who was involved in a local land dispute. Seán McNamara, the head of the 6th battalion, planned the attack, to take place on 3 January 1920. McNamara and four Volunteers took up positions on the left side of a crossroad along which the RIC were due to travel; four other Volunteers were stationed on the opposite side of the road thirty yards away. The RIC arrived at 10.30, marching in close formation instead of being spread out in pairs. The patrol had also been strengthened with the addition of a fifth member, 'Special Constable' Flannery, who had officially retired from the RIC but still volunteered for part-time duty. When the leading RIC men drew opposite Seán McNamara's position, he opened fire:

> Owing to the darkness, perhaps, and due to the fact that all my men were having their first appearance in an ambush, most of the police survived the initial outburst of fire and took shelter straight away. They

threw two hand grenades which exploded fairly close to myself but did no damage. Mixed through their rifle fire they used Verey lights, which were entirely new to us and exceptionally upsetting too. In a short time the engagement became almost a hand to hand encounter. So close did we come to one another that one policeman struck the barrel of his rifle against mine, and in the exchange of shots which followed my cap was blown off and I damaged the uniform of that particular policeman by putting a bullet through it. As far as I can now remember I would say we kept up the engagement for about ten minutes – when the supply of cartridges which we had was exhausted I ordered a retirement. The Verey lights and the rough bushy country through which we had to re-treat made this a tough job for inexperienced men, but it was managed without any casualties other than scratches from blackthorn bushes and torn clothes.

The RIC were shaken by the attack and, unable to see the IRA in retreat, fired blindly in several directions. Two of the RIC men had been wounded, including 'Special Constable' Flannery, who immediately ended his part-time policing duties.

During 1919 republican raids and ambushes had been so successful in making Clare impossible to police that in many areas the RIC were armed with Verey flares to summon reinforcements, along with high calibre military weapons including Lee Enfield rifles and Mills bomb hand grenades. When faced with these weapons the IRA simply withdrew out of their range and continued to harass the RIC at a distance. As foot patrols were becoming increasingly dangerous the RIC were equipped with military service Crossley Tenders, but the blocking and trenching of roads by republicans limited their usefulness. The RIC had always acted as a paramilitary police force, being much more heavily-armed and concerned with political issues than their police counterparts in Britain. However, the increasing militarisation of the force was an admission that the situation throughout Ireland was quickly spiralling out of control. The RIC were increasingly used as guides and reinforcements for the British army.

In January 1920 the British army and RIC posts in Cooraclare were evacuated. The IRA learned that the furniture of a married member of the RIC was still in the town and would probably be removed by the police within a few days. Seán Liddy, the local IRA company commander, decided to use the occasion to attack the RIC. The republicans in the area were poorly armed, having only three rifles and no ammunition. It was decided to attack the RIC using a few shotguns and a punt gun, a large antique weapon used for shooting large numbers of birds along riverbanks and marshes. On 19 January six Volunteers took up their attacking positions as the RIC van and four armed police came to collect the furniture. When the IRA opened their attack the punt gun had been overcharged with too much gunpowder, shrapnel and lead shot. It was only fired once at a range of about five yards and succeeded in shattering the windscreen on the RIC van before the gun burst. The other Volunteers had scarcely opened fire on the stunned policemen with their shotguns when their two scouts signalled that an RIC patrol was approaching from the opposite direction, and the republicans began a hasty withdrawal.

As the RIC closed on their position one of the republican scouts, Michael Darcy, was lagging behind the others. When the RIC spotted him retreating they concentrated their fire on him and in a panic Darcy rushed into a deep part of the Cooraclare River and drowned. Some of the retreating Volunteers made an attempt to rescue him but were prevented by a burst of rifle fire from the RIC. Michael Darcy's body was not recovered until the next day. At the inquest into his death the jury condemned the RIC for not coming to his aid and for preventing his rescue by the Volunteers.

The existence of the breakaway 'independent brigade' began to pose problems for the IRA in the Mid Clare brigade area. The 'independent brigade' had not been active in attacking the RIC or British army and had failed to act on intelligence information it was given from republican sympathisers. The breakaway group had become involved in land disputes and their actions sometimes confused the local population into thinking that they were members of the IRA. The Mid Clare brigade accused the 'independent brigade' of causing trouble in Kilmaley, Connolly, Inagh and Ennis. At a brigade council meeting it was decided that the breakaway group should be suppressed and their weapons seized. Martin Devitt organised thirty Volunteers from the 4th and 5th battalions to move into the Connolly–Kilmaley district to disarm the 'independent brigade'.

During one week the Volunteers seized six shotguns from them and warned the leaders of the brigade about their behaviour. When the Volunteers were returning by cart with the captured weapons they ran into a British army convoy. As the Volunteers approached Crowe's Bridge that evening, some at the front of the column dismounted from their carts to climb a steep hill, leaving their weapons behind them. These Volunteers were surprised by a British army lorry which appeared on the Cloonanaha by-road near Crowe's Bridge. The republicans took shelter at the roadside without being able to retrieve their guns. The British army were equally taken by surprise; three of the soldiers left their vehicle to examine the contents of the carts, seizing the guns from the first before moving on to examine the next. As the soldiers approached, Martin Devitt and three other Volunteers opened fire. The soldiers returned fire as their vehicle reversed towards Inagh. After the encounter Martin Devitt decided to retreat from the area and sent the carts away by road while the remaining Volunteers were led to Cloonagh and dismissed.

The British vehicle the IRA had encountered at Crowe's Bridge had been carrying Colonel Murray White, the British military commander in Clare, on a tour of inspection. Colonel White assumed that his escort had encountered a large IRA force on its way to attack an RIC or British army barracks, and immediately ordered a large force of British soldiers to search the area. Hundreds of soldiers and RIC men were mobilised, but by the time they arrived the Volunteers had already gone into hiding. Although the IRA had not suffered any casualties during the attack, they had lost three shotguns and one rifle. Martin Devitt was annoyed at the loss of the weapons and planned an ambush on an RIC patrol at Crowe's Bridge a week later. His brother Patrick remembered his determination to capture more arms: 'My brother vowed that ere long he would recover at least as many guns from the enemy.' The Inagh company of the IRA had noticed that a cycle patrol of four RIC men regularly left their barracks at Inagh and travelled towards Connolly through Fermoyle, not far from Crowe's Bridge. Devitt decided to ambush them to capture their arms.

On 22 February Devitt sent his brother to Andrew O'Donoghue in Kilfenora to collect rifles and ammunition for the ambush. Patrick Devitt carried these back to McGoffs' house outside Inagh where he met his brother, Ignatius O'Neill and Patrick Lehane from Lahinch. The four IRA men left McGoffs at 9 a.m. the next morning and arrived at Fermoyle an hour later. Scouts from the Inagh company were posted between Fermoyle and Inagh to signal the approach of the RIC cycle patrol which consisted of four men – Sergeant Giles and RIC Constables Glynn, Hughes and O'Connell. Martin Devitt and Patrick Lehane were waiting to attack the police from behind a low fence 100 yards from the road. Patrick Devitt and Ignatius O'Neill were 200 yards away behind a hedge some 100 yards from the crossroads. From here they had a good view of the road and were to act as a covering party for Martin Devitt and Lehane.

The RIC patrol approached the ambush site cycling two abreast, but on this occasion the distance between the two pairs of policemen was 350 yards rather than the fifty-yard spread that the IRA expected. As soon as the first two RIC men came into view O'Neill and Patrick Devitt opened fire. The two policemen were unharmed and threw themselves off their bicycles, taking cover in a trench on the opposite side of the road. When the RIC men at the rear of the patrol heard the shots they took cover behind a fence facing Martin Devitt and Patrick Lehane's position, just out of view of the IRA covering party. By now both sides were manoeuvring back and forth, firing shots and trying to get into a better position. Sniping from the republicans became so intense that one of their bullets severed the chin strap on Constable Glynn's hat. O'Neill and Patrick Devitt could see no target and held their fire and position for twenty minutes until the shooting subsided. O'Neill suggested to Patrick Devitt that he should move closer to the road to find out what was happening. Devitt saw the first two policemen's rifles and bicycles lying on the road but could see no sign of the policemen, until a sheepdog came along the road and peered into the trench until something scared it and it raced off. Devitt guessed that the hiding policemen had frightened the dog and he moved back up the hill to report to O'Neill. When he rejoined O'Neill the pair moved under fire to the position where Martin Devitt and Patrick Lehane were last seen. The covering party could find no trace of their two comrades and O'Neill decided to remain there and try and locate them while Patrick Devitt moved back to his original position.

From the covering position Patrick Devitt saw O'Neill racing towards him under fire, towards the furze bushes on the top of the hill. O'Neill had seen Martin Devitt being shot and had gone to his assistance. O'Neill himself was wounded in the thigh as he advanced and found Devitt dead. O'Neill was retreating back to safety when Patrick Devitt saw him and came to his aid. As Patrick approached he heard O'Neill shouting at him to 'Clear out of here!' Devitt rushed to the nearest house, the home of one of their scouts named Meaney, where he found O'Neill and Lehane:

> In the house I found O'Neill sitting on a chair and blood flowing from him. He had been badly wounded in the thigh. He greeted me with the sad, 'Oh Paddy, Martin is knocked out.' Lehane was also in the kitchen. O'Neill told me that Martin's body was lying alongside the fence a bit away from where we had left himself and Lehane that morning and that if I attempted to go near it the police would 'blow my head off'. After remaining in Meaneys' for about ten minutes or so – we were then seven or eight hundred yards from the road as the crow flies and discussing our next line of action – O'Neill insisted that Lehane and I should clear out of the place.

Patrick Devitt and Lehane travelled across country to Cullinagh, three miles from Ennistymon where they parted company. Devitt met Séamus Coneally, a member of the 5th battalion, and told him about his brother's death. Coneally went to Ennistymon to arrange a car to take O'Neill, who was still at Meaneys' house, to safety. As Devitt was making his way home he decided to change direction and return to Fermoyle to make sure that O'Neill was safe:

> As I approached Inagh I saw a big concentration of RIC and military there, so I avoided them and got into Deas' house in the vicinity of that village. In that house I met a school master named Cuddihy who knew me but did not let on that he did. He and the Deas assured me that O'Neill was safe and that my brother's body was in the hands of the Inagh Volunteers. I then went back to my home in Cahersherkin where I made no reference to my own people about the day's happenings. On the following day my father heard about the death of his son when he went to Ennistymon on some business errand.

Martin Devitt's body was hidden in a disused limekiln by the Inagh company of the IRA and was placed in a coffin the following night. A meeting of the Mid Clare brigade's staff was held and decided that Devitt's death should be kept secret from the British forces and his body hidden until the situation had calmed down and he could be given a proper burial. That night Volunteers from all over the Mid Clare brigade assembled at Inagh and marched behind Devitt's coffin from Inagh to Cloonagh where the parade was dismissed before the coffin was hidden away. Patrick Devitt and twelve other senior members of the Mid Clare brigade stayed behind to carry the coffin on their shoulders to a bog at Russia where Devitt was buried in the early hours of the morning. Every IRA member present was warned to keep the details and location of Devitt's body strictly secret.

A few weeks afterwards a convoy of RIC and British soldiers under the command of the RIC District Inspector Mooney drove directly to where Devitt's body was buried and removed the coffin. A public inquest was held and afterwards Martin Devitt's body was turned over to his family. The parish priest of Ennistymon refused to allow Devitt's remains inside the parish church. Instead the coffin was taken to the local workhouse for the funeral. The three Clare brigades of the IRA arranged a large military funeral and parade as a final mark of respect. The British army monitored the proceedings but did not prevent an IRA firing party shooting a volley at the graveside.

The capture of Devitt's body by the British forces started a number of rumours and a great deal of speculation in the area about the discovery. Word reached the IRA that a British spy had been present at the burial and passed on the location of Devitt's body to the British forces. It is more likely that careless talk reached the ears of the RIC or else that one of the IRA members objected to Devitt's covert burial for religious reasons. Peadar O'Loughlin, the brigade quartermaster, replaced Martin Devitt as vice-O/C of the Mid Clare brigade.

Between 1919 and spring 1920 the IRA in Clare ambushed ten RIC patrols and attacked or raided five barracks. The majority of these actions had been planned to capture RIC weapons and only the attacks at Cooraclare, Kilfenora and Kilmihil were deliberate attempts to kill RIC men. Two RIC constables had been killed in Clare and by March 1920 nineteen other policemen had been killed in the rest of Ireland. The RIC had begun withdrawing from rural barracks, as republican attacks increased, to larger police barracks in towns and villages or to larger British army barracks. Sinn Féin had declared a social boycott of the RIC which was implemented in many parts of Ireland.

Policing throughout the country was becoming increasingly dangerous and for the first time in their careers many RIC constables had to face the possibility that they could be shot. As the pressure mounted on the force, a wave of resignations began. While some RIC men only resigned out of concern for their personal safety, others had to make the difficult decision to resign because of their principles. The first resignations took place in 1918 when a small number of principled RIC constables refused to enforce the British government's plans for compulsory conscription in Ireland. In 1919, ninety-nine members of the force resigned and 234 took early retirement. Many who resigned from the force for genuine political reasons had to make great sacrifices; these were young men with families who were losing their livelihoods with little hope of finding other employment.

The IRA had succeeded in making it impossible for the RIC to police the country. British-imposed law and order was collapsing throughout Ireland, with the Sinn Féin-organised Dáil courts and the

IRA's republican police force filling the vacuum. The British government needed to act quickly to regain control of the situation. Thousands of soldiers had already been sent to Ireland to suppress the republican rebellion, but if the army replaced the RIC as the main force fighting the IRA, the British government would be exposing itself to the charge that they were fighting a war and that the IRA were a legitimate army and not a criminal gang of murderers and thugs. The RIC had always prided itself on being a semi-military force and this made the complete militarisation of the force rapid, as the previous distinct roles of soldier and policeman became fused. The policemen of the RIC became soldiers, British soldiers became policemen, and ex-soldiers became a strange new hybrid.

To keep up the pretence that the IRA was a criminal organisation the British government decided to reinforce the RIC as their main weapon against Irish republicanism. New recruits with military experience would have to be found to rebuild the RIC's falling numbers. The IRA had wanted to spark an all-out war with the British forces in Ireland and by March 1920 the British government were ready to give it to them.

6

Keeping Down the Irish

Said Lloyd George to McPhearson, I'm giving you the sack
For keeping down the Irish you haven't got the knack.
I'll send over Greenwood, he's a much sterner man,
And we'll keep down the Irish with the bold Black and Tans.

From 'The Bold Black and Tans', a song popular with members of the force

On 25 March 1920 Christopher O'Sullivan, a reporter with the *Limerick Echo*, was returning by train from Dublin. At Limerick Junction he encountered a group of RIC constables wearing a poorly fitting mixture of very dark green, RIC uniform and British army khaki. The policemen spoke with English accents and in dress and stature they seemed very different to the usual RIC recruits. Writing in the weekend edition of the *Limerick Echo*, O'Sullivan described his meeting with the new RIC recruits: 'He measured up to about 5'6' and could scarcely weigh 10 stone. I would associate him with the Pallasgreen Scarteen Hunt, to judge by the colour of his cap and trousers.' The Pallasgreen Scarteen Hunt O'Sullivan referred to were a famous pack of hunting dogs from the Limerick/Tipperary border known as 'The Black and Tans'. O'Sullivan's name for the new RIC recruits stuck and quickly became popular. The first Black and Tans had arrived in Ireland.

The British Ministry of Labour had estimated that after the war there were 167,000 unemployed ex-soldiers in Britain, angry young men who had both military training and combat experience. They were supposed to have returned from the war to 'a land fit for heroes' but instead they found themselves back where they had begun – unemployed with poor welfare provision, living in poverty in slum conditions and abandoned by the wealthy politicians who had sent them to die as cannon fodder. With rising unemployment, ex-soldiers became increasingly disillusioned with the British political system and, inspired by the role of soldiers in the Russian Revolution, they joined militant trade unions, left-wing political parties and political ex-servicemen's organisations like the Soldiers', Sailors' and Airmens' Union or the National Federation of Discharged and Demobilised Sailors and Soldiers, which called for the public ownership of land, the abolition of the House of Lords and its replacement with a democratically elected second chamber.

With the political vacuum caused by the continued existence of the war coalition government, the frequent outbreak of strikes and social unrest in British cities and the crisis caused by the republican revolution in Ireland, there was a very real danger that the ex-soldiers' protests could spark a revolution in Britain. The British establishment were so terrified by this prospect that they set up a new domestic intelligence group, A2 Branch GHG GB in early 1919 to ensure the loyalty of ex-servicemen's associations. A2 Branch recruited military officers such as Jack Byrnes, a sergeant major in the army, to infiltrate these organisations, spy on their members, contest positions of leadership and then sabotage them. Byrnes posed as a militant demobilised soldier to infiltrate different left-wing ex-servicemen's groups in London. He eventually became the secretary of the Soldiers', Sailors' and Airmens' Union and the London Workers Committee. Byrnes successfully sabotaged both groups by exploiting existing feuds and by publicly accusing other leaders of being British government spies. (In December 1919 Byrnes was sent to Ireland to gather information on republican leaders but was captured by the IRA; he was executed in March of 1920.) The British government needed to get rid of these ex-soldiers in a hurry, and since they were unwilling to address the social causes that led to the protests, their natural solution was to use these men again to suppress the revolution in Ireland.

In May 1919, faced with the crisis in the RIC, Walter Long, MP, wrote to Field-Marshal Lord French, the British viceroy in Ireland, suggesting that these unemployed ex-soldiers could be recruited as RIC 'temporary constables' to strengthen the police force to fight against the IRA. The new RIC inspector general, T.J. Smyth, readily agreed to Long's idea and on 27 December authorised recruitment for the RIC in Britain. Six days later the first of a wave of new recruits joined the RIC. In January 1920 the RIC recruited 110 ex-soldiers; they were sent to Ireland after their initial training that March. Almost all of these new recruits were sent to Cork, with the remaining seven sent to Limerick. It was probably this first batch of Black and Tans that Christopher O'Sullivan had encountered at Limerick Junction.

The new recruits were supposed to be regular RIC men subject to police discipline and authority. However, when the first of them joined the force, the RIC were unable to equip them with regular dark green RIC uniforms. The new recruits were not subject to the RIC's physical regulations and many were too short to fit the existing stock of police uniforms. Due to the republican boycott of the RIC, tailors refused to make more uniforms for the new policemen and they had to supplement their dress with khaki or tan-coloured British army uniforms. Their peculiar dress and behaviour immediately set the Black and Tans apart from the regular RIC in the minds of the Irish public.

Shortly after the arrival of the first Black and Tans in Ireland the British government began another recruitment campaign to enlist ex-British army officers as members of the auxiliary division of the RIC. The Auxiliaries, or 'Auxies' as they became known, were created at a conference of the British cabinet on 11 May 1920. Winston Churchill proposed that ex-British army officers should be recruited as 'barracks defence sergeants'. Recruitment began shortly afterwards. They held the rank of temporary cadet and were in effect police sergeants. Like the Black and Tan's the Auxiliaries were supposed to be regarded as regular policemen but unlike the Black and Tans they had their own separate command headed by Brigadier General Crozier.

The Auxiliaries were affected by the same uniform shortage and initially wore the same mixture of police and military uniform as the Black and Tans, except that they wore Scottish Tam O'Shanter hats with the letters TC on their epaulettes which stood for 'temporary cadet'. When the shortage of uniforms was over late in 1920 some auxiliary companies were issued with dark blue British police uniforms but still retained their Tam O'Shanter uniform hats.

Like the Black and Tans, the Auxiliaries were armed with Lee Enfield rifles and Mills bomb hand grenades. They were usually armed with two .45 Webley and Scott revolvers, one strapped in a holster to each thigh. Auxiliary Bill Monroe remembered that a mixture of bravado, drunkenness and horseplay often resulted in accidents: 'Some of us were influenced by western films and wore our revolvers in holsters low slung on the thigh which looked very dashing but which were the cause of quite a number of shot off toes – as the enthusiasts attempted to emulate the cowboys of Texas.'

Upon arriving in Ireland the Black and Tans and Auxiliaries quickly became notorious for their campaign of terrorism designed to bludgeon the Irish into submission. This earned the Black and Tans a hated position in Irish history similar to that of the Nazi Gestapo and SS units in Europe. For sixteen months the British forces were given a free hand in Ireland to commit theft and robbery during their 'police searches'. They often followed this with arson, burning thousands civilian homes, and whole cities and towns like Cork and Balbriggan. The Tans and Auxiliaries were also at liberty to torture their prisoners and to murder Irish republicans and civilians.

Some of the atrocities attributed to the Black and Tans and Auxiliaries were actually carried out by regular British troops such as the 1st battalion of the Essex Regiment who regularly committed war crimes in the west Cork area. By 1920 the Irishmen who remained in the RIC were mostly staunch unionists who opposed republicanism more than British troops, who had little interest or understanding of Irish politics. After two RIC men were killed in Tuam on 20 July 1920 the RIC garrison in the town ran amuck, smashing windows, setting fire to businesses, throwing hand grenades and threatening to shoot civilians – the RIC men involved were all Irish but their rampage was attributed to Englishmen in the Black and Tans. It should also be remembered that it was Irishmen in the regular RIC who murdered Thomas MacCurtain, the Sinn Féin mayor of Cork. While the Black and Tans' reputation for indiscriminate violence and murder is well deserved, the popular enduring belief that they were 'the scum of English prisons released specially to cause murder and havoc in Ireland' is not true.

First of all the Black and Tans and Auxiliaries were not all English, or even British – at least 14 per cent of new recruits to the RIC were recruited in Ireland. The Black and Tans and the Auxiliaries were an overwhelmingly British force with 66 per cent of the new RIC recruits English, 14 per cent Scottish and about 5 per cent Welsh. Other Black and Tans were recruited from throughout the British Empire, particularly Canada, Australia and New Zealand. One Black and Tan who was arrested by the regular RIC in Naas on 13 January 1921 for being drunk and firing his revolver in the air turned out to be Mexican. However, at least 19 per cent of the Black and Tans and 10 per cent of the Auxiliaries were Irish. Not all of these Irish Black and Tans and Auxiliaries were hardened Orangemen and unionists; the majority were Catholics from Munster, Leinster and Connaught. Fifteen Claremen joined the Auxiliaries and another forty-six joined the RIC as Black and Tans; the majority of these were Catholic ex-soldiers.

Some 300,000 Irishmen served in the British army during the First World War, and according to British government figures there were still 21,000 unemployed ex-British army soldiers in Ireland in 1920. For many of these men a career in the RIC was the only job available. Initially recruitment was slow among ex-soldiers until summer 1920 when the pay of the RIC was increased to ten shillings a day plus expenses for a temporary constable or Black and Tan. Temporary cadets or Auxiliaries were paid a whole pound a day plus expenses. These were very high rates of pay at the time and encouraged many Irish ex-soldiers to join the RIC, despite the obvious risks. Many of these Irish recruits to the Black and Tans were mercenaries motivated by the high rate of pay. Other Irishmen who enlisted genuinely supported British rule and felt it was their duty to serve the British government by fighting the IRA.

The Black and Tans and Auxiliaries were not specially released from English prisons to join the RIC; they were mostly British army veterans of the First World War. The idea that the Black and Tans were all convicted criminals came from the British secret service's recruitment of a criminal named J.L. Gooding for intelligence work in Ireland. Gooding was a very successful con man who had convictions for forgery, theft, larceny and embezzlement spanning thirty-four years. In 1918 he was sentenced to five years in jail for fraud. Using his alias, Frank Digby Hardy, he wrote to the British viceroy in Ireland, Field-Marshal Lord John Denton Pinkstone French, claiming he could use his experience as a con man to get information about the IRA's arms and ammunition hidden throughout Ireland. Gooding was released from prison having served less than a year of his sentence and was enrolled in the British secret service.

IRA intelligence network managed to get a copy of Gooding's letter offering his criminal services to Lord French, and publicly revealed his activities in Ireland. Exposed, and his mission in tatters, Gooding fled back to Britain. The next morning newspapers published his story under the headlines 'English spy unmasked' and 'Treachery at its vilest'. Gooding's criminal career, release from prison and involvement with the British secret service were so widely reported that it's hardly surprising, given the murders and war crimes of the Black and Tans, that many Irish people believed that the British government had released thousands of criminals to serve in the RIC.

Ex-British army soldiers could apply to join the RIC or its new auxiliary division at any British army recruitment office in Britain or Ireland, or at RIC recruitment offices in Dublin, Glasgow, London and Liverpool. Between January 1920 and June 1921 9,000 Black and Tans and 2,000 Auxiliaries had joined the RIC. In the same period unemployment in Britain rose from 2.4 per cent to 14.8 per cent. Most of the ex-soldiers who joined the Black and Tans and Auxiliaries knew very little about the political situation in Ireland, Sinn Féin or the IRA and they cared even less. They were motivated by money and not an ambition to do their duty 'for King and country'.

Because most of the Black and Tans saw the war in Ireland as a financial opportunity rather than a patriotic struggle against the IRA, they took a very relaxed approach to their duties and were not anxious to expose themselves to danger in combat. Douglas V. Duff, a Black and Tan who fought against the IRA at an ambush near Oughterard in Galway, made no patriotic illusions about where his loyalty lay:

> Under the blast of machine gun and rifle fire the 'Shinner' musketry died away completely, but as soon as we attempted to advance they opened such a heavy fire that we were glad to crawl back into our ditch again. Remember we were mercenary soldiers fighting for our pay, not patriots willing and anxious to die for our country; most of us had been that already in a far more important 'scrap' and had seen exactly how much that sort of thing was worth or even appreciated by the people at home. Our job was to earn our pay by suppressing armed rebellion, not to die in some foolish, though maybe spectacular 'forlorn hope' … Until nearly three o'clock the fight went on, still without a casualty on our side. It was amusing to look down the bank side; men lay in all positions, some chewing steadily at bread and cheese, others drinking out of the necks of bottles that the tenders brought up from the inn at Oughterard while every now and again one fired a magazine full at some spot on the opposite hillside where one thought movement had occurred.

The fact that most of the RIC's new recruits were mercenaries with no strong feelings about British rule in Ireland meant that the IRA could occasionally find Black and Tans and Auxiliaries who were willing to sell intelligence information to the IRA. Dick Foley, a member of the Dublin brigade of the IRA, met Major Reynolds, a member of F company of the Auxiliaries stationed at Dublin Castle, who was willing to provide information in return for money. Foley passed this information on to Michael Collins, who ordered Frank Thornton to sound out Major Reynolds and assess whether he could be trusted:

> I met Reynolds regularly in different public houses and gave him certain jobs to do, which he did successfully … At the beginning, however, we were not too satisfied about his trustworthiness, and on every occasion that I met Reynolds either Dolan or Joe Guilfoyle was conveniently nearby and were armed. However, as time went on, Reynolds became more useful and secured quite a lot of very valuable information in the

form of photographs of the murder gang – F Company, Q Company and other companies of the Auxiliaries.

Major Reynolds was later transferred to Clare and continued to supply the local IRA with information.

A very small number of the Irishmen who joined the RIC as Black and Tans and Auxiliaries developed republican sympathies as the war progressed and were ready to act as IRA agents. Charles Browne, the adjutant of the 7th Cork battalion of the IRA, remembered one such Auxiliary who actively supported the republicans in the Macroom area:

> Contact was made by our intelligence service with an Auxiliary officer named Patrick Carroll, a native of the West of Ireland. [A first cousin of John McBride, executed in 1916.] He agreed to give any information he could obtain regarding enemy activities and as an earnest of good faith brought out from time to time over six revolvers with ammunition, which he handed over to our agent Miss Gretta Graham, Middle Square, Macroom. He also provided information of intended enemy activities and refused to accept any sort of compensation.

Relationships between the Black and Tans, the Auxiliaries and regular RIC men were poor. Regular RIC constables resented the better pay the Black and Tans received and were often jealous that Auxiliaries held rank over them as temporary cadets and feared they would remain in the police force and be promoted as permanent RIC sergeants, even though they had a shorter service record and less experience. Other regular RIC men were also shocked by the Black and Tans' behaviour and lack of discipline. RIC constable John Tagney claimed: 'They were the lowest form of humanity … They were roughnecks.' In his experience the regular RIC 'had no friendship for them, and had nothing more to do with them then necessary'.

In Clare one Black and Tan was arrested for threatening to shoot his RIC sergeant. Another six Black and Tans were disciplined for threatening their own orderly sergeant and shooting at a regular RIC constable. An Auxiliary was charged in Ennis with larceny, having stolen the boots from a wounded RIC man to sell them. The Black and Tan members of the RIC in one police district in Clare stole £5 from the RIC garrison in another. Two RIC men were shot in a pub by G company of the Auxiliaries who had been sent there based on information supplied by the Black and Tans, to the effect that there were two Volunteers drinking there.

The Black and Tans' and Auxiliaries' relationship with the British army was little better according to Major General Douglas Wimberly, who was stationed in Cork with the Cameron Highlanders:

> Finally as matters became really bad the government brought into southern Ireland irregular Volunteer forces of semi soldiers and semi police called 'Black and Tans' who were largely recruited all over Britain from ex-temporary officers and men who had served in the Great War, of a type who would not, or could not, settle down in civil life and some of whom were undoubtedly no more or less than real thugs. They were totally undisciplined by our regimental standards, and members of this curious force undoubtedly committed many atrocities, and in retaliation dreadful atrocities were in turn committed on them by the Sinn Féin bands roaming the countryside. They seemed to make a habit of breaking out of their barracks illicitly and killing men they thought were suspect rebels, and in this way the habit spread surreptitiously even to a few army officers and men.

The Black and Tans and Auxiliaries who arrived in Ireland received very little police training; some of them spent less than a week at the Gormanstown camp before taking up duty with the RIC. This meant that they had to rely on their military experience from the British army and ensured that the RIC acted as a paramilitary force incapable of conducting normal policing or restoring order. The average Black and Tan received twelve to fourteen training lectures, instruction in drill, rifle revolver and bombing practice over a two to three-week period. The average training concentrated on the military and combat aspects of their job and ensured the new RIC recruits acted as soldiers and paramilitaries in police uniform. The Auxiliaries received up to six weeks' training, again concentrating on rifle, revolver and bombing practice. Their policing lectures taught them the difference between a misdemeanour and a felony and detailed a policeman's power of arrest, but this instruction in legal affairs was of little value given the new role of the RIC as a combat force. During their training the Black and Tans and Auxiliaries were taught very little that would be useful in fighting the IRA in guerrilla warfare.

Black and Tan Alfred Smith from Hackney, London gave an interview to the British press detailing his experiences in Ireland:

> The general mode of operations was as follows. A wire was received that a crime had been committed. The bugle went and we fell in, fully equipped. Every man had his rifle ammunition and a pair of handcuffs. How we turned out didn't matter so long as we were there. Then, generally thirty to fifty men were called on to proceed to a certain place. Instantly there was a scramble by everyone in the camp for the motor lorries already drawn up, engines running, near the gate. More often than not half the camp managed to get in. The other half followed as best they could. In the lorries we found cans of petrol and bombs. These we divided up between us, and as soon as we got near our destination we began to warm things up. The first thing we did on arrival was to find the public house. Then we spilled out petrol over everything, exploded a bomb in it and went on to the next houses. These we had pointed out to us and we went methodically through them, giving people five minutes in which to clear out. On this work I say nothing. The men did not object to it. What they did object to was that we worked without officers, and in the excitement of the moment many excesses were committed which, had there been good discipline, could have been avoided.

The pretence that the Black and Tans were ordinary policemen quickly evaporated when they went on duty with regular members of the RIC like Constable John Tagney:

> They knew absolutely nothing about police duties. On one occasion there was a county inspector whose duty it was to visit the barracks. He was trying to instruct these fellows, and we were all in the barracks, for we had to go to school with him. And he asked this fellow what was his power of arrest, and he said he didn't know. He tried to make it simpler

to him. He said: 'If you see a man on the street and asked his name and address and he refused, what would you do?' And the Black and Tan said: 'If I met a man on the street and asked his name and address and he refused, I would lift him right under the jaw, and the next thing I would use my bayonet. That is what I would do to the man.'

The Black and Tan's reply to the county inspector is a good example of the blunt, brute force approach the Black and Tans and Auxiliaries used in their attempt to restore 'law and order' in Ireland.

Constable Eugene Banton, who had fought against Thomas Ashe's force of republicans at Ashbourne in 1916, was stationed at Navan when the first Black and Tans were posted to his barracks to reinforce the RIC:

> They were a low down lot of dirty scoundrels, and it was believed that they were mostly jailbirds and men of bad repute. One fellow called Richards was a right desperado. He was a Scotsman. Davis, who drove the Crossley lorry – commonly known as Crossley tenders – was a decent man. He was English. He had rigged up a sort of box set into the floor of the tender in which he always carried about a dozen bombs. One day Richards and he had a row, or should I say a serious difference of opinion. That night the tender was out on patrol and on arriving back at barracks had just entered back into the yard. I was holding a stable lantern at the gate to give them light to enter. The entrance was a bad one from the barrack lane. The tender had stopped in the yard and the occupants, except Richards, had jumped off and moved away. Richards took one of the bombs out of the box and, drawing the pin from it, let it fall at the driver's feet [Davis] in front of the tender. It exploded, destroying both of Davis' legs. I was very lucky that I did not receive some of the splinters. It was only the woodwork at the front of the tender that saved me. The following morning Richards was brought up before the county inspector in his office. He was paid off and sent back to Scotland. That was the only disciplinary action that was taken against him.

The British government decided to appoint a high-ranking British army officer as 'police adviser' to supervise and coordinate both police forces in Ireland – the RIC and the Dublin Metropolitan Police. Four days later Major General Tudor was appointed to this newly created position as effective head of all the British police forces in Ireland. Tudor was not interested in the political dimension of the IRA's campaign or in the Irish political situation. He saw himself as a soldier who had been given a military job to do. While other British army officers began to realise that the military situation in Ireland was out of control, and that it was urgent to open political negotiations with Sinn Féin, Tudor thought that it would be possible to crush the republican revolution if the British government gave the RIC a free hand to use extreme measures to deal with the IRA. General Tudor called on the British government to replace all civic courts with military tribunals, to introduce mandatory identification cards and passports and restrict changes of residence. Tudor also called for the deportation of Irish prisoners to Britain, the introduction of public flogging and the imposition of collective fines on the entire population wherever there was IRA activity. Tudor thought the RIC had become useless as a police force but believed it could still play an important role if he could transform it into a military force.

General Tudor's plans to militarise the RIC were reinforced by the appointment of other senior British army officers to high-ranking positions in the police force. These officers were eager to give the Black and Tans and regular RIC constables a free hand to combat the growth of Irish republicanism and actively encouraged them to use a campaign of terrorism and violence against anyone suspected of republican sympathies. The British government supported and even encouraged this campaign of terrorism conducted by the RIC by turning a blind eye to Black and Tan atrocities. General Decie, a British army officer, was appointed a divisional commander of the RIC after the formation of the Auxiliaries in 1920. Constable John Tagney was present when the general visited his barracks: 'There were six Black and Tans present when General Decie came to the barracks and he was questioning them about what they knew about Sinn Féiners and the movement that was going on in the southern part of the country. And in case they were able to identify a person with Sinn Féin sympathies passing the barracks, or going near the barracks, to bayonet him and not to waste good powder but just to bayonet him.'

General Decie's incitement of the RIC to kill suspected Irish republicans on sight was outdone by the advice of Lieutenant Colonel Gerard Smyth, DSO, the divisional commander of the RIC in Munster, to a group of regular RIC constables at Listowel:

> If a police barracks is burned or if the barracks already occupied is not suitable, then the best house in the locality is to be commandeered, the occupants thrown into the gutter. Let them die there – the more the merrier. Police and military will patrol the country at least five nights a week. They are not to confine themselves to the main roads, but to take across country, lie in ambush, and when civilians approach shout 'Hands Up!' Should the order not immediately be obeyed, shoot and shoot with effect. If persons approaching carry their hands in their pockets, or are suspicious-looking, shoot them down. You will make mistakes occasionally and innocent persons may be shot, but that cannot be helped. No policeman will get into trouble for shooting any man.

General Neville Macready, the commander of the British forces in Ireland, had issued a proclamation condemning reprisals in August 1920. A month later he drew up official regulations for carrying out the burning of civilian houses and commented that if a member of the RIC put on a mackintosh coat and false beard to go out and commit reprisals he was 'damned glad of it'.

With ex-military officers now in charge of the RIC encouraging a campaign of terrorism among the ordinary ranks of the force, the Black and Tans were free to carry out acts of violence with little fear of recrimination. A general RIC order issued on 18 December 1920 meant that any officer wishing to submit unfavourable reports about their subordinates needed to have the report read and signed beforehand by those concerned. It was clear that new RIC commanders like Decie and Smyth would not enforce normal standards of police discipline, and because the Black and Tans were the enforcers of British 'law and order' in Ireland they were now effectively above the law. This situation was made worse by the Black and Tans' experiences during the First World War. Most had been brutalised by their experiences during the war, and many were mentally unbalanced and suffering from 'shell shock', a situation made worse by drunkenness in their ranks. Large quantities of drink were readily available to the Black and Tans and Auxiliaries, and their high rate of pay meant that they could easily afford to buy drink in their barrack canteens, though more often than not they simply demanded it for free at gunpoint from local publicans. When Brigadier General Crozier took command of the auxiliary division of the RIC in July 1920 he found that within two weeks the Auxiliaries had already run up an unpaid bill of £300 for alcohol in their barrack canteen and from there the situation only worsened:

> The average consumption of liquor in the auxiliary division totalled £5 per head per week or £30,000 a month in canteens alone and when it is considered that the police often demanded free drinks from publicans as the price of 'protection', till they got too drunk to 'protect', when they helped themselves, it is no exaggeration to say that the great deal of that £4,000,000 damages [caused in Ireland during 1920 and 1921] ... was attributable to excessive drinking of alcoholic beverages.

The Black and Tans and Auxiliaries were not one-dimensional characters like the 'bad guys' in Hollywood films, but none of this changes their well deserved reputation for committing violence.

In Ballina, County Mayo, a group of Black and Tans arrested a local tailor named Michael Tolan because of his republican sympathies. Tolan was not a member of the IRA and had been disabled since birth. He was taken from his home and beaten and tortured by the Black and Tans before they tied him to the back of their armoured car and dragged him along the road behind it to the streets of Ballina to Shraheen bog where he was murdered and his body hidden. On 29 September 1920, 200 Black and Tans and Auxiliaries descended on the town of Balbriggan in Dublin after the shooting of RIC Head Constable Peter Burke. They burned down four pubs, a factory and nineteen private houses; a further thirty houses were looted or vandalised, causing a total of £160,000 worth of damage. At 1 a.m. they raided the homes of two Volunteers, James Lawless and Jim Gibbons; both were dragged to the corner of Quay Street, bayoneted and shot dead.

Black and Tan violence was not always directed against republicans. Irish unionists could be victimised as easily by Black and Tans who cared little about Irish politics, knew even less, and regarded all Irishmen as Sinn Féiners. On 24 July 1920 the Black and Tans burned down the business premises of G.W. Biggs, a Protestant unionist from Bantry, because he had written a letter published in *The Irish Times* pointing out that there was no sectarian persecution of Protestants in Bantry. Colonel O'Callaghan Westropp, another Protestant unionist, from Clare had his hay barn and cattle shed burned and received a death threat from the 'Anti-Sinn Féin Gang' after writing letters to the press and making speeches condemning atrocities by the Black and Tans.

In July 1920 a group of Black and Tans raided the Cork Federation of ex-British Servicemen's club, wrecking furniture, stealing money and beating the ex-British soldiers who had been drinking inside. A month later on 15 August a Black and Tan named Cyril Henry Nathan was assassinated by the IRA in Limerick. When his comrades in the RIC heard about Constable Nathan's death around thirty Black and Tans went on a drunken rampage through Limerick. They fired their weapons at random and started smashing windows in civilian homes. They followed this by carrying out random raids to try and find Constable Nathan's killers. In one unionist household they began smashing up furniture, mirrors and ornaments, including a portrait of King George V. The Black and Tans then commandeered a car and loaded it with petrol in an attempt to set O'Connell Street on fire, in the process burning down five shops and two houses. One Black and Tan was shot and wounded by his comrades and before the night was finished they also shot an English ex-British army veteran. Another group went to Limerick railway station where they dragged an engine driver from the train and cleared the passengers out of the carriages, firing shots in the air as they went, and gave three loud cheers before driving away. Outraged by this behaviour, one unionist landowner, 'The O'Connor Don', declared: 'Tell

Mr Lloyd George, if the government don't turn these damned Black and Tans out of the country we'll soon all be damned republicans.'

On 30 March 1920, just five days after the first Black and Tans arrived in Ireland, IRA headquarters issued the following proclamation: 'Whereas the spies and traitors known as the Royal Irish Constabulary are holding this country for the enemy, and whereas said spies and bloodhounds are conspiring with the enemy to bomb and bayonet and otherwise outrage a peaceful, law-abiding and liberty-loving people, wherefore we hereby proclaim and suppress the said spies and traitors, and do hereby solemnly warn prospective recruits that they join the RIC at their own peril. All nations are agreed as to the fate of traitors. It has the sanction of God and man.'

7

The Risen People

Fear ye the risen people. They that have hungered and held
Ye that have bullied and bribed, tyrants, hypocrites, liars!

Taken from a version of Patrick Pearse's poem 'The Rebel'

Between February and April 1920 the military situation in Clare was quiet, and the republicans seemed to be gaining the upper hand in the conflict. The IRA began to tighten up its organisation and training and the Dáil courts began to meet openly in some parts of Clare. The RIC continued to withdraw to larger barracks, fearing republican attacks. Apathy and low morale struck the RIC as the number of resignations from the force continued to grow. Now only the most aggressively unionist members carried out their duties and actively pursued the IRA.

As Easter approached, IRA headquarters issued orders that all abandoned barracks were to be burned as a republican show of strength to commemorate the fourth anniversary of the Easter Rising. Under cover of darkness the Gort company of the IRA crossed into Clare and met with the Crusheen company to destroy the evacuated barracks along the Clare/Galway border. The IRA's Mid Clare brigade was so enthusiastic in setting fire to the abandoned barracks at Lahinch that a number of Volunteers were badly burned. At Bodyke, the Tulla company could not destroy the barracks in the village by burning, in case they damaged the houses attached to it, so they set to work with crowbars and pickaxes. RIC barracks were also destroyed at Ballydora, Bunratty, Carron, Fanore, Kilfenora, Knock, Mullagh and Quilty. In a single night the IRA destroyed around 350 abandoned barracks, burned a number of courthouses and raided dozens of income tax offices and customs and revenue posts. This was a major embarrassment to British rule in Ireland, as it showed that the IRA was the dominant force in many parts of the country. The IRA raids on tax offices, in which official documents were seized, meant that the British government could not collect income tax in Ireland. Sinn Féin-controlled county councils refused to help British officials to assess the taxes due, and city councils refused to give them any information. On 23 March the government appointed General Neville Macready commander in chief of the British armed forces in Ireland, hoping that he would be able to gain control of the situation.

As the IRA's military campaign continued, the prisons in Ireland and Britain were filling up with republican prisoners who refused to be treated as criminals by the British legal system. Prison protests and hunger strikes continued apace with the republican campaign. On 7 April, 100 republican prisoners in Mountjoy went on hunger strike for prisoner-of-war status, led by Clareman Peadar Clancy. Hamar Greenwood, the British chief secretary in Ireland, said the hunger strikers would be allowed starve and their demands would not be met under any circumstances. Detectives from G division of the Dublin Metropolitan Police were called to Mountjoy to identify the leaders of the hunger strike and break the republican prisoners. Peadar Clancy identified one of the detectives called Henry Kells and managed to smuggle this information to the IRA's intelligence network in Dublin. On 13 April Detective Kells was assassinated by the IRA.

Kells' assassination focused national media and political attention on the hunger strike, and Clancy's claim that men were about to die electrified the situation. Once again the British authorities tried to use the Catholic Church to break the spirit of the republican prisoners. One of the IRA prisoners, Todd Andrews, remembered Catholic priests visiting the prisoners on hunger strike using their religious and social position to try and force them to end the strike:

> I had a visit from the prison chaplain. I thought he was going to sympathise with my dangerous plight and offer me the last sacraments. Instead he warned me that I was wilfully endangering my life, which was an immoral

act totally forbidden by the Commandments. He did not use the word suicide but that is what he meant … I am sorry he did not ask me if I wanted to go to confession; being in a state of grace since the previous Saturday I could have had great pleasure in refusing his ministrations. However, I assured him that I was not going to take food and that he was not helping by pressuring me to change my mind. I never saw him again … The chaplain was the only one of the prison staff who kept his nerve and did his duty, although in our estimation 'doing his duty' was merely doing the dirty work required by his British employers. He continued to demoralise the prisoners by hints of eternal damnation if they died of hunger.

Not only were a majority of the Irish people in support of the prisoners, including the socialists and the Irish Transport and General Workers' Union, who organised a one-day general strike in support of the strikers. The republican prisoners' demand for prisoner-of-war status was met that evening, just hours after the deputy prime minister had told the House of Commons and the world's media that they would never yield to the hunger strikers. With the prisoners' demands met, Clancy decided to raise the stakes even further by refusing to call off the hunger strike until all the republican prisoners were released. Fearful of creating another republican martyr, the British government granted the release of the 100 republican prisoners in Mountjoy after eight days of hunger strike. The Mountjoy hunger strike gave the republican organisations throughout Ireland a huge boost at little cost, and weakened the British will to govern Ireland. Peadar Clancy walked out of the prison as a republican legend, but also as a marked man to the British authorities, who saw him as the architect of their humiliation and they swore revenge.

On 14 April, the night that the hunger strikers in Mountjoy were released, a group of about thirty Sinn Féin supporters, mostly young men and women, gathered at Canada Cross in Miltown Malbay in celebration. IRA Volunteer Ned Lynch was nearby when the RIC and British army attacked them:

A crowd was singing and celebrating, mostly Sinn Féin supporters. I was on the run at the time and was watching proceeding about one

yards away at Kinucanes' shoe shop. Eight armed soldiers left the RIC
post and with Sergeant Hampson headed for the crowd. With revolvers
drawn and soldiers bearing arms, they called on the crowd to disperse
and opened fire. Volunteer John O'Loughlin fell in the stampede beside
a blazing tar barrel. Myself and local blacksmith Pat Maguire rushed to
O'Loughlin's aid and removed the unconscious Volunteer to Kinucanes'
after Maguire had been shot through the thigh. Another Volunteer,
Dido Foudy, was despatched for spiritual aid and medical help. Thomas
O'Leary and Patrick Hennessy were killed and seven wounded. I retreated to O'Neills' in Ballard for the night.

IRA Volunteer John O'Loughlin died of his wounds despite Ned Lynch
and Pat Maguire's initial efforts to save him.

The British attorney general in Ireland, Denis Henry, excused the
massacre, claiming that the Sinn Féin supporters had provoked the RIC
and British army. The British forces in Miltown Malbay were confined
to barracks for a few days following the massacre, and the local IRA
companies patrolled the town. The three dead men were given military
funerals at Ballard graveyard, which was attended by thousands of
people from all over Clare. As news of the shootings spread, the civilian
population of Clare became very hostile towards the RIC. Many businesses
refused to sell them food or fuel and the police initially responded by
commandeering their requirements at gunpoint. In Miltown Malbay the
boycott of the RIC and British army was so effective that they began to
travel to Ennistymon to get supplies.

Three days after the funerals the British authorities ordered a coroner's
inquest into the shootings but the families of the three dead men would
only allow the IRA to exhume their bodies. The British solders involved
gave evidence at the enquiry that they had only opened fire after they
were first shot at from the crowd. Every RIC member of the patrol
questioned supported this claim, except RIC Constable McDonnell,
who swore that there had been no violence from the crowd and that all
the other RIC men were deliberately committing perjury. Paddy Lynch
represented the families of the deceased at the enquiry. He produced
evidence showing that RIC Sergeant Hampson, the commander or

the joint RIC and Highland Light Infantry patrol on 15 April, had planned and ordered the massacre. Local publicans and traders swore that Hampson was drunk on the night of the shootings. He had been overheard telling the RIC and British soldiers to 'get ready' and another RIC constable was heard saying that it was all right to kill Sinn Féiners. Sergeant Hampson was the first member of the patrol to open fire when he was just eight yards from the crowd, and had killed one man. The other members of the patrol then opened fire, killing the second man and wounding seven others. The RIC register for the Miltown Malbay barracks showed entries reporting patrols by Sergeant Hampson, the six other RIC constables and British soldiers, but these had made no reference to the shootings or the fact that three people had been killed and many wounded.

Post-mortems carried out by Dr Hillery showed that two of the dead men had been shot in the back. On 7 May the inquest's jury returned a verdict that three members of the RIC, Sergeant Hampson and RIC Constables Thomas O'Connor and Thomas Keenan, were 'guilty of wilful murder without any provocation'. Six soldiers of the Highland Light Infantry were also found guilty of the same charge. This was the fifth inquest within three weeks to charge members of the RIC and British army with murder. The coroner's court issued warrants for the arrest of the nine members of the British forces found guilty to District Inspector Mooney of the RIC. Even though the coroner's court findings were binding by British law, the authorities decided to ignore the guilty verdict and the soldiers and RIC were never brought to trial.

On 21 April Private Thomas Sibthorpe of the Royal Highland Light Infantry was shot dead at the British army barracks at the old jail in Ennis. The inquest into Private Sibthorpe's death returned a verdict of suicide but the press reports of evidence given by his comrades suggested foul play.

Shortly after the burning of the abandoned barracks at Easter, the first Black and Tans began arriving in Clare. IRA Volunteer Liam Haugh recalls their arrival in Kilkee: 'The first two of these to appear in the area excited more curiosity than aught else. As a few of the RIC moved out, the Black and Tans moved in. Their hostility increased in proportion to their numbers. Police tenders appeared more often on the roads. Some assaults were committed on well known Sinn Féin sympathisers.' In addition to the arrival of the First Black and Tans, a Royal Navy destroyer landed fifty British soldiers from the Royal Marine Light Infantry at Kilrush as an additional garrison to fight the republicans. Though the arrival of the Black and Tans and extra soldiers increased the strength and firepower of the British forces throughout Clare, they were like fish out of water. The majority of Black and Tans had little knowledge of Irish politics and, with no experience of intelligence work, relied completely on veteran members of the RIC to act as their eyes and ears guiding them on police raids and searches. The IRA needed to direct their campaign against the RIC to cripple and blind the force but the police increased their security measures, remaining in large well-defended barracks and only travelling in large groups. This posed problems for IRA Volunteers like Liam Haugh: 'RIC patrols in country districts having now been suspended, and the Volunteers not yet given consideration to methods of coping with the occasional lightning passage of a police tender, it was decided that if anything effective were to be accomplished with the means at hand, the police must be attacked in the village streets.'

Republican intelligence reported that four RIC men in Kilmihil went to mass every Sunday. The RIC and British army barracks were 400 yards apart at opposite ends of the village. The IRA decided that this was one of the only opportunities they could get to attack the police in the area and three republicans, Seán Breen, Martin Melican and John O'Dea, volunteered to carry out the attack. Early on Sunday 18 April the Volunteers, armed with revolvers, moved into position with some of the party taking cover behind low stone walls a short distance from the church. As the congregation was leaving the three Volunteers left their hiding places and moved behind the three RIC men. RIC Constable Martyn noticed that he was being followed and turned around as Seán Breen drew his revolver, shooting Sergeant Patrick Carroll dead at point blank range. As Breen did so the other IRA Volunteers opened fire and Constable Collins fell to the ground wounded. Seán Breen pursued the third policeman, Constable Martyn, who was retreating towards the barracks through the congregation. As Breen closed his ground on the policeman Constable Martyn turned and shot him through the forehead, killing him instantly. The soldiers in the British army barracks were alerted by the sound of gunfire and rushed to the scene, forcing the IRA to retreat without their fallen comrade.

The British soldiers recovered Breen's body and brought it to his uncle's home in the village under military guard the next day when a civilian inquest was held into Breen's death. Breen's body was then handed over to his relatives for burial at Kilmihil graveyard. On Monday night the local company of the IRA escorted Breen's body to the church. The next day over 500 Volunteers, under the command of John Flanagan, marched through the village behind Breen's coffin and assembled at the graveside but the large British army and RIC presence prevented them from firing a volley over the grave. As the police numbers increased with the arrival of the Black and Tans in Clare, a small number of RIC detectives stationed in Ennis became the most active members of the force in monitoring republicans and gathering information on the IRA. One of these detectives named Swanton remained the main thorn in the side of the Mid Clare brigade; he was particularly hostile to the IRA and regularly watched all the passengers entering and leaving Ennis railway station in the hope of identifying local republicans. Five Volunteers were detailed to follow and assassinate Detective Swanton and another detective who accompanied him on his errands. On 24 April William McNamara and four other Volunteers waited at the crossroads opposite the entrance to the Christian Brothers school for the two detectives to return from the train station:

> As we were waiting for our quarry, Keane, acting as scout, reported to us that only Detective Swanton was coming. Swanton had noticed Keane on his trail and was on the alert; when he saw us standing at the cross-roads he began to run. We opened fire after him and the next thing we

saw Swanton falling on the road. After falling he never made a move and, thinking he was dead, we moved off. About two hours after this attack I was arrested in my own home by the RIC.

Detective Swanton was seriously wounded in the attack but survived and later resumed his detective work with the force.

Republicans were not idle while the RIC gathered information on them. Patrick Mulcahy, a clerk in Ennis post office, was busy monitoring RIC and British army communications and passing information to the Mid Clare brigade of the IRA:

> During 1919 and 1920, the police and military kept in touch hourly by phone with all outposts. A favourite 'annoyance operation' by Volunteers was to cut the telephone wire. This always resulted in intensive enemy activity. In order not to dislocate civilian communication, I prepared telegraph pole diagrams and, by marking the wires to be cut, ensured that only police and military wires were interfered with … Another form of assistance was the taking of important police letters passing through the post. The bulky official envelopes were seldom important, but I became familiar with the handwriting of RIC confidential clerks, DIs and CIs. Letters in their handwriting were always of interest. I could also recognise disguised handwriting on envelopes addressed to the police and invariably took such letters. They usually contained information of Volunteer activity from some local spy or, sometimes, a disgruntled Volunteer. One such capture resulted in the banishment of one man from Clare. Usually, however, such letters were unsigned, but contained correct information. During this time I was assisted greatly by the stupidity of the RIC and military, who discussed the most secret plans over the telephone.

In late May, Seán Finn, the commander of the IRA's West Limerick brigade, contacted Michael Brennan to ask him to participate in an attack on Kilmallock RIC barracks. On 27 May Brennan crossed the Shannon by boat from Cratloe to Pallaskenry where he met Seán Finn and played a prominent part in the attack, which completely destroyed the barracks by fire despite the RIC's dogged resistance. After returning, Brennan attempted to repeat the success of the operation with an attack on Sixmilebridge barracks. His plan was to blow a breach in the wall of the barracks using a gelignite landmine and to storm the building with hand grenades supplied by the IRA in Dublin. If this failed the IRA could resort to the tactics used at Kilmallock by using hand grenades to blow a hole in the roof and set the building on fire by throwing petrol followed by flaming torches through the roof. Members of the West Limerick brigade crossed the Shannon to take part in the attack while companies of the East Clare brigade would stage attacks on Feakle and Broadford barracks to draw the British forces away from Sixmilebridge for the duration of the attack. None of the Volunteers in the East Clare brigade had any experience using gelignite and Michael Brennan contacted Ernie O'Malley who was with the IRA in Tipperary to help them construct the mine.

On 2 June Ernie O'Malley cycled to Sixmilebridge to supervise the building of the landmine with Michael Brennan. Within a few hours Brennan and the others building the mine became violently ill from the poisonous fumes given off by the gelignite; most were unable to stand, never mind attacking an RIC barracks, and the operation was abandoned. The cancellation orders were not sent out in time to reach the other IRA companies at Broadford and Feakle, however. Volunteers from Scariff and Mountshannon, under the command of Thomas Tuohy, had already received orders from Michael Brennan that 'All roads leading to Feakle to be well blocked and be firing on the barracks by ten o'clock'. The Feakle company had already blocked roads by building stone barricades and felling trees across them when Henry O'Meara, Joe Nugent, Thomas McNamara, Thomas Tuohy and his brother Michael took up their positions behind a low stone wall across the road from Feakle barracks. A hundred yards away another group of Volunteers, armed with shotguns, remained hidden in case the RIC attempted to leave the barracks to attack Tuohy's group:

> The attack began at ten o'clock sharp. It opened with the hand grenades, eight of which were thrown onto the barracks roof, all of them exploding. We then began firing on the windows with the rifles and kept up the

fire for ten minutes. Vigorous return fire came from two machine guns and rifles, which lasted actually until six o'clock next morning. We left our positions ten minutes after the attack began, rejoined the shotgun party and went to Rochfords' yard in east Feakle where the arms were collected and all the men dispersed.

At Broadford the local IRA sniped the barracks for half an hour before withdrawing.

Early in June the Mid Clare brigade found another weakness in the routine of the British forces. Joe Barrett and the brigade's leadership had adopted new tactics to deal with the developing military situation: 'The coming of June found the police sheltering behind their steel shuttered windows, watchful, but for the most part, immobile in their rural localities. On the other hand our men were drilling and organising, but they urgently needed arms and ammunition to press home the fight with greater vigour. Our brigade officers were examining ways and means to repair this want.'

Two members of the Ennis company of the IRA, Liam Stack and Michael Malone, noticed that every day a patrol of seven British soldiers from the Royal Highland Light Infantry marched from their barracks at Ennis jail down O'Connell Street to guard the military transport depot on Carmody Street and always returned by the same route to their barracks in the old jail a few hundred yards away. Joe Barrett and the officers of the 1st battalion decided to keep the soldiers under surveillance and if their routine remained unchanged to attack and disarm them. Seán O'Keefe kept watch on the patrol for over a week. The IRA decided to disarm the soldiers on 23 June, the evening before the Spancil Hill horse fair. The republicans felt that this would provide a good cover as Volunteers loitering in the area would not attract attention from the RIC or the British army. Joe Barrett began special training for the operation at Dromconora Woods outside Ennis. The twenty-one Volunteers who were trained to disarm the soldiers came from rural areas outside the town because there was less likelihood that they would be recognised and identified. Eight Volunteers from the Ennis company were to cover the attackers' withdrawal and lead them through the streets of the town. A third IRA group were waiting in cars to remove the captured rifles from the area as quickly as possible.

At 4 p.m. on the day before the Spancil Hill fair the IRA took up their positions among the crowds gathering in the town. Michael Nugent from the Barefield IRA company and a number of other Volunteers brought horses to the corner of Carmody and O'Connell Street where members of the attacking party were pretending to haggle. Around the corner from Darcys' pub Volunteers John Joe Egan, Jack Mellet and Mick Kennedy were waiting in cars to take the rifles from the scene of the attack. Joe Barrett took up position in front of Darcys, which gave him a clear view of both streets and the approach of the British army patrol.

When the second pair of British soldiers passed the corner, John Joe Egan started his car and the blast of Joe Barrett's whistle sent the attacking party of the IRA, armed with revolvers, springing into action. Each group of soldiers was held up, grabbed from behind and disarmed. Only the corporal offered any resistance, but Seán O'Keefe subdued him with a number of blows to the head and he was quickly disarmed. The entire attack was over in two minutes and Joe Barrett blew his whistle again to signal its completion. The captured soldiers were marched into the yard behind Darcys' pub where they were relieved of their equipment, helmets and 300 rounds of ammunition. They were locked in a shed in Darcys' yard while the republicans loaded the seven captured rifles and equipment into the waiting cars, which were driven away to Kilmorane where another IRA party under Patrick Costello was ready to hide them at the brigade dump. A fourth car with no arms or ammunition was driven by Joseph Tierney from the site of the attack towards Kilrush as a decoy. An army armoured car that had been sent to follow the three cars loaded with arms mistakenly followed Tierney's car towards Kilrush instead.

News of the IRA's action spread quickly at the Spancil Hill horse fair the next day and Joseph Barrett claimed it was a major boost to the morale of the Mid Clare brigade:

It was a neat piece of work, carried out efficiently and expeditiously

under the very noses of the garrison in the old jail … The manner in
which the operation had been conducted and its complete success greatly
enhanced the prestige of the IRA in the area. It had been witnessed by
many people from the town and district, and though several attackers
were well known to the onlookers, not one of them was betrayed.

A week later the Mid Clare brigade decided to put the seven rifles they
had captured to use against the British military. Reports had reached
them that a lorry of British soldiers frequently accompanied a mail car
travelling from Ennis to Kilrush and the IRA decided to ambush them
at Decomade, Lissycasey on 19 June. The IRA hoped to capture more
rifles from the British army as well as the post from the mail car to
check it for information being sent to the RIC. As the ambush began,
Joe Barrett's brother, Michael, pushed a horse cart between the two
vehicles separating the military lorry from the mail car, but the lorry
reversed, pushing the shafts of the horse cart out of the way and allowing
the mail car to pass. The lorry then drove to a covered position and the
soldiers dismounted, engaging the IRA in a running battle. After about
twenty minutes the soldiers were gaining the upper hand and the IRA
retreated under fire.

In June Sinn Féin had won control of twenty-nine of the thirty-three
county councils and 172 of the 206 rural district councils in Ireland during
the local government elections. These councils passed formal resolutions
pledging allegiance to the Irish Republic and Dáil Éireann and ended all
contact with the British Local Government Board. Belfast was the only
unionist-controlled city in Ireland. Sinn Féin controlled twenty-three
councils in Ulster while the Unionists controlled twenty-two. The unionist
response to this was to try and force a nationalist and republican exodus.
On 19 July armed unionist mobs began a four-day pogrom in nationalist/
republican areas of Derry, killing nineteen, wounding fifty, burning houses
and looting shops. On 20 July this purge was extended to the Belfast
shipyards where Catholics, known republicans and socialists, including a
number of Protestant republicans, better known to their Orange attackers
as 'rotten Prods', were attacked and warned not to return to their jobs. The

unionist mob continued on towards the city's nationalist areas where they continued rioting for five days, leaving seventeen dead and 200 injured.

At the beginning of July the West Limerick brigade of the IRA crossed the Shannon by boat and handed over General Lucas of the British army as a prisoner to Michael Brennan. Lucas had been captured on 26 June by Liam Lynch and the IRA's 2nd Cork brigade. The IRA initially hoped to exchange the general for Robert Barton, a member of the IRA who the British planned to execute. However, the British government dismissed the idea, claiming Barton was a far more important figure to the IRA than Lucas was to the British army. Lucas talked freely with his IRA captors about the military situation in Ireland and confessed to Thomas Malone that if he were an Irishman he would have joined the IRA. The general was held prisoner at Sheehans' house in Templeglantine and later moved to Dores' house in Shanagolden. Maintaining an armed guard over the general was costly in terms of the IRA's time and manpower so the West Limerick brigade decided to do what the North Cork brigade had done before them and pass the general along to someone else.

Michael Brennan experienced the same inconvenience of looking after General Lucas:

> His presence completely immobilised us, as we daren't do anything that would involve raiding by the British. In addition he was an expensive luxury as he drank a bottle of whiskey every day which I hated like hell to pay for ... I kept appealing to GHQ to get rid of our prisoner but all I got was news that East Limerick would take him over soon ... We had realised by now of course that nobody wanted Lucas, as his presence held up all activities. We also knew that GHQ and the Dáil government were very embarrassed by him. Threats had been made publicly that he would be held against other prisoners and obviously we couldn't play this game indefinitely against the British. When a Dublin visitor commented: 'Why the hell doesn't he escape?' I saw the solution of the difficulty. We spent three days in Caherconlish and then moved to a vacant house near Herbertstown, Bruff. We took Lucas for long walks across country and I noted with satisfaction that he studied the topography carefully from every hilltop. Up to this we had always left a

man outside his bedroom window at night and when his room was on the ground floor we withdrew this man. At first nothing happened; he may have suspected a trap, but when we got up the second morning our prisoner was gone.

The general had made his way across country to the main Limerick to Tipperary road where he was eventually picked up by a British army lorry. As the lorry drove towards its barracks it was ambushed by a group of Volunteers led by Seán Treacy. Two British soldiers were killed and Lucas was wounded during the attack. He was taken to the county infirmary in Limerick to recover and was interviewed by the British press. Some elements of the press were eager to publish stories of the general's torture by the IRA but when they questioned him he simply replied: 'I was treated as a gentleman by gentlemen'. When he recovered, the general was asked by the military to prepare an assessment of the IRA's strength and organisation. He was impressed by the IRA's discipline, determination and efficiency; he stated that the British forces faced a much graver military situation in Ireland than they realised and that it would take a much larger force of British garrisons and a bitter struggle to defeat the IRA.

On 21 July the Ennistymon company of the IRA disarmed a British army patrol as it left the Ennistymon workhouse to collect its laundry in the town. The soldiers were surprised by six Volunteers armed with revolvers. Six soldiers and their corporal were disarmed, and released shortly before their IRA attackers made off with their rifles and ammunition. The next day the IRA in Ennistymon made another attempt to disarm British soldiers, but this time they were not so lucky. Michael Conway, Séamus McMahon and a third IRA Volunteer held up two British officers in the town at gunpoint. One of the officers drew his revolver and shot Michael Conway dead. McMahon was wounded but managed to escape with the other Volunteer.

Late in July, Patrick Buckley, an RIC constable from north Kerry stationed at Sixmilebridge, made efforts to contact the IRA. Buckley had decided to resign from the RIC in protest at British atrocities in

Ireland when he realised that he could strike a far greater blow for the Irish Republic if he could help the IRA to capture his barracks. Pat Reidy, a Volunteer with the Mid Clare brigade, met Buckley while he was on patrol in Sixmilebridge. Buckley told Reidy how badly the barracks was defended and how easily it could be captured. Reidy passed this information on to IRA intelligence and Michael Brennan arranged to meet Buckley to discuss the possibility of raiding the barracks for arms. Brennan convinced Buckley to help the IRA capture the barracks by leaving the window over the front door open when he was on duty. Michael Brennan's first attempt to capture the building was a failure, when by chance one of the RIC men inside the barracks noticed the window that Buckley had opened.

On 5 August the IRA made another attempt to capture the barracks. This time Buckley had arranged to leave the front door of the barracks unlocked. At midnight the IRA met at Convent Cross, a mile from Sixmilebridge, and sentries were posted on all roads leading to the village. The Volunteers removed their boots and crept towards the barracks door with their revolvers drawn. Pat Reidy guarded the door while Michael Brennan lifted the latch and entered, followed by the other Volunteers. Seán Murnane headed for the RIC constables' quarters while Brennan went to tackle the barrack's sergeant, Sergeant Porter:

> I sent my three or four companions to capture the guard and two men in bed and I went along to the sergeant's quarters myself. On Buckley's plan I found his room easily and the light of my torch on his face woke him. He ignored an order to put up his hands and when I repeated it he snatched a revolver on the table beside him and levelled it at me. I found it impossible to fire at a man in bed, so I took a chance and hit his gun hard with my own. I was lucky and his gun rolled on the floor. After this he surrendered. I was warned that he would be tough and he certainly was.

The IRA tied up the RIC and searched the barracks, seizing official police documents, valuable intelligence information and police equipment. The IRA's main haul was the RIC garrison's arms, six .45 Webley revolvers, six carbine rifles and a large quantity of ammunition. Before leaving, the IRA cut the telegraph wires leading from the barracks to prevent the RIC calling for assistance. No damage was done to the building during the raid and none of the police were harmed. Sergeant Porter was so disturbed by the raid that he tried to commit suicide by cutting his throat a few days later.

The British authorities responded to the raid on Sixmilebridge barracks by sending fourteen lorries of British soldiers and Black and Tans to search Kilkishen for republican suspects. As the British forces surrounded the village, IRA Volunteer Joseph Clancy had a narrow escape:

Martin McNamara, Jack Curley, Michael Neville and myself were having a meal in Boyles' public house at the time. We were all 'on the run' and each of us was armed with a revolver. We were warned in time to get out by the back door into the fields but were observed by the raiders, who turned machine gun and rifle fire on us. McNamara and myself became separated from the others and we ran along by a hedge for about 200 yards, when McNamara was wounded in the knee. However, we kept going, with the enemy still on our tracks, and traversed about three miles through the country until we crossed the Owenogarney River, which was waist high at the time, and got into the wood on the Belvoir estate where we eluded our pursuers.

By summer 1920 raids by British forces meant that active IRA Volunteers had to leave their homes to avoid capture. As the first British reprisals and murders began, Volunteers had to think of the dangers their presence could pose to their families. Many Volunteers' names and addresses were known to the British forces and because these men were officially wanted by the RIC they went 'on the run', hiding in republican safe houses or sleeping rough in the countryside. In an effort to strengthen the IRA, general headquarters issued orders to local brigades to form active service units or 'flying columns', large mobile forces of well-armed Volunteers which could combat the motorised patrols of the British forces while making full use of the men who had been forced to go 'on the run'.

Michael Brennan selected Joseph Clancy, an ex-British soldier who had joined the IRA, to train the East Clare brigade flying column:

> I had been appointed brigade training officer by reason of my post on the brigade staff and because of my experiences in the First Great War ... As brigade training officer I took in hand personally the drilling of each company according as I moved about the brigade area with Brennan. I always had a rifle or two with which I was able to give lectures on the rifle, its mechanisms and care, how to load it and how to aim with it. I also gave instructions on the use of small arms and bombs. In this way every Volunteer of average intelligence in the East Clare brigade could in an emergency be called upon to use the rifle or revolver by the end of 1920.

Art O'Donnell was appointed commander of the West Clare brigade's flying column organised that August:

> It was suggested that two picked men from each company be brought together, bringing with them all available equipment for special training with a view to establishing an effective mobile column, and this suggestion was accepted. Instructions were issued to each company commander to select two of the best men in his company and send them with equipment to Tullycrine ... Many company captains did not comply with the instructions and instead put the matter before a full meeting of the company, the selection being invariably by drawing lots. As a result, many men were selected who had no intention of going on active service, some actually claiming exemption on the grounds of some imaginary physical defect. When the full column had mobilised, Commandant Liddy asked if I would take charge and I agreed. I set about examining the possibilities of each and found that only about a dozen would be suitable. I billeted them all, however, in the locality and arranged a quiet spot to meet the next morning. Liam Haugh, a returned American and an American ex-army man, took them on hand at shooting practice.

The first Sunday in August the column assembled at Simon O'Donnell's house in Tullycrine. Liam Haugh trained them in the use of the Lee Enfield rifle and members of the column practised shooting a .22 rifle. The Volunteers mobilised again the following Monday and Tuesday, and were lectured on the basic tactics. As they prepared for a fourth day of training, O'Donnell's house was raided by a large combined force of RIC and British soldiers:

> Up to this time, all activities enjoyed immunity from enemy intelligence. The Volunteers as a whole would not, or could not, conceive the possibility of the enemy inducing anybody to set the spy. The known pro-British element within the area were few and scattered; they were, besides, kept at more than an arm's length and were known to be inactive. All the greater, therefore, was the consternation when, on the forenoon of the fourth day, a large force of military and police from Kilrush swooped down on O'Donnell's. About ten of the column who had remained in the neighbouring houses overnight easily escaped.

The West Clare brigade's flying column was temporarily disbanded as a result of the raid while the IRA concentrated on discovering how the British forces had known about the training camp. It was known that the raid was ordered by Detective Constable John Hanlon who was stationed at the barracks at Kilrush. Detective Hanlon must have received information from a spy but the IRA were unable to discover who it was. The West Clare brigade decided to assassinate Detective Hanlon, knowing that local British intelligence would be in chaos without him.

Hanlon was very careful about his security arrangements and seldom left Kilrush on duty. According to Liam Haugh, the Kilrush company of the IRA were 'a squeamish lot' and were reluctant to shoot Hanlon. So two Volunteers from outside Kilrush, Paddy Clancy and Michael Melican, were given the job instead. Clancy and Melican entered the town and took up position near Hanlon's home on Moore Street. As the detective approached, the Volunteers crossed the street to shoot him, but at that point a woman with a pram was walking alongside Hanlon. The gunmen hesitated, allowing the detective to reach his home safely. On 10 August the IRA made a second attempt to shoot the detective. Six members of the IRA armed with revolvers met at Tullycrine Grove to commandeer a car to travel to Kilrush. After a while a black Ford van approached. It appeared to be an ordinary business van, and as it approached, one of the Volunteers stood on the road waving his revolver as a signal to stop. The van came to a halt and the other republicans dashed to the back door only to find themselves staring down the muzzles of six rifles held by half a dozen equally surprised RIC men. The six Volunteers fled through the fields while the RIC beat an equally inglorious retreat in the opposite direction.

On 21 August Liam Haugh was passing through Kilrush on his bicycle when he saw Detective Hanlon on Moore Street. Haugh followed Hanlon into Walshes' pub and shot him dead in the kitchen. A number of British soldiers and RIC policeman were patrolling Kilrush at the time but the shot that killed Detective Hanlon was not heard outside and Haugh had safely left the town before the British discovered Hanlon was dead. After Detective Hanlon's killing, the British carried out widespread searches in Kilrush and the surrounding countryside. Volunteer Patrick Burke was arrested and beaten mercilessly by an RIC patrol having been found with a revolver, for which he was sentenced to two years in prison. His health was broken by the poor treatment he received from the prison authorities and he died shortly after his release.

About this time, the republicans in Clare suffered another loss when IRA Staff Captain Joe McMahon from Kilmaley was killed. McMahon worked as a carpenter in County Cavan and had been attached to the IRA's South Cavan brigade. He was trying to develop a homemade explosive for use in landmines when he was killed on 15 August 1920 by an accidental explosion. His body was brought back to Kilmaley for burial. There was a large force of British soldiers at the graveyard to stop the IRA giving the deceased military honours. As the last shovel of earth was placed on McMahon's grave, the soldiers left and a small group of Volunteers stepped out from behind the churchyard wall and fired their revolvers over the grave.

After a number of appeals from Michael Brennan to IRA head-quarters for arms and ammunition, a crate containing thirty hand grenades was sent to the Mid Clare brigade. The brigade's quartermaster, Seán Murnane, had the crate smuggled by train to Ballycar station near Newmarket on Fergus. The grenades had been made at an IRA armament factory in Dublin, they were twice the size of the regulation British army grenades and before they had even arrived in Clare the local Volunteers had already heard rumours of their destructive power.

Michael Brennan decided to use the grenades to attack the barracks at Scariff. The barracks was a large stone-built two-storey building situated in the village square. The front door of the building was in the centre with a window on either side; sandbagged defences and hundreds of yards of barbed wire protected the door. All the windows were loop holed with bullet-proof steel shutters. On the right of the barracks was Stephen Duggan's pub; to the left was Moloneys' shop. Two RIC sergeants and twelve constables and Black and Tans guarded the building. IRA intelligence reported that members of the RIC garrison regularly drank in Stephen Duggan's.

Michael Brennan's plan was to occupy a number of buildings around the barracks and send a group of six Volunteers up a laneway behind the pub to capture the police drinking inside. Another group was to enter Moloneys' shop, get on to the roof and throw heavy weights from there through the roof of the barracks. Buckets of petrol would then be thrown through the hole and ignited with grenades. As the barracks' roof was being attacked Brennan was to blow a whistle as a signal for the remaining Volunteers to open fire, keeping the police inside under pressure. The date fixed for the attack was 18 September.

Michael Brennan ordered a large mobilisation of Volunteers from the Bodyke, Feakle, Meelick, Mountshannon, Newmarket, Kilkishen, Tuamgraney and Scariff companies outside Scariff village. Michael Gleeson transported the crate of grenades from Dublin with a number of rifles borrowed from the O'Callaghan's Mills company to an empty house in Coolreagh about two miles from Scariff. The Bodyke company of the IRA mounted a guard over the arms until the East Clare brigade's flying column arrived to take the weapons.

Michael Brennan assembled the Volunteers and warned each rifleman to check his ammunition for any marked 'ZZ'. British soldiers and Black and Tans had been dropping clips of .303 rifle ammunition and hand grenades while on patrol in Clare towns. The British forces knew that the IRA were short of ammunition and that any dropped by them would quickly find its way into republican hands. The grenades were rigged to explode as soon as an Volunteers using them removed the pin, and the .303 rifle ammunition would burst when fired, making the rifle useless and injuring whoever used it. Thomas Tuohy, a member of the Scariff company, was present when Brennan warned the Volunteers about the ammunition:

> Prior to the commencement of the attack, when the column was about to move into Scariff Mick Brennan requested every man who had a rifle to examine the .303 ammunition and discard any bullets marked 'KN' or 'ZZ'. He explained that these bullets had been specially charged by the British so as to explode the breech of the rifles and thus damage the gun and cause injury to the man using it ... I was engaged in checking my ammunition, about fifty rounds, when I noticed two youthful Volunteers who had been detailed to hold up all traffic bound for Scariff engaged in an arguments with the occupants of an outside car who wanted to get through. I went up to them and took a more stern attitude towards the very persistent driver. As I was about to finish the examination of my ammunition, orders were given to move off and I left the job unfinished.

At 8 p.m. the Volunteers moved into Scariff under cover of darkness. Two groups took over Conways' house on the north side of the square and Rodgers' house on the north-west corner, which overlooked the barracks sixty yards away. Pat Duggan's drapery shop, a two-storey building diagonally across the square from the barracks, was taken over by Michael Brennan's group as his headquarters for the attack. Joseph Clancy and William McNamara had entered Moloneys' shop next to the RIC barracks, ready to attack it from the roof. They were armed with three 14lb weights on ropes to smash through the slates of the barracks' roof and the crate of grenades to destroy the building. At 9 p.m. Patrick Brennan led a group of six Volunteers down the laneway behind Duggan's pub. As they were about to enter, Michael Hehir fired an accidental shot from his revolver. The party rushed through the back door, but the RIC men and Black and Tans drinking in the bar and sitting on the bench outside had been alerted by the shot and scrambled to get back inside their barracks.

Thomas McNamara and the other Volunteers opened fire as the RIC and Black and Tans ran from the pub: 'A single shot rang out. This alerted the police in front of the barracks and they all made a rush through that building. Simultaneously we fired on them. The O/C of the IRA party, Michael Brennan, happened to be outside Duggan's drapery shop at the time and he also fired on the police, two of whom were wounded.' At the same time one of the RIC sergeants who was returning to the barracks was shot at by another group of Volunteers in the village. The sergeant was badly wounded but hid and escaped capture. The twenty-five IRA riflemen stationed at the drapery shop and Conways' and Roches' houses opened fire on the barracks. Patrick Brennan's group moved from the pub into the square and joined in the attack. When the IRA opened fire on the RIC, William McNamara and Joseph Clancy got to work on attacking the barracks from the roof of Moloneys' shop:

> McNamara and I first of all removed some slates from the roof of Moloneys' house to get out on the roof. We were not long in doing this, nor did breaking a hole in the roof of the barracks occupy much time. With this accomplished each of us threw four bombs through the hole into the barracks. None of the bombs exploded. The sniping continued until about eleven o'clock, but the police, who were replying vigorously with their rifles, were determined not to surrender.

The RIC sent up flares to signal for help from the British army in Tulla. Joseph Clancy's group in Moloneys' shop requested petrol to pour through the hole in the barrack roof to try and set it on fire but Michael Brennan refused permission because the fire could easily spread and destroy either of the business premises. The sniping attack continued for some time as it was now hoped that the IRA's rifle fire on the barracks would force the RIC to surrender. Thomas Tuohy continued firing at the barracks from his window in Rodgers' house until he mistakenly used one of the doctored 'ZZ' rounds:

As the attack progressed I used the checked rounds and then proceeded to use the ammunition in the other pocket. One of these bullets, as we had been warned, exploded and damaged the ejector of my rifle and slightly injured me in my right eye ... On returning home that night the eye was treated by members of Cumann na mBan and though it continued to be a bit tender I did not bother going to a doctor. It never ceased to give me trouble and after some years became worse until ultimately I lost the sight of that eye. When eventually I did receive medical treatment I was informed that the other eye was also affected and as I make this statement I am practically sightless.

After two hours of fighting it was obvious that without working grenades the IRA would not be able to capture the barracks and any further sniping would only be a waste of ammunition. After 11 p.m. Michael Brennan blew his whistle as the signal for the IRA to end the attack and withdraw. Joseph Clancy decided to try the grenades one last time:

Just before the call off of the attack was given I went back to the roof and flung three more grenades into the barracks, but these also proved to be duds. As I was engaged in throwing these bombs the other men who were in the building with me withdrew from the place, leaving me locked in.

Clancy tried to climb off the roof, fell and was injured. He was placed on a handcart and taken back to the main party of the IRA where Michael Brennan ordered them to disperse.

The East Clare brigade were depending on the reputation of the explosive power of the grenades from Dublin to destroy the barracks, because of Michael Brennan's reluctance to set the barracks on fire in case it spread to neighbouring houses and businesses. Brennan reported the failure of the bombs to IRA headquarters in Dublin and claimed that a technical fault was found when the grenades were tested. However, Michael Gleeson offered a more likely explanation: 'Next day, as the unused bombs were being removed to a little dump, which we had constructed, we examined them and found the explanation of those which had been thrown into the barracks to explode. The detonators had not been inserted.'

The day after the attack a large number of RIC and Black and Tans entered Scariff, accompanied by two armoured cars. Michael and Patrick Brennan, who were still in the area, sent word to Joseph Honan, Seán O'Halloran, Paddy O'Donnell, Michael Brady and Arthur O'Connor to meet them on the Ennis side of Scariff Bridge, 100 yards across the river from Scariff town hall. Michael Brennan's group were waiting along the docks opposite the town hall when republican scouts reported that sixteen Black and Tans were approaching the hall with cans of petrol. Brennan moved his men into a firing position:

> We had apparently arrived just as petrol had been spilled over several sections of the floor, as within a few minutes flames appeared in different parts of the hall. There was no point in waiting for the others of our party and we fired five or six shots through the windows of the hall, firing the police instantly onto the floor. They were now faced with the position that the hall was on fire and there was no way out except against the fire of our rifles. They did the only thing possible – keeping flat on the floor (we were on a hill about 100 yards away and we could almost fire onto the floor through the windows) they crept around and beat out the fire. We dropped an occasional bullet through the windows to make matters more complicated, but as always we had to be very sparing with our ammunition. We intended crossing the bridge to look for the others, but just as we left our position an armoured car appeared on the bridge and fired Verey lights. We were only about fifty to sixty yards from the car in the open field and, as our only chance, we dropped flat and lay perfectly still. The car opened fire across where we lay with a machine gun, but as the bullets were clearing us we concluded we weren't seen. When the light and fire died down for a moment we sprinted for a low loose wall, jumped it and took cover behind it. The Verey lights and machine gun fire continued for some time, but it was wild firing and our only real danger was from splinters of stone broken by bullets off our protecting wall. We didn't reply to the fire, as our rifle bullets would have been useless against the armoured plating of the car. The fire from the town hall had been completely extinguished and the Black and Tans sneaked out under the protection of the 'barrage' from the car. Having done its job, the car moved away up the street and we walked off.

That same night RIC Constable Jason Duffy was killed at Boston near the Galway border when an RIC foot patrol opened fire on an RIC Crossley tender that was approaching with its headlights turned off, killing Constable Duffy.

About week after the IRA's attack the RIC barracks was evacuated. This was an important victory because a large area of north-east Clare and southern Galway between Woodford (in County Galway), Tulla and Killaloe was free of British forces except for a dozen RIC constables and Black and Tans stationed in Feakle. The nearest enemy posts to Bodyke were the British army at Tulla, seven miles away, and the RIC and Auxiliary posts at Killaloe, twelve miles away. All roads capable of taking British lorries were blocked by digging deep trenches, building stone barricades or felling trees. The area became a safe haven for IRA Volunteers 'on the run' and IRA activity and training in the area was unchecked by the British forces.

On 14 September Volunteers from the West Clare brigade assembled at Kilmurry McMahon to ambush a British military convoy that regularly travelled through the area. A deep trench had been dug across the road in the hope of stopping the British vehicles. The main body of the republicans, armed with shotguns and revolvers, were posted on higher ground to the east of the road. A smaller section of three Volunteers, Patrick Hassett, Paddy Haugh and Joe Kelly, under the command of William Shanahan were stationed in the hedges at the western edge of the road. Shanahan and Hassett were armed with rifles, in support of Haugh and Kelly who were armed with hand grenades, which they were to throw into the British lorries when they became stuck in the trench. The convoy approached the site earlier than expected, surprising two republican scouts who were running to get into position when they heard the sound of approaching vehicles. The British soldiers immediately halted their lorries 200 yards from the ambush site, dismounted and opened fire on the republican scouts. The soldiers were so far outside the ambush position that the republicans were unable to attack them. As the British began to spread out in an encircling movement William Shanahan realised the danger to the main group of Volunteers armed with shotguns and revolvers which would be useless against British soldiers with Lee Enfield rifles at a long distance. Shanahan and Hassett advanced along the roadside hedge until they were in a better position to attack the soldiers before opening rapid fire on them, keeping them engaged long enough to allow the rest of the Volunteers to withdraw to their headquarters at O'Donnells' house in Tullycrine. Seeing that their comrades were safe, Shanahan and Hassett withdrew and joined them in O'Donnells' that evening.

In the Mid Clare brigade's area the IRA's activities had not yet broken the British government's control over such a large area, and widespread military activity and intelligence gathering by British forces continued. In September the Mid Clare brigade captured two British spies who were operating in the Ennistymon area. In the early autumn a British army officer dressed in civilian clothes came to the garage where IRA Volunteer Thomas McDonough worked in Ennistymon and hired a car and a driver for the evening:

I recognised him at once as a Captain McLean who had been stationed in Lahinch with a detachment of Scottish Horse a year previously. He did not, of course, give his name or say what business he was on. I was detailed to drive him. Before going out with him I consulted [John Joe] 'Tosser' Neylon who said: 'By all means go with him, keep an eye on what he is doing and report back.' For three days I drove him to various parts of county Clare including Kilfenora, Ballyvaughan and Lisdoonvarna. On one day he was alone with me; on the other two he had a companion with him also in civilian clothes … I gathered that McLean was trying to give me the impression that he was a commercial traveller, for he made calls at shops and hotels He asked me various questions such as the names of places we drove through and the names of people living in certain houses. My answers were vague, either telling him that I did not know or giving him incorrect information, but I noticed that the routes chosen by him brought us to the vicinity of the homes of active Volunteers including that of Seán McNamara, commandant of the 6th battalion, and then a 'much wanted' man by the British forces. Often on the tops of hills or on high ground he, McLean, would ask me to stop and he would get out and view the countryside.

Each night he returned to Ennistymon and each night I reported the day's proceedings to Neylon.

It was now obvious that Captain McLean and his companion Captain Collins were gathering information to plan a 'round up' of leading IRA members in the area, so the IRA decided to capture and interrogate the two officers. They were disarmed and arrested by Volunteers in Ennistymon on 19 September and taken to Ballinalacken Castle for interrogation. There they were interrogated for a number of days and released, having given an assurance that they would leave Ireland immediately. The Mid Clare brigade passed all the information on to IRA intelligence. The pair were exceptionally lucky not to have been executed; had they been captured after the shocking events in the Milltown area the following week, they almost certainly would have been. The IRA's war against British rule had not yet reached boiling point in Clare. While the republicans were becoming increasingly organised and daring in their military operations throughout the county, British murders and reprisals by the RIC, Black and Tans and the army had not taken place on any significant scale, but all that was about to change. On 22 September the full fury of 'the Black and Tan terror' was unleashed in Clare.

8

Another Black Page in British History

It is a black page in the history of powerful and free nations when they look on in craven silence at the spectacle of children massacred in their homes because of the loyalty of their fathers to freedom.

The hypocritical words of former British PM Lloyd George – who had ordered British murders and atrocities in Ireland – denouncing Fascist atrocities in the Spanish Republic in 1936

In early autumn 1920 Anthony Malone and the other officers of the 4th battalion were ordered by the brigade council of the Mid Clare brigade IRA to prepare an ambush for British motor patrols in the Miltown Malbay and Ennistymon areas. IRA intelligence reported that a patrol of regular RIC men and Black and Tans travelled in a Crossley Tender from Ennistymon to Miltown Malbay at 10.30 each Wednesday morning. The brigade council decided to attack the patrol the following Wednesday, 22 September.

The countryside along the RIC's weekly route was examined and an ambush site was selected at Rineen, about two miles from Miltown Malbay on the Ennistymon road. The site was a low cliff where the West Clare Railway rose sharply above the road commanding a good view of Lahinch and the surrounding coastline to the west. A curve in the road forced vehicles travelling from Ennistymon to Miltown to slow down as they reached the ambush site.

The operation at Rineen was to be the first major attack on the British forces in the area and the officers of the Mid Clare brigade decided to use a large force of Volunteers from eight companies in the 4th battalion to take part in the attack. The morning of the attack each of these IRA companies was to supply seven Volunteers to form the attacking party or to act as scouts and messengers. On 21 September John Joe Neylon was detailed to select seven men from the Ennistymon company to take part in the ambush:

> On the night previous to the attack I paraded the Ennistymon company and called for Volunteers to take part in it without disclosing any details of what was about to come off. Nearly every man present – and there was a parade of about seventy strong the same night – volunteered. I had to select only seven and that was a difficult job indeed. When I had made my selection I instructed these men to report to Lehanes at Lahinch that night and went off myself on a bike to see Ignatius O'Neill with whom I had some other business to discuss.

Ignatius O'Neill was still recovering from the wounds he had received at the Crowe's Bridge ambush and was staying at safe house at Lisdoonvarna. The officers of the Mid Clare brigade had decided not to include O'Neill in the attack because he was still recovering from his wounds, and so kept all information regarding the planned attack at Rineen from him. When John Joe Neylon met him that night, O'Neill had heard of the preparations for the attack and was furious:

> O'Neill met me with a violent reception. He was raging mad because he had heard from some source that we had decided to bring off the ambush without asking him to take part. He described the battalion officers as 'a shower of bastards', and accused me of being a 'double crosser'. In order to placate him I said: 'All right the ambush is coming off and you'll have to take charge.' Although he did not want to be in charge I Insisted that he should and outlined to him what our plans were and told him of the arrangements which had been made. As far as I remember he made no change in them. We arrived in Lahinch about three or four o'clock in the morning and there found between sixty and sixty-five men assembled. All the companies had supplied the seven men they were asked to do and, in addition, there were the officers of the battalion staff.

At 4 a.m. O'Neill and Neylon led the Volunteers towards Carrig at Ballyvaskin; there the Moy company of the IRA scouted the route to

Rineen while the members of the attacking party followed on foot. Thomas McDonough drove a number of Volunteers from Ennistymon to meet the main IRA force at the final assembly point about a mile from the ambush site at Rineen. By six that morning fifty members of the IRA had assembled for the ambush. O'Neill posted sentries guarding the roads to Miltown Malbay and Lahinch while the main force of the IRA settled down for a brief rest along the boreen leading from the railway line down to the roadway. O'Neill and Neylon reviewed the ground with the different company captains and discussed the advantages and possible problems posed by their chosen position. Both the RIC and British army had a habit of suddenly changing the formation and strength of their transport patrols; if the strength of the RIC's patrol was increased to more than one lorry, the attacking formation would have to be changed quickly. A number of signallers were posted along the hilltops near Rineen and Thomas Moroney was placed in charge of the scouts posted on the roads leading to the ambush site. Their job was to watch for the approach of the patrol and give advanced warning of a change in its strength or the arrival of British reinforcements. As daylight approached, O'Neill assembled the remaining forty Volunteers and with the help of John Joe Neylon and Patrick Lehane divided them into three different attacking parties. O'Neill repeatedly explained to them in detail the plan of the operation until he was satisfied that each individual IRA Volunteer and section leader knew what their task was.

To the north and west of the IRA's position at Rineen, open ground and fields swept towards the sea. To the south and east of the railway line small fields gave way to open bog land leading towards Miltown Malbay. Ignatius O'Neill made an inspection of the IRA's arms and rejected a number of old shotguns. The remaining arms included the six Lee Enfield rifles, three carbine rifles, a large number of shotguns and a few revolvers. Anthony Malone and Patrick Kerin were given rifles and ordered to take up position behind a low fence twenty yards directly to the north of the road; two other riflemen, Stephen Gallagher and Seán Bourke, were stationed about 200 yards further west towards Miltown Malbay. These four had orders to prevent the RIC and Black and Tans leaving the lorry and taking cover in the fields, or from attempting to retreat towards the sea and back to Lahinch.

O'Neill gave the remaining rifles to John Joe Neylon, David Kennelly, Dan Lehane and Michael Dwyer. Peter Vaughan, an experienced ex-American soldier who had served on the western front during the First World War, was equipped with two hand grenades. These five men were to form the main attacking force and were stationed at the north-western end of a small by-road which connected to the Lahinch road. The main body of Volunteers were stationed about fifty yards further up this by-road where it crossed the railway line. This group commanded a good view of the ambush site, being in a raised position about forty feet above the level of the road at a distance of thirty yards. They were mostly armed with shotguns and were to act as a secondary attacking force with orders to cover the position of O'Neill's group. A number of large furze bushes had been cut to provide camouflage for these men. At O'Neill's command, a single rifle shot from John Joe Neylon was to be the signal to open the attack. The riflemen in the first attacking group had orders to shoot the driver of the lorry to prevent it breaking out of the ambush position. Peter Vaughan was to throw his two grenades into the back of the RIC lorry. If the IRA came into difficulties they were to fall back to the railway line crossing the hill at Rineen and use it as a secondary line of defence while they retreated. It was now past 7 a.m. and the republicans settled down to a long wait before the expected arrival of the RIC patrol.

That morning eleven miles from Rineen, the 2nd battalion of the IRA's West Clare brigade were also waiting in ambush. Captain Alan Lendrum, an ex-British army officer from Tyrone, had been appointed acting resident magistrate at Kilkee by the British authorities. Captain Lendrum occasionally travelled to and from court in an RIC Crossley Tender with a number of Black and Tans for security, but more often he travelled alone in his Ford car. The 4th battalion of the West Clare brigade watched his movements for several weeks and decided to hold up Lendrum at gunpoint and commandeer his car. On the morning 22 September while the IRA lay in ambush at Rineen, William Shanahan and a few other IRA Volunteers waited for Captain Lendrum at a level railway crossing at Caherfeenick two miles north of Doonbeg. As Lendrum drove towards the level crossing the gates were closed by the two Volunteers and he was ordered at gunpoint to surrender his car. Captain Lendrum drew his automatic pistol but was mortally wounded before he had a chance to fire. One of the IRA Volunteers drove the ex-British officer's car from the scene while William Shanahan took the mortally wounded Captain Lendrum to an outhouse in a nearby field. Shanahan, thinking Lendrum was already dead, took him to a lake, tied a weight to him and threw him into the water, where the unconscious captain died of drowning. This action was to have serious consequences for the IRA ambushers at Rineen later that morning.

Arriving back at Ennistymon having driven some Volunteers from the town to the ambush site at Rineen, Thomas McDonough reported for work at Roughans' garage when he saw the patrol of RIC and Black and Tans preparing to travel to Miltown Malbay: 'I was standing at the garage door and watched a lorry of police move off from the barracks across the road. It was driven by a Black and Tan named Hardiman and manned by I think six RIC men including Sergeant Hynes and Constables Kelly, Harte and Hodnett, all of whom I knew well.' As the Crossley Tender roared out of Ennistymon towards Miltown Malbay, a young IRA Volunteer watched the RIC and Black and Tans disappear in a cloud of dust from his work at Roughans' shop and was overheard saying to himself: 'They are going now, but will they ever come back?'

After 11 a.m. the IRA ambushers hidden at Rineen heard the sound of a train coming from the south and hid from view behind ditches until the train had passed. As the Volunteers scrambled back into position, the scouts watching the road from Lahinch signalled the approach of the RIC. John Joe Neylon could hear the sounds of the patrol approaching when the IRA's scouts reached him and O'Neill with reports that the enemy force was much larger than expected:

About noon, word was received from the scouts that the three lorries were coming from the Ennistymon side. O'Neill had a quick consultation with myself and a few of the officers beside him. He had expected only one lorry and the plans had been made accordingly. His force was mainly composed of raw material and the ground did not lend itself to quick deployment. In the circumstances he decided, in view of the scouts' message, to withhold fire. When only one lorry passed he realised a mistake had been made by one of the scouts.

The message 'Police lorry coming' had been misinterpreted by one of the IRA's scouts as 'Three lorries coming'. The result was that the RIC's Crossley Tender was allowed to pass through the ambush without a shot being fired.

Realising the mistake, O'Neill despatched Jack Clune, an IRA Volunteer from Inagh, to cycle to Miltown Malbay, report on the activities of the RIC patrol and report back immediately if it appeared that the RIC and Black and Tans had seen the Volunteers waiting in ambush and were calling for reinforcements. O'Neill moved the riflemen in the first attacking party into a more suitable position to attack the Crossley Tender on its return from Miltown and made a few more changes to the IRA's other positions while he waited for Clune to return. Two hours later Clune reported back that the RIC patrol had not detected the ambush and their lorry was parked outside the RIC barracks in the town facing the direction of Rineen. Clune's information was confirmed when one of the republican scouts signalled the return of the police lorry. A few minutes later the Crossley Tender re-appeared. It passed about ten yards beyond the laneway to O'Gormans' house on the northern side of the road when O'Neill gave the order to Neylon to fire the opening shot. Patrick Vaughan stood up and threw his first grenade at the police lorry; his second grenade missed and landed on the northern edge of the roadway, exploding harmlessly. Already the Volunteers in the first and second attacking parties had opened fire, blasting the RIC and Black and Tans in the back of the vehicle with rifle and shotgun fire.

Within seconds of John Joe Neylon firing the opening shot the attack had ended:

Immediately all the party opened up. The attack was over in a matter of seconds. There was no reply from the lorry and our fellows rushed towards it to find five dead police men lying inside. One of the police managed to get off the lorry and had gone about 300 yards towards Miltown when he was seen and shot by Donal Lehane of Lahinch in a field near O'Connors' house.

A short distance away on the northern side of the road Anthony Malone had joined the first attacking section in taking aim at the driver:

The pre-arranged signal shot was fired. There was an immediate volley from the different positions. I fired three or four rounds at the men sitting in the cab and next I saw the driver slump over the wheel as blood pumped from a wound in his neck. He seemed to be staring directly at Kerin and myself. The men on the other side of the road poured several rounds into the Tender and, in a matter of minutes, the attack was over.

As soon as the firing stopped O'Neill gave the order to cease fire and search the vehicles. The IRA searched the Crossley Tender and recovered six Lee Enfield and carbine rifles, six .45 Webley and Scott revolvers, a number of Mills bomb hand grenades and almost 3,000 rounds of .303 ammunition. After the weapons and ammunition were recovered the lorry was set on fire. Patrick Kerin rushed on to the roadside with Anthony Malone and searched the bodies of the dead RIC men and Black and Tans for intelligence papers and official documents: 'When the firing stopped, Malone and myself rushed over to the Tender. I searched one of the dead men and, from correspondence which he had received from lady admirers in London, I learned that his name was Reggie Hardman, obviously a Black and Tan.' Reginald Hardman was the first Black and Tan killed in Clare; he was twenty-one years old and came from East Finchley in London. He had served in the Royal Artillery Regiment before joining the RIC. The other five members of the patrol were all regular RIC men – Constable Michael Harte from Sligo, Constable John Hodnett from Cork, Constable Michael Kelly from Roscommon and Constable John McGuire from Mayo died at the scene, while Sergeant Michael Hynes from Roscommon was fatally wounded in the ambush and died two days later.

While the Crossley Tender and the bodies of the dead RIC men were being searched, Volunteers sat on the roadside smoking and talking until Dan Kennelly, who had served in both the British army and RIC, urged the men to get back up the hillside to safety quickly. The IRA shared out quantities of the captured .303 ammunition and began moving back up towards the railway line crossing the hill. Séamus Hennessy heard the sound of lorries approaching from Lahinch. He shouted to Stephen Gallagher, who had gone to collect the rifle and ammunition from the now dead RIC man who had tried to escape from the ambush, to hurry back towards the hill. Next Hennessey shouted a warning to a group of Volunteers who had halted below the first hill and indicated in the direction of the noise. A few minutes later a British army lorry came around the bend in the road below the railway. The driver stopped when he saw the blazing RIC Crossley Tender and the soldiers jumped out and rushed up the hillside towards the railway line. Moments later a second British lorry halted a short distance behind the first and more British soldiers poured out to pursue the IRA.

Ten lorries of British soldiers had left Ennistymon to search for Captain Lendrum who had been killed by the West Clare brigade at Caherfeenick near Doonbeg earlier that morning. As they approached Rineen they heard the distant gunfire from the ambush and saw the smoke rising from the burning Crossley Tender and Volunteers crossing the hillside. When the British soldiers came into view advancing towards the IRA, the republican scouts let out a warning cry of 'Military!' and O'Neill gave the orders to retreat across the railway line back towards Ballyvaskin. A small group, including Ned Lynch, Michael O'Keefe and the Bourke brothers, who had been separated from the main force of the IRA, made off towards the sea shore in the opposite direction without being noticed by the enemy.

As the soldiers gained ground on the main force of the IRA scrambling over the hilltop O'Neill and John Joe Neylon stood their ground along the railway line to cover the others' escape:

Those who had already been making their way towards the top of the hill, as well as the party who were starting to do so, all came under heavy fire – rifle and machine gun – from the newly arrived troops … As the big majority of our men had only shotguns, they were of no use in meeting the British forces who in a short time had reached the hilltop a quarter of a mile or so east of the scene of the ambush. There was only one course open to us and that was to use the riflemen to fight a rear-guard action while the others with the shotguns were making their way to cover and safety on the Ballyvaskin side. Unfortunately only a few of the riflemen were available for this purpose. They included O'Neill himself, Michael Dwyer, Patrick Lehane and myself. The other men with rifles had gone off in different ways and it was not possible to collect them. The four of us took up positions in a field adjacent to Honans' house and engaged the military, who were using a machine gun behind a stone wall at the corner of a field about 300 yards almost due east.

Their opening volley felled the leading British soldier advancing towards them, and his comrades took cover in the heather. The four riflemen spread out and commenced rapid fire, returning the captured British .303 ammunition to its previous owners at a generous rate. This gave the British the impression that they were facing a much larger group of riflemen. Séamus Hennessy was heading towards a gap in a bank when Patrick Vaughan shouted a warning: 'Don't go out that gap, for they're like to set the gun on it. Roll over the bank when I shout.' When Vaughan gave the word, the shotgun men tumbled over the bank while the soldiers on the hill raked the gap of the bank and its edges with machine gun fire.

While O'Neill and Neylon's group were firing on the soldiers in an effort to halt their advance, Patrick Kerin and the other Volunteers continued their retreat towards Ballyvaskin across open ground:

We went in extended formation and had gone 100 yards or so when we came under heavy machine gun fire from the north-east. The military had reached the top of Dromin hill and placed a machine gun in position 400 yards away from us. Our party at this stage were in the middle of a ten-acre field through which ran a stream in the direction of Ballyvaskin. Pat Frawley and myself made for the stream. On the way I was stunned by a bullet which passed between my ear and head. Recovering after a few seconds, I got into a shallow drain where I remained for ten minutes or so, and then dashed twenty or thirty yards further on to a cock of hay. There I found Pat McGough, O/C of the Inagh company. With him I got as far as a low stone wall. The firing was still fierce and was coming mostly from a machine gunner. Here we began to time the machine gun burst and reckoned that a pan was being changed. We dashed across another fifty or sixty yards of open ground behind another stone fence where we met two more of our crowd, Dave Kennelly and John Crawford. Kennelly, who had a rifle, was in an exhausted state and enquired if any of us were in a condition to return the fire. Crawford had a carbine which he captured from the Tender, but the 'cut off' had jammed. This I put right by forcing it with my teeth, and we both opened fire. I exhausted all the ammunition I had, a total of fifty-two rounds. Our fire enabled the men in our vicinity to retreat in more safety and, when my ammunition was finished, we went after them.

On the side of Dromin Hill, John Joe Neylon's group were coming under increasing pressure as the rest of the Volunteers reached Ballyvaskin. They had concentrated their rifle fire on the machine gun crew and thought they had wounded one of them because the fire halted for a short period but longer than a normal stoppage. When the machine gun resumed firing, a second volley from the four riflemen silenced it again, Neylon and his comrades used this opportunity to retreat. As they scrambled down the hillside the British soldiers' fire was so close that Neylon had his leg grazed by a bullet which passed through the leg of his trousers:

> O'Neill was wounded in the thigh early at this stage of the fighting and as we retreated he had to be removed. This was done by Michael Dwyer, who carried him on his back. Gradually we made our way towards Ballyvaskin taking advantage of whatever bit of cover was available ... ultimately the whole party got into the Ballyvaskin country and dispersed.

With the British soldiers in hot pursuit the republicans had no time for an ordered retreat and broke up into a number of smaller groups which would be harder for the British to pursue. Local farm labourers who had been making trams of hay near the edge of the bog when the running battle started helped carry the two wounded Volunteers to safety and sent for doctors to Miltown and Lahinch. The wounded were then placed on stretchers and carried across country to Moy. Patrick Kerin and Michael Curtain expected British forces to arrive in the area at any time and hid their rifles and the papers they had taken from the RIC men's bodies in a stone wall near Molohans' house. It was now after four o'clock and the British military had sent for reinforcements as soon as they had arrived at the ambush site at Rineen two hours earlier. O'Neill and Curtin were the only IRA members wounded in the withdrawal, though neither was wounded seriously. However, the British forces suffered much heavier losses; in addition to the six dead members of the RIC several British soldiers had been wounded.

O'Neill had expected the British forces to carry out raids and reprisals in the area following the ambush and had asked Andrew O'Donoghue, commandant of the Mid Clare brigade's 5th battalion, to meet the ambushing party at Ennistymon to mount fresh attacks on the British forces and prevent them carrying out reprisals. O'Donoghue travelled to Ennistymon with six Volunteers, but because of the chaotic withdrawal from Rineen no members of the 4th battalion were there to meet them.

When the last of the Volunteers reached Ballyvaskin they looked back towards Rineen to check if the British were still in pursuit. Instead they saw the first clouds of smoke rising from burning houses near the ambush site, as the soldiers began taking revenge on the local civilian population. When the soldiers realised that the IRA had narrowly escaped they returned to their lorries on the roadside at Rineen. On seeing the bodies of their dead comrades they flew into a rage and descended on Honans' farm, the nearest house to the ambush site, and set it on fire. They returned to their lorries and drove the short distance to O'Gormans' farm in whose fields the RIC man who had attempted to escape had been shot. The O'Gormans were dragged from their home, abused and terrorised by the soldiers before their home was also set on fire. As the soldiers drove from O'Gormans' blazing house they spotted

Seán Keane, an elderly man out in his fields building a rick of hay. They shot and mortally wounded the old man, who died on 1 October.

After dark, a mixed British army and RIC raiding party arrived at the home of Dan Lehane, at Cragg in Lahinch. His eldest sons, Patrick and Donal, had taken part in the Rineen ambush. At gunpoint they questioned Dan Lehane about his sons' involvement in the IRA and arrested his fourteen-year-old son Jimmy. Dan Lehane gave them curt answers before finally telling them to 'go to hell'. They beat him and dragged him to the gates of the nearby railway crossing and shot him through the throat within view of his horrified wife and son. Two RIC men were about to shoot his son Jimmy when a British military officer intervened. Dan Lehane died of his wound early the next morning; a few hours later the RIC returned and burned his home to the ground.

The British search parties sent to look for Captain Lendrum in the Doonbeg area gave up their search at nightfall and began raiding and burning roadside houses at Bealatha, Cree, Doonbeg and Kilkee. On their way back to Ennistymon they stopped again at Doonbeg and Miltown Malbay to burn stacks of turf and fields of crops.

The silent darkness on the streets of Ennistymon was broken by the sound of Crossley Tenders, as RIC reinforcements and Black and Tans arrived in the town. They were enraged by the official police report on the Rineen ambush which claimed that the IRA had mutilated the bodies of the six dead policemen. The Black and Tans began their atrocities shortly after nine o'clock when they set the town hall on fire. An hour later an RIC sergeant and a force of twenty RIC men and Black and Tans arrived at the home of Tom Connole, the local secretary of the Irish Transport and General Workers' Union. Connole's house was surrounded by the RIC while a number of them broke down his door. The sergeant arrested Connole, threw him into the street, and tied his hands and feet. The police threatened to shoot his wife when she attempted to fetch a coat for him. She was forced from the house and refused permission to get a shawl to wrap around herself and her four-month-old child. At gunpoint she was taken to a neighbour's house leading her four-year-old son by one hand and carrying her infant in the other. The RIC set fire to his home and executed Tom Connole in the street, shooting him in the head at point blank range. Before leaving they took his body and threw it into the blazing building, while his wife watched from a neighbour's window. To make the act even more horrific the RIC and Black and Tans involved in Connole's murder were all sober at the time. Early the next morning a piece of his blood-stained skull was found on the street near his home and his charred corpse was found inside the remains of his house.

The RIC and Black and Tans broke into Flanagans' shop and stole a large amount of spirits and then began knocking on the doors of a row of houses giving the occupants seven minutes to leave their homes before they set them on fire. True to their word the policemen returned seven minutes later and set Flanagans' and the first four houses on fire. As the RIC set to work burning Flanagans' house, Susan Flanagan pleaded with them to spare the house because she was unable to remove her invalid sister who was still inside. One of the RIC men replied: 'We don't give a damn if you have five invalid sisters, we're going to burn.' Susan Flanagan dragged her sister down the stairs and carried her out of the house on her back to the bottom of the garden while the house went up in flames. After this the RIC took a break to loot more alcohol and then returned to Michael Vaughan's house where without warning they threw an incendiary bomb through the window. As the occupants – an elderly woman, a mother and her child – fled from the house they were fired upon. As the RIC and Black and Tans were leaving the burning buildings they captured and shot dead P.J. Linnane, a fifteen-year-old boy who had been sent by his mother to warn an elderly neighbour that her home was in danger of being burned. The next day his body was found near the local barracks with four bullet wounds.

The RIC made their way back through the town setting fire to Davitts' drapery shop and looting Madigans' pub, drinking their fill before leaving to set more buildings on fire and shoot randomly at anyone they saw fleeing or attempting to quench the fires. Some of the local people stayed in the town to try and put out the fires but others fled to the surrounding countryside as the RIC's campaign of terror spread. At one stage a few British soldiers stationed in Ennistymon made attempts to put out the fires set by their comrades in the RIC, to prevent the whole town from being destroyed. With the town well ablaze, a group of RIC travelled to Lahinch and repeated their usual round of looting and burning. They raided seven homes and set fire to them. A farmer from East Clare, Joseph Samon, who was on holiday in Ennistymon, was shot dead by the RIC while helping a woman out of one of these houses. Next the RIC turned their attention to Flanagans' shop, where Patrick Lehane was hiding in the attic. Having wrecked the shop and looting its goods the Black and Tans and RIC set fire to the building and Patrick Lehane was burned alive in his hiding place.

At midnight the two forces left their barracks in Miltown Malbay determined to make the townspeople suffer for the ambush. A number of them had been demanding free drink in the local pubs for several hours, before emerging onto the streets. Drunken Black and Tans fired indiscriminate volleys through the streets, while the RIC threw hand grenades at shop fronts, splintering the woodwork and shattering the windows. A group of RIC men broke into the hardware shop belonging to Ignatius O'Neill's father and set it on fire. In an orgy of arson attacks the RIC then proceeded to burn Collins' pub and the home of Michael Hayes. A second group of RIC arrived in the town by Crossley Tender and joined the local forces in breaking into several pubs and homes in search of drink. They then began looting houses and shops in the town, still firing their guns and smashing windows at random. When they were sufficiently drunk and tired of looting, they again turned their attentions to arson and burned Michael Marrinan's home, Jones' grocery shop and bar and Caseys' drapery shop. The British forces ended their rampage at 5 a.m. and returned to barracks, leaving several buildings in the town still blazing. As the fires spread, some members of the British army stationed in Miltown Malbay attempted to keep the rapidly spreading fires in check, but by then it was too late; the damage had already been done. By morning eight houses were destroyed by fire and many others had suffered serious damage; the streets were a mass of rubble, charred wood, broken glass, empty bottles of spirits and charred shop goods.

According to Anthony Malone the Rineen ambush and the British forces' reprisals had a strong effect on local people and IRA Volunteers:

> The ambush had as far as our battalion area was concerned two very direct results. The enemy became more hostile and active, but he used large convoys when travelling. The people became very much embittered against him and adopted a more defiant attitude towards the military and Black and Tans. The women and the older people did not hesitate to show their feelings when they encountered these forces in the course of raids and searches. As far as the IRA organisation itself went, the men became keener at their drill and showed more enthusiasm in the different duties which they were called upon to perform, e.g. road cutting, scouting and despatch carrying.

Far from being random acts of cowardly drunken violence, the British attacks on the people of Ennistymon and Miltown Malbay were premeditated. The RIC and Black and Tans had organised supplies of petrol, extra hand grenades and reinforcements for their rampage of arson and killing. RIC drivers and Crossley Tenders had to be made available for these reprisals, while Irish members of the RIC guided the Black and Tans and British soldiers to their destinations and prepared lists of houses to be burned.

The atrocities committed by the British forces were widely reported in British newspapers and were raised in parliament by Mr Arthur Henderson, MP, who moved the resolution, 'That this house regrets the present state of lawlessness in Ireland, and the lack of discipline in the armed forces of the crown, resulting in the death or injury of innocent citizens and the destruction of property; and is of the opinion that an independent enquiry should at once be instituted into the causes, nature and extent of the reprisals on the part of those whose duty is the maintenance of law and order.' Unsurprisingly the resolution was opposed by the British government. Sir Hamar Greenwood, the British government's chief secretary for Ireland, claimed that the RIC and British soldiers who murdered five people and attempted to burn three towns in a single night were 'brave men' who had been driven wild by alleged republican atrocities. The House of Commons voted against Henderson's resolution.

However, Field Marshal Sir Henry Wilson expressed outrage at the reprisals, not because he was upset by the killings of innocent Irish people, but because he was unhappy with the way the killings were conducted, commenting: 'If these men ought to be murdered then the government ought to murder them.' Killing republicans was perfectly acceptable to Wilson as long as they were 'murdered' in an official fashion by the British government. Winston Churchill was also pressuring the government to make the British campaign of 'murder' in Ireland official and respectable by calling for the execution of republican prisoners. Five weeks later both men got their wish when IRA Volunteer Kevin Barry was hanged in Mountjoy prison. He was the first of twenty-four republicans officially executed by the British government.

Having had their terrorist acts excused in parliament, the forces threatened to resume their murderous campaign against the people of west Clare. On the morning of 26 September, the residents of Kilkee found notices pinned to their doors threatening that if Captain Lendrum was not found by noon the following Wednesday the villages of Cooraclare, Doonbeg and Mullagh would be burned in reprisal. To show that this was not an empty threat, a police patrol of RIC and Black and Tans arrived in Kilfenora and looted a number of shops in the village and shot a number of cattle before leaving. Liam Haugh, the commandant of the IRA's West Clare brigade, decided to mount a number of ambushes to prevent the RIC and army carrying out their threat. On Tuesday 28, the night before the British deadline, the IRA blocked the roads in the area by building stone barricades and cutting trenches across them. The IRA laid a number of ambushes at night and posted snipers during daylight for the next two days, preventing the RIC and British army from burning the villages. Captain Lendrum's body was removed from its watery grave a few days later, and was placed in a roughly constructed coffin. On 1 October the coffin containing Lendrum's body was placed on the railway line near Craggaknock railway station. Four days after the body was returned, a large force of soldiers and RIC raided the carpenter's shop where his coffin had been made. Luckily the carpenter was not home at the time, and he went on the run shortly afterwards. It was obvious to the IRA's West Clare brigade that a spy was still active in the area.

In East Clare there had been no let up in the IRA's campaign despite the widespread British raids following the attack on Scariff barracks. Michael Brennan had received information that a five-man RIC foot patrol regularly policed the village at night. Joseph Honan and nine other Volunteers from Scariff and Tuamgraney assembled at Malones' yard in Tuamgraney on 24 September and marched to O'Callaghan's Mills. Here they were met by Michael Brennan, Joseph Clancy and eight Volunteers, armed with revolvers. The republicans marched to the outskirts of Broadford. Michael Brennan had assigned the Volunteers their positions when Martin Vaughan, the groups scout, reported that there was no RIC foot patrol but a number of the regular RIC were drinking in Will O'Brien's pub and two Black and Tans were out of barracks courting local girls.

Joseph Honan and the other republicans remained in position for a few more minutes before they spotted two RIC men returning to their barracks:

> We waited for a short time after hearing Vaughan's report and about 9 p.m. we saw the RIC leaving O'Briens' and coming towards us. We moved to meet them, walking lightly down one side of the street. When the police were within a few yards Michael Brennan advanced on to the middle of the road.

In the darkened street Michael Brennan was at first uncertain as to whether the approaching men were RIC or civilians:

> It was very dark, but they stepped in front of us and peered into our faces. As they did I saw a reflection of light from a window glinting on the peak of one of their caps and I realised they were RIC men. I pulled a gun at once and fired at one of them and James Hogan followed suit. Both men turned and ran down the street. We followed until an over-enthusiastic

youth in our party started blazing after them with a shotgun from behind us. We were in much more danger from him than from the men he was firing at.

The IRA broke off their attack as the two policemen disappeared down the street. Before the Volunteers moved out of Broadford, Michael Brennan and Joseph Clancy entered O'Briens' pub further down the village, where they found another RIC man about to leave by the back door. Brennan and Clancy fired at him but he escaped and made his way back to his barracks safely. As the first two RIC men to be attacked by the IRA fled to safety, one of them, RIC Constable Michael Brogan, who was severely wounded, became disorientated and took cover under a cart parked on the side of the street where his body was found the next morning.

On 29 September Michael Brennan, Michael McMahon, Alfred Rodgers and Martin Gildea met in John Ryan's house:

Each man had a rifle and a revolver. After a meal they opened up a conversation with me on the subject of where they would get something to shoot. On my suggestion it was decided to go into O'Brien's Bridge about three miles away where there were usually Black and Tans and RIC drinking in the public houses in the daytime. We left my place about three o'clock in the evening and going cross country over Ardtaggle Hill we entered O'Brien's Bridge on the east side of the village. The RIC barracks was about 100 yards off towards the south. We then walked up the village street, taking a quick look into each pub we passed. In the last pub, John Ryan's, fifteen or twenty yards from the barracks, we saw through the window the uniformed caps of three policemen. Personally, I believe that on the same day Brennan was in the mood that if this opportunity had not presented itself he would have gone right into the RIC barracks rather than leave the place without getting one of the enemy. At any rate he decided to attack the police in Ryans' with revolvers and, ordering me to take over custody of his own and the other three rifles and to remain on guard at the door, he led the others into the bar, flanked by McMahon and Rodgers with Gildea in the rear. He fired as the door was opened by one of the others and then they all began shooting. Two of the police were killed outright, but the third man got away through the rear. The police got no chance to fire, but Brennan himself was wounded in the wrist by one of his own men. I gave each man back his rifle – except Brennan, who was now not fit to use it – and we left the village by the route through which we had entered it, going on then to Ardtaggle.

Brennan and his comrades had shot RIC Constable John Downey, from Cork, killing him instantly, while Constable John Keefe, a native of Clare, died from his wounds shortly afterwards.

The 6th battalion of the IRA's East Clare brigade had set three ambushes on different roads near the Feakle garrison of the RIC but on each occasion the force failed to travel through the ambush site. On their fourth attempt the IRA were not content to leave empty-handed and they held up the local postman who was taking mail to the barracks. His sack of mail was taken for intelligence investigation and the postman was released unharmed. Following this an RIC foot patrol began travelling to the post office to collect the mail. The post office was three-quarters of a mile outside Feakle village. Each morning an RIC sergeant and five constables travelled to the post office in three pairs, a few yards apart. The first pair to arrive waited on guard outside while another RIC man went in to collect the mail. This patrol was kept under surveillance by a small group of local Volunteers, who reported its strength and movements to Thomas Tuohy, the vice-commandant of the 6th battalion, on 6 October:

Joe Nugent, Feakle, the battalion quartermaster, came to me to report that on the two previous days six policemen had come on foot from the barracks to the post office for the mail round ten o'clock in the morning and that they walked in pairs about seven or eight paces apart. On hearing this I instructed Nugent and my brother Paddy to notify certain picked men in the Feakle district to appear in Rochford's field, Feakle, after the circus which was to be held that night in the village. All the men selected turned up and totalled about thirty. I sent half of them through the different townlands in the parish to collect arms and ammunition, and with the remainder I got into Tadhg Kelly's house, Feakle east, which had been vacated by himself and his family as he had heard of our intention to attack the police. About 2 p.m. all the men sent to collect the arms had completed their mission and rejoined us. All told we had twenty guns, four rifles, fifteen shotguns and one automatic short 'Peter the Painter' [C96 Mauser pistol].

The Feakle post office was situated on the Gort Road almost directly opposite the graveyard. About fifty yards from the post office the Feakle road forked off towards Tulla at Keatings' house, a small one-storey cottage. Nugents' house, a large two-storey building, stood on the opposite side of the road between the fork in the road and the post office. Thomas Tuohy posted five Volunteers armed with rifles and shotguns commanded by his brother Michael. Pat Houlihan, armed with a rifle, was in charge of three shotgun men who occupied the post office shortly before the RIC patrol was due to arrive. Six other Volunteers, armed with shotguns, were waiting at the windows of Nugents' house under the command of Joseph Tuohy. One Volunteer, Patrick Broady, was behind a recess in a wall of the Gort Road to guard the entrance to a laneway which led to Tadhg Kelly's house.

Thomas Tuohy commanded the other IRA section in Keatings' house, He was armed with the Mauser automatic pistol and was accompanied by three shotgun men:

About nine o'clock that morning I sent a scout, Martin Moloney, Killenena, into the village to keep an eye on the police barracks until he saw the patrol leaving. After ascertaining their strength and formation he was to walk quickly in front of them and when he got to a bend in the road half a mile from Nugents' he was to sprint as quickly as he could to me with the information. Moloney was a champion sprinter at that time While he was away I brought the party from Kellys' house to the back of Nugents'. Moloney returned after three-quarters of an hour and his report indicated that there was no change in the size and formation of the patrol. Each section then moved quickly into the positions which had been assigned to them. In the course of ten minutes or so the patrol came along headed by Sergeant Doherty and Constable Stanley. As these two passed by Jack Tuohy at one of the windows in Nugents' he fired at Stanley, contrary to orders. On the previous night he had been held up inside the village when he got a bad beating from Stanley. The middle pair, Constables Murphy and McFadden, on hearing the shooting made for the fence opposite Keatings', while the last two did not enter the ambush position at all but retreated back to the barracks. Constables Murphy and McFadden, who dropped their rifles, got into the fields where, taking advantage of thick cover, they managed to remain concealed until we left. At a pre-arranged signal nine of the attacking party came out on the road where they collected four carbines, one .45 revolver, 300 rounds of .303 and twenty-four rounds of .45 ammunition and one Mills bomb. A coded message which was intended to be sent from the post office to RIC headquarters in Tulla was found on the sergeant and this was forwarded to the vice-O/C of the brigade, Tom McGrath.

The IRA's burst of fire following Jack Tuohy's premature shot had killed Sergeant Francis Doherty from Leitrim and Constable Stanley from Cork. The second pair of RIC men, Constables Murphy and McFadden, had both been wounded, but they managed to get back to their barracks. Having searched the two dead policemen's bodies for weapons and papers the IRA began looking for Murphy and McFadden. The republicans combed the area for twenty minutes until Fr O'Reilly, a local Catholic priest with republican sympathies, arrived to administer the last rites to the dead RIC men. The noise of shooting from the ambush scene had been heard at the barracks in Feakle and two RIC men were immediately sent on bicycle to report the republican attack to the British military's headquarters at Tulla, over six miles away. An army cavalry unit stationed there was despatched to intercept the IRA. Fr O'Reilly had seen the two RIC men cycling towards Tulla and as he approached the ambush scene he shouted a warning to the Volunteers who were still searching for the two constables. Thomas Tuohy immediately called off the search and the IRA withdrew from the ambush site along the Scariff Road.

They had gone about half a mile when they saw the cavalry and groups of soldiers with bloodhounds converging on the hills above their ambush position. However, instead of pursuing the main IRA force, the British soldiers began following the trail of the unarmed Volunteers who had left the ambush scene when the attack ended. The army failed to catch them and the main group of the IRA escaped from the area to their safe houses at Coolnagree.

The IRA, expecting the forces to carry out reprisals on the local civilian population that night in revenge for the attack and Thomas Tuohy, took action to prevent this:

> A consultation was held among the principal officers and it was decided to occupy a number of houses in Feakle village that we expected to be burned that night. We were approaching the village at about eight o'clock; the leading column was only a quarter of a mile away when flames were seen rising from three houses – Considines', O'Briens' and Fr O'Reilly's. Realising that we had been forestalled it was agreed right away to send back the reinforcements. I kept as many men as I had arms for, about thirty altogether, on the Coolnagree hills for the ensuing three days, sleeping in the open and getting food from the houses round about, until a despatch arrived from the brigade O/C ordering me to 'refrain from further attacks as for certain reasons he did not want Feakle turned into a battleground'.

On the night of the ambush ten Black and Tans and a group of regular RIC, led by their district inspector, arrived in the village at 6.30 and made straight for Fr O'Reilly's house. They ordered Fr O'Reilly outside and beat him with their rifle butts and later returned to burn his house. The British forces shot and wounded Thomas Moloney, the local postmaster, and then set fire to the post office, Tadhg Kelly's home, Nugents', Rochfords', McNamaras' and Tuohys'.

As the republican struggle against British rule in Ireland continued, Catholic priests with republican sympathies like Fr O'Reilly were the exception. The majority of Catholic priests and the hierarchy of the Church actively supported British rule and often used the pulpit for political rather than spiritual purposes by actively condemning the IRA's actions, while ignoring the reprisals and atrocities committed by British forces. Only a week before this ambush Bishop Fogarty of Killaloe used his sermon at mass as another opportunity to publicly criticise the IRA:

Recklessness is not patriotism, but madness. Hot headed action on the part of irresponsible individuals is wholly to be deprecated as injurious to the national cause and serving no other purpose than a pretext to those who are but too anxious to get one for brutally victimising innocent people, as is now done.

Thomas Tuohy and the other members of the 6th battalion of the East Clare brigade faced repeated condemnation from the local Catholic priest, Fr Michael Hayes, who had regularly denounced republicanism and castigated local Volunteers and members of Sinn Féin from the pulpit and even actively collaborated with the British forces:

After the Feakle ambush the local parish priest, Fr Hayes, a violent imperialist who regularly entertained members of the enemy forces, strongly denounced the IRA from the pulpit. He referred to us as a murder gang, and declared that any information which he could get would be readily passed on to the British authorities and that he would not desist until the last of the murderers was strung by the neck. This denunciation led to unpleasant consequences and for some time services at which he officiated were boycotted by most of the congregation.

The boycott of Fr Hayes's services grew to such an extent that when Bishop Fogarty of Killaloe visited the parish there were only six people attending mass.

Fr Hayes was not the only British collaborator in the area. It became obvious to IRA intelligence after the Feakle ambush that there were several British spies active in the village and that Fr Hayes was using his housekeeper, Johanna Slattery from Tipperary, as a means to pass information to the British forces. Her activities quickly came to Thomas Tuohy's attention:

One day, about 23 October 1920, as she was returning as a passenger in a motor car from Limerick the car was held up a few miles from Feakle by three or four of the local Volunteers, who made her a prisoner and took her off towards Scariff. That night she was conveyed by boat across the Shannon and left in her native county with a warning never to return. The Black and Tans and RIC threatened several people in the district with death if she was not released immediately. A fortnight later she was brought back under a heavy escort of police, military and Auxiliaries and left with the parish priest. From that time onwards she gave no more trouble and was not interfered with.

Miss Slattery was extremely fortunate not to have been executed. The East Clare brigade decided it would make for bad propaganda if they executed a female spy; similarly if Fr Hayes had not been a Catholic priest he would certainly have been abducted and executed for his collaboration with the British forces. He was eventually removed from Feakle and posted as the parish priest of Sixmilebridge. Even with these two British spies publicly exposed and isolated the IRA had still not broken the network of informers and collaborators in the area.

As the East Clare brigade was busy trying to break the British spy network in Feakle, the Mid Clare brigade of the IRA had found a republican sympathiser inside the RIC garrison at Ruan who was willing to defect. Seán Casey, the adjutant of the Mid Clare brigade's 2nd battalion, had been approached by RIC Constable Bill Carroll from Roscommon who was stationed at Ruan barracks. Carroll claimed that he wanted to defect to the IRA and could get Volunteers inside the barracks. The IRA had to be careful in their dealings with Carroll as the possibility remained that his approach was part of a planned British ambush to trap the IRA.

Seán O'Keefe and a number of other IRA officers were detailed to interview Carroll and assess if he was a genuine defector:

Carroll impressed us as being a sincere type of young man who was sorry for having found himself in the RIC at that stage. He declared himself in sympathy and said he attempted to resign from the police force. He was then asked to describe the internal layout of the Ruan RIC station, how the garrison operated at night time and give details of the military equipment of the station. He also mentioned that he would be on night duty on the third week of October along with an elderly RIC man named Wilmot, and that Wilmot would be leaving the station every morning about half past seven to get milk from a neighbouring house owned by people named Callanan. There was a general discussion at the meeting on the information supplied by Constable Carroll and it was decided there to attempt the capture of the barracks.

Following the meeting with Constable Carroll, Frank Barrett carried out a night time examination of the Ruan barracks and the surrounding area with Seán Casey. On 15 October Barrett had completed his arrangements for the attack and sent word to Constable Carroll, through Seán Casey, that the attack would take place three nights later. The barracks at Ruan had been a thorn in the Mid Clare brigade's side for some time. It was an important part of the British system of defence; situated six miles from Ennis, it controlled one of the main approaches to the town and was a great hindrance to the movement of IRA arms, ammunition and supplies through the area. The barracks also served as a clearing house for gathering and processing intelligence information. It was a two-storey solid stone building manned by a sergeant and thirteen constables. The building was surrounded by a stone wall and an almost impenetrable barrier of barbed wire seven feet high. Barbed wire screens also sloped down from the upper storey of the building and all the windows were covered with bullet-proof steel shutters and sandbags.

Constable Carroll told Frank Barrett that every morning when Constable Wilmot left the rear of the barracks to collect milk from Callanans' 100 yards behind the barracks he pushed aside part of the barbed wire entanglements which stretched from the outer barbed wire defences to the block of out-offices containing a fuel shed and toilet. This section of barbed wire was left open until Wilmot returned a few moments later. The IRA's plan was to capture Wilmot when he left at half past seven and enter the barracks compound through the gap he had left open behind him. Once inside the barbed wire, Constable Carroll would open the barracks door and thirty Volunteers armed with revolvers would enter, capture the sleeping RIC men and destroy the building. The village of Ruan is about four miles from Corofin, which was garrisoned by a force of RIC and Black and Tans. Ennis had a very large garrison of British military and RIC; these forces had motor transport and could be in Ruan within the hour if they were alerted. Members of the 1st and 5th battalions of the Mid Clare brigade were responsible for blocking the roads leading to Ruan. A large force would be needed to capture Ruan barracks and Frank Barrett mobilised selected Volunteers from the 2nd, 3rd and 4th battalions to form the main force to carry out the raid.

The Volunteers selected for the attack assembled at 10 p.m. on 17 October at a disused house near Barefield owned by the Costello family. The 5th and 6th battalions had mobilised their Volunteers for the attack at O'Briens' house in Kilfenora the previous night; so many of their men had mobilised that Seán McNamara had to select a number of them to go to Ruan the next night and ordered the rest to mobilise on the 18th in Kilfenora and hold themselves ready to act as a reserve force. At Costellos' over fifty men had mobilised, including Seán Moroney and Mick Tuohy from the Mid Clare brigade who had been told about the planned operation by Laurence Allen. Barrett assembled all the Volunteers present and explained to them the exact details of the planned action. At 4 a.m. they moved off towards Ruan led by an advance party of ten Volunteers. Those from the 1st and 5th battalions were already at work blocking the roads leading to Ruan. To prevent British forces rushing to Ruan or attempting to encircle the IRA, a widespread system of roadblocks was put in place. The outer line of defence was a far-flung ring of twenty stone barricades built across all the roads leading to Ruan, some of them as far as ten miles from the village. Inside these barricades the IRA constructed a second series of roadblocks on the roads leading directly to Ruan. Each of these road blocks was guarded by a section leader and Volunteers armed with shotguns.

Half a mile from the barracks the IRA stopped at a wood on the Dromore estate, took their boots off, and marched silently into Ruan in stockinged feet. It was still dark at six o'clock when the different IRA sections took up their positions behind the outer wall of the barracks. Hidden from view of the barracks windows, the IRA waited for over an hour in a tense silence for Constable Wilmot to leave on his morning errand. Just before 7.30 they heard movement inside the barracks yard.

In the still morning air Frank Barrett could clearly hear the noise of the back door being shut and the barbed wire entanglement being pulled open. A moment later Constable Wilmot appeared; he had gone about thirty yards when he was held up by Peter O'Loughlin and two other Volunteers, Jim Quinn and Frank Keane.

Within seconds of Wilmot's capture the first sections of the raiding party rushed down the concrete passage and through the gap in the barbed wire entanglements to the back door of the barracks. Constable Carroll had watched the capture of Constable Wilmot and immediately opened the door and led the republicans inside. William McNamara led his section up the stairs with his revolver drawn and entered the first of two dormitory rooms which housed the eleven RIC constables:

> In less time than it takes to tell, we were in the upstairs rooms where the police were fast asleep. In the room in which I was, one of the police, Constable Lougheed, jumped out of bed on being awakened and appeared to be making an attempt to get his rifle from the rack over his bed when a shot rang out which mortally wounded him. Another policeman was slightly wounded in the leg. In the other room Sergeant McCarthy, who was in charge of the garrison, also made an effort to fight, but he was deprived of his revolver before being able to use it.

Seán O'Keefe's section, which entered the other upstairs room, also met resistance from the RIC but this was subdued without any further killing:

> In the room where I entered with my section the occupants were all asleep and were roused by shouts of 'Hands up!' One constable named Ruddy did not comply and threw himself out of bed. He was fired at and wounded, but this bullet also wounded another constable named Farrelly.

Constable John Lougheed was carried to the barracks yard, but died from his wounds within minutes. The eleven other RIC men were ordered to dress, taken downstairs at gunpoint and led to a nearby house where they were made as comfortable as possible. In their search of the barracks the

IRA captured fourteen Lee Enfield rifles, fourteen .45 Webley and Scott revolvers, two shotguns, one automatic pistol, two Verey light flare pistols, twenty-four Mills bomb grenades, 1,000 rounds of .303 ammunition and 700 rounds of .45 ammunition.

When the barracks had been thoroughly searched the building was set on fire. As the first flames took hold, Ignatius O'Neill arrived by car with three other Volunteers from the 4th battalion of the Mid Clare brigade. One of these Volunteers, Frank Molyneaux, a chemist from Ennistymon, was taken to the three injured RIC constables and he dressed their wounds. The remaining RIC men were being held as prisoners in front of the barracks when O'Neill arrived. William McNamara from Ennis was one of their guards. 'Most of the RIC did not appear to be unduly upset over the fate that had befallen them, but Sergeant McCarthy was very annoyed and refused to give an undertaking that there would be no reprisals.' On hearing this O'Neill couldn't resist the temptation to give them 'a small dose of their own medicine'. Frank Barrett watched as O'Neill gave the RIC men the order to 'fall in' for foot drill:

> All complied with alacrity, with the exception of the senior sergeant who obstinately refused to be drilled by an IRA officer. O'Neill, a former Irish Guardsman … was not the type who would readily tolerate disobedience to a military command that he might utter. The recalcitrant sergeant was possessed of some rudiment of wisdom, however, for he did not persist in his attitude and sulkily 'fell in' with the others before it became necessary for O'Neill to apply some persuasion. Up and down the narrow road marched the bewildered police, their nailed boots on the road re-echoing in the crisp October air. Half the village watched in astonishment as the peelers 'jumped to' in response to orders bawled out by O'Neill.

When O'Neill had finished drilling the RIC, Constables Wilmot and Carroll were separated from the group, who were told that the pair were being kept as hostages to prevent reprisals by the British forces. The RIC were told that Wilmot and Carroll would be shot and the houses of local unionists burned if the RIC engaged in reprisals for the burning of the barracks. The real reason for taking them hostage was to deceive the British as to Carroll's part in the attack and provide cover for his defection to the IRA. With the demolition of the barracks completed by fire, the RIC sergeant and his men were again warned about the consequences of reprisals; they were then taken to houses in the village and given breakfast. They were warned not to leave these houses for an hour. The IRA was dismissed by Barrett and broke up into different sections which departed for safe houses in their own areas.

Bill Carroll was to be posted as an IRA Volunteer in the Ballyvaughan area of the Mid Clare brigade's 6th battalion. Seán McNamara and the other members of the battalion withdrew from Ruan, taking Carroll and Wilmot with them as 'hostages' to Diffleys' house at Carron in north Clare:

> At Carron we held a mock court-martial for Constable Wilmot's benefit. The 'court' decided to release him and to 'detain' Constable Carroll as a hostage. Constable Wilmot was told he was to convey word to his authorities that if there were any reprisals by the British troops as a result of the Ruan attack that Constable Carroll would be executed. We had the problem of ensuring that Constable Wilmot would get back safely to some RIC station so we decided that it would be best that he should be taken to Gort in County Galway. This task was left to myself to arrange. One of the most reliable men in the battalion, Mick O'Loughlin of Ballyvaughan, had a motor car and I got him to drive myself and Constable Wilmot from Carron to Tirneevin Cross about three miles from Gort. Before parting from his guard at Carron, Constable Wilmot insisted on shaking hands with all his captors and was most profuse in his thanks for the good treatment he had received.

While the Mid Clare brigade's ruse had prevented reprisals in the Ruan area, British raids and reprisals continued in Miltown Malbay. The British raided houses of known republicans, deliberately destroying furniture and property in the course of police searches and terrorising local people in an attempt to force them to give information about the IRA. Volunteer Ned Lynch's family suffered at the hands of British soldiers who used these searches as a disguise for their criminal activities:

On 21 October 1920 I had paid a visit to my parents and was told by a neighbouring girl that two members of the Royal Scottish Regiment [Royal Highland Light Infantry?] were looting local houses. After a while two soldiers arrived at the door where I met them and enquired for their business. The taller of the two said they were raiding for arms and tried to push past me. I told him there were no arms in the house and they were acting without authority. He carried what I first thought to be a revolver but on closer scrutiny noticed it was a glass one painted black which I knew had been looted sometime previously from Blakes' pub in Miltown. I hit him a heavy punch in the right arm which caused him to drop the 'shot of malt', as the toy gun was known to us locally, and it broke in pieces on the doorstep. Just as this happened one of the neighbours arrived accusing the soldiers of having stolen £10 from him whereupon the bigger soldier tried to break away. I tripped him and we searched him thoroughly, recovering other articles he had looted but not the money. The second soldier [Private Buchannon], who was less truculent, was also searched but offered no resistance and after receiving directions from my brother made off for the military post. The bigger soldier had run 200 yards from the house through the fields and was firing at us and shouting what he would get done to us. He arrived at the military post before his companion and said we had attacked them with pitchforks and that his companion was killed. The taller soldier, McPhearson, returned with a mixed group of crown forces and wounded a farm labourer, O'Grady, and beat up the Lorries, who were of ex-British army stock. Myself and my brothers had left the farm and only my mother and father were at home and were coming out of the haggard when the gang arrived. McPhearson without a warning aimed his rifle at my father, Charles, and sent a bullet through the old man's heart, killing him outright. The gang carried on into the country for a mile or two and McPhearson was going to shoot a neighbour and my brother John until an RIC man named Cooney intervened.

The British authorities ordered that the Lynch family were not to bury their father until they held an inquest into his killing, as a question about the shooting had been raised in the British parliament. Charles Lynch's body was kept in his family home until the following Sunday, when it became obvious that despite the attention his murder had received in the press and the British parliament, the British government would never admit their forces stationed in Ireland contained murderers and criminals.

In late October Thomas Tuohy and members of the East Clare brigade's 6th battalion arrested Martin Counihan, a civil servant from Feakle who they had been monitoring since the ambush of the RIC patrol at the village post office that October. Counihan had come to the attention of the IRA when he passed comment in public naming Volunteers he had seen leaving the ambush site that morning. He began frequenting areas where wanted Volunteers were on the run and wandering the roads outside Feakle village watching groups of Volunteers who were digging trenches to hinder British motor patrols. He visited the barracks regularly late in the evenings, and on the morning following each of his visits to the barracks large areas were surrounded and searched by the RIC and British soldiers.

Based on these observations Thomas Tuohy was convinced Counihan was a spy and would have to be arrested and interrogated. This took place on 28 October:

> It was decided that Martin Counihan should be arrested at the first convenient opportunity and court-martialled. A week afterwards while four Volunteers were engaged digging potatoes at Annagh, Feakle, they noticed Counihan's pony coming towards them, apparently to take a load of turf from Ernagh bog. These Volunteers were Jack and Joe Tuohy, Dromore, Eddie Fennessy, Coolgarse and my own brother Paddy. The pony was being driven by Counihan's daughter and sitting inside the creel was Martin Counihan himself. Making masks out of an apron worn by a girl that was helping them at the potatoes, they got on to the road and held up the cart. They removed Martin Counihan despite a heroic resistance made by his daughter, who in her efforts tore the mask off Joe Tuohy's face. They marched Martin Counihan to Coolreagh, sending word in the meantime to me of their capture. Miss Counihan returned home and on her way reported the incident at the RIC barracks. In a short while the local RIC and military from Tulla arrived in large numbers in the district and cordoning off a big area began exhaustive searches. While these operations were in progress I and a company captain and two lieutenants were proceeding with the

court-martial. He admitted having given information to the RIC about the IRA, adopted a defiant attitude and said he would, whenever he got the chance, again notify the police of anything he heard or saw concerning the IRA. He was sentenced to be shot and the sentence was carried out that night. I was in charge of the firing party. Though he received the contents of two shotgun cartridges and five .45 revolver bullets, two of which through the head, he managed to make his way to Bodyke three miles away, where he died. Four houses were burned in the area as a reprisal for Martin Counihan's shooting, Tuohys', Dromore, Rochfords' and Kellys' of Feakle and McNamaras' in Laccaroe. A reward of £500 was offered by the RIC for information which would lead to the capture of Joe and Jack Tuohy of Dromore.

In November 1920 G company of the auxiliary division of the RIC were sent to Clare. They commandeered the Lakeside Hotel at Killaloe, on the Ballina side of the River Shannon, as their headquarters. G company consisted of 100 Auxiliaries under the command of Lieutenant Colonel R.I. Andrews. Straight away they set out to terrorise the local population into submission. On the night of 1 November thirty Auxiliaries announced their arrival in the county by launching an arson attack on the people of O'Brien's Bridge. At gunpoint they ordered six families out of their homes and fired shots over their heads as they fled. The Auxiliaries ordered the women and children to clear away while they lined the men and older boys up against a wall on the pretext of searching them. These men and youths were placed under guard as the Auxiliaries poured petrol over their homes and set them on fire. On their first night in Clare the Auxiliaries completely destroyed three houses, severely damaged several others and caused an estimated £13,000 worth of damage.

On Monday 14 November the Auxiliaries suffered their first casualties in Clare. An RIC Crossley Tender driving at high speed to prevent ambush crashed full force into a stone pier at the gateway to Dromoland Castle, killing RIC Constable Driscoll from Cork, RIC Constable Roper, an Auxiliary from England, and RIC Constable Fleming, an Auxiliary from Laois. The following night the British forces in Clare suffered another loss when Private Dailey, a soldier in the Royal Scots regiment, was killed in Ennis. His death was reported as an accidental shooting but the nature of his wound (bullet entering the mouth and exiting the back of the head) strongly suggests suicide.

After the republican attack on Scariff RIC barracks, the local garrison was evacuated to Killaloe to strengthen the British forces already stationed there. The former commander of the RIC at Scariff, Sergeant Brennan, was bitter that the IRA's attack had forced the abandonment of his barracks and when the Auxiliaries arrived that November Brennan and his men were eager for revenge. The sergeant found willing accomplices in G company of the Auxiliaries and he used his local knowledge to lead them on raids and searches to capture Volunteers he believed had been involved in the attack. The locations of the raids and the specific questioning by Brennan and Auxiliary officers made it obvious that they had received information about which Volunteers had been involved in attacking Scariff barracks.

Joseph Clancy was sent to warn three Volunteers who were hiding in a disused building close to Williamstown house, but they paid little heed to his warnings. The support of the local people for the republican struggle and the efficiency of the IRA's warning system lulled these three Volunteers into a false sense of security which was to prove fatal. On Tuesday 16 November the Auxiliaries sailed the *SS Shannon* across the lake and approached Williamstown house by stealth, surrounded the building and arrested the caretaker, Michael Egan, who lived alone in a house in the yard. They questioned him about the Volunteers who were hiding in the area but he refused to give them any information. He was beaten and arrested by the Auxiliaries. However, Egan's loyalty to the republicans was in vain. Michael McMahon, Alfred Rodgers and Martin Gildea were captured while sleeping and disarmed. They had their hands tied and were brought aboard the *Shannon* with Michael Egan.

An hour later the Auxiliaries returned with the second pair of prisoners, John Conway and his brother Michael, who had been captured separately. John Conway was taken aboard the *S.S. Shannon* where he saw his brother and the four other prisoners tied up on the deck. As the boat set out from the pier the Auxiliaries continued questioning the three Volunteers, who kept repeating to them that Michael Egan was not involved with them, but their protests fell on deaf ears. It was getting dark when the boat reached the pier by the Lakeside Hotel:

> My brother Mick and I were put down the hatch, and the other four were taken off and into a big room in the hotel. They called it the day-room. The other four were there before us and they were handcuffed ... As we came in Auxies in uniform took them out of the dayroom one by one. They kept them out a good long time. Alfie Rodgers was the last to be brought back and he was pumping blood from the nose and face ... Mick and myself were taken out into a small room where the colonel – Andrews was his name, I think – cross questioned us and threatened us. He showed us revolvers and ammunition and said they were found with the lads. He tried to get us to say that we were friends of Mike Egan, and that we knew the boys had been staying at Williamstown House for the last three weeks. We had nothing to tell them unless we started telling lies ... As we were brought in the four boys were taken out. After about a half hour Mick and I were given a blanket each. We were taken out along a long passage and into a small room where there wasn't a bed or a chair.

The three Volunteers and Egan were taken by lorry from the Lakeside Hotel onto the bridge crossing the River Shannon between Killaloe and Ballina. They were ordered out of the trucks by Sergeant Brennan and the Auxiliaries, who began torturing them and beating them with fists and rifle butts. This continued for seven or eight minutes, during which time the prisoners' screams were so loud that they woke a number of people in the nearby houses. The men could be heard crying and appealing to be allowed see a priest before they were tied together in the centre of the bridge. There was silence for a moment before the local people heard the first burst of rifle and machine gun fire. The RIC and Auxiliaries had raked their four prisoners with gunfire at point blank range before one of their officers had walked up to each of the dead and dying men with a revolver and fired a number of shots into their temples.

Back in the Lakeside Hotel John Conway could hear drunken Auxiliaries and RIC men celebrating:

> There was an awful hullabaloo away at the other end of the passage – shouting and roaring, dancing and drunken men singing 'When Irish Eyes are Smiling' … Suddenly the door was burst in on us and Auxies shouted at us to get up quickly. Each of us was marched out between two Auxies; I was first, up to the bridge … The bridge was packed with Auxies, Tans and Peelers. We were marched across it. We hadn't gone far when the Auxie flashed a light and told me to walk over the body, stiff he called it. I knew it was the body of one of the four boys. About twenty yards further on there was another, and then another. The last body was right over the canal arch. There was a Crossley Tender at Shannon View hotel with its lights on facing us, and I saw by its light that that was Martin Gildea. He was dead. He was handcuffed and his face was bloody. We were halted near the Tender. The Tans used to come over to us, look into our faces and threaten us. While we were there we saw them throw the body of Martin Gildea into the back of the Tender just like you'd throw in a dead pig. After that we were marched up the hill by the same Auxies to the RIC barracks and taken into the dayroom. As we got into the barracks the Tender passed us and went in the archway with the bodies. There was a Black and Tan officer, Gwynn was his name, I heard, in the dayroom. The Auxies handed us over to him and told him he would be responsible for us. The dayroom was full of Tans … After a while they threw us into the black hole. We were beaten then and it was by two Irish Peelers; they struck us, knocked us down and leaped on us … Some time afterwards a Peeler came in with a baton in his hand. He drew at my face and I pulled back, but he got me on the point of the left cheek bone and gave me a very sore black eye.

John Conway and his brother were taken from the barracks at Killaloe later that day and interned without trial in Limerick prison.

At 3.30 that evening the RIC sent four identical telegrams to the parents of the murdered men reading: 'You are informed that your son … was shot dead when escaping from custody last night. Signed Gwynn, District Inspector RIC.' When the relatives of the four men arrived to claim their bodies later that evening, they were refused the right on the grounds that a military enquiry would have to be held into the killings. The relatives were not permitted to see the bodies. The following day the families returned; they had arranged coffins and hearses to remove the bodies from the barracks. Dennis Sparling successfully negotiated with the British forces for the men's families to claim their remains, but the RIC refused to let the hearses pass over Killaloe Bridge half a mile away. RIC District Inspector Gwynn insisted that the RIC would shoulder the coffins to the hearses, but the four men's relatives were appalled by the idea that their murderers would have any hand in their removal. The RIC relented and the coffins were removed by the relatives and were brought to Scariff church where the bodies lay in state overnight.

Inside the church the coffin lids were removed to allow the men's families and their IRA comrades to see the remains. When the last of the mourners had left the church the bodies were examined by the coroner and his jury. Shocked by what he saw, the coroner insisted that Dr Holmes carry out an autopsy. It revealed that each of the bodies had at least seventeen bullet wounds, fired at very close range into the front of the men's bodies. Alfie Rodgers' and Martin Gildea's bodies both showed singeing of the hair around bullet wounds on their temples. Their hair had been arranged by the RIC to cover gaping exit wounds behind their eye and ear on the opposite side of their heads, indicating that they had been finished off execution style with a revolver. The wounds inflicted on Michael McMahon and Michael Egan were intended to be fatal but not to cause death instantly.

Volunteer Pat O'Donnell helped remove the four bodies from their coffins for the autopsy:

> Alfie's hair was singed at the temples where there was a gaping wound made, I'd say by one or more .45 bullets fired at point blank range. When I tried to lift Martin Gildea my hand ran through the back of his head. The hair was singed and there was a dreadful wound in his temple as if more than one bullet had been fired into the spot. All the bodies were riddled and we were all satisfied from the wounds that the first shots were aimed low down and that the weapons, while being fired from, were gradually raised up. All the bullets went straight through the

bodies. There was an expression of a painful lingering death on Brod's [Michael McMahon's] face.

The four men's funerals took place on the Saturday morning; as the funeral mass was ending the British forces arrived in four Crossley Tenders. They surrounded the church and the RIC and Auxiliaries set up a security cordon and began searching the relatives and mourners. The four men were buried side by side in a prepared grave in Scariff churchyard. The three Volunteers could not be buried with republican military honours because of the heavy presence of British troops.

The British-censored newspapers reported that the four men had been killed while attempting to escape, even though they had been shot while handcuffed and in the RIC's custody, on a bridge which had a British checkpoint at each end. The coroner's inquest returned a verdict of wilful murder against the British forces stationed at Killaloe but it was never reported in the British press. A number of pamphlets were circulated in an effort to bring the details of the murder to public attention in Britain and Ireland, including one by Captain Grey, an ex-British army officer and unionist living at Killaloe, who was horrified by the murders. The Killaloe murders were eventually raised in the British parliament, but were dismissed by the government. Following the publication of Captain Grey's pamphlet he was intimidated by the RIC and forced to flee his home. Brigadier General Crozier, the commander of the Auxiliaries, went to Killaloe to investigate the killings and became convinced they were murders; he later claimed one of the Auxiliaries dismissed from G company was paid to remain silent about the killings by the British government: 'A blackmailer who had been dismissed from the force and sent to England by me was regularly paid to keep his mouth shut about the Killaloe Bridge murders.'

Thomas McMahon and other members of the East Clare brigade were convinced that the three Volunteers had been betrayed by an informer. 'There is no doubt whatever that these unfortunate men were betrayed to the enemy by someone living in the locality. Because of another happening I am convinced that there was a spy or spies there at the time, though it

William Smith O'Brien (seated). This photo was taken while O'Brien was in captivity awaiting trial. *Photo courtesy of Kilmainham Jail Museum.*

Peadar Clancy, from Cranny, County Clare. This mug shot was taken by the British military immediately after the Rising. *Photo courtesy of Kilmainham Jail Museum.*

Dundalk jail, 1915.
(Back row, left to right) Diarmuid Lynch, Ernest Blythe, Terence MacSwiney, Dick McKee, Michael Colivet; (front row, left to right) Frank Thornton, Bertie Hunt (Clare), Michael Brennan (Clare).

Members of the East Clare Battalion *c.*1914. *Author's collection.*

Execution at Kilmainham Jail 1916. Photograph staged on location by the Khaki and Green War of Independence re-enactment group. *Author's collection.*

'The man with the strange name'. Éamon de Valera addressing a Sinn Féin rally at Killaloe during the East Clare by-election of 1917.

British army officer forcibly searches a defiant Irish civilian, 1917. Such scenes were commonplace during the East Clare election. *Photo courtesy of Kilmainham Jail Museum.*

General Election.   Manifesto to the Irish People.

(AS PASSED BY CENSOR.)

The coming General Election is fraught with vital possibilities for the future of our nation. Ireland is faced with the question whether this generation wills it that she is to march out into the full sunlight of freedom, or is to remain in the shadow of ▮▮▮▮ imperialism ▮▮▮▮▮

▮▮▮

Sinn Fein aims at securing the establishment of that Republic.

1. By withdrawing the Irish Representation from the British Parliament and by denying the right ▮▮▮▮▮▮▮▮▮▮▮▮▮ of the British Government ▮▮▮▮▮▮▮▮▮▮▮▮▮▮▮ to legislate for Ireland.

▮▮▮

3. By the establishment of a constituent assembly comprising persons chosen by Irish constituencies as the supreme national authority to speak and act in the name of the Irish people, and to develop Ireland's social, political and industrial life, for the welfare of the whole people of Ireland.

4. By appealing to the Peace Conference for the establishment of Ireland as an Independent Nation. At that conference the future of the Nations of the world will be settled on the principle of government by consent of the governed. Ireland's claim to the application of that principle in her favour is not based on any accidental situation arising from the war. It is older than many if not all of the present belligerents. ▮▮▮▮▮▮▮

▮▮▮

Sinn Fein stands ▮▮▮▮▮▮▮▮ for the Nation; it represents the old tradition of nationhood ▮▮▮▮▮▮▮▮▮▮▮▮▮▮▮▮▮▮▮▮▮▮▮▮▮▮▮▮▮▮▮▮▮▮▮▮ reasserting the inalienable right of the Irish Nation to sovereign independence; reaffirming the determination of the Irish people to achieve it, and guaranteeing within the Independent Nation equal rights and equal opportunities to all its citizens.

Believing that the time has arrived when Ireland's voice for the principle of untrammelled ▮▮▮▮▮▮▮ self-determination should be heard above every interest of party or class, Sinn Fein will oppose at the Polls every individual candidate who does not accept this principle.

The policy of our opponents stands condemned on any test, whether of principle or expediency. ▮▮▮▮▮▮▮▮▮▮▮▮▮▮▮▮▮▮▮▮▮▮▮▮▮▮▮▮▮▮▮▮▮▮▮▮▮▮ Any attempt to barter away the sacred and inviolate rights of nationhood begins in dishonour and is bound to end in disaster. The enforced exodus of millions of our people, the decay of our industrial life, the ever-increasing financial plunder of our country, the whittling down of the demand for the " Repeal of the Union," voiced by the first Irish Leader to plead in the Hall of the Conqueror to that of Home Rule on the Statute Book, and finally the contemplated mutilation of our country by partition, are some of the ghastly results of a policy that leads to national ruin.

▮▮▮
▮▮▮
▮▮▮

▮▮▮▮▮▮▮▮▮▮▮▮▮▮▮▮▮▮▮▮▮▮ By declaring their will to accept the status of a province instead of boldly taking their stand upon the right of the nation, they supply England with the only subterfuge at her disposal for obscuring the issue in the eyes of the world. ▮▮▮▮▮

Sinn Fein goes to the polls handicapped by all the arts and contrivances that a powerful and unscrupulous enemy can use against us. ▮▮▮▮▮▮▮▮▮▮▮▮▮▮▮ of Sinn Fein to secure the freedom of Ireland the British Government would destroy it. Sinn Fein, however, goes to the polls confident that the people of this ancient nation will be true to the old cause ▮▮▮▮▮▮▮▮▮▮▮▮▮▮▮▮▮▮▮▮▮▮▮▮▮▮▮▮▮▮▮▮▮▮▮ and whose demand is that the only status befitting this ancient realm is the status of a free nation.

ISSUED BY THE STANDING COMMITTEE OF SINN FEIN.

Sinn Féin Election Manifesto 1918, as passed by the British censor, with a quarter of the text deleted.

Soldiers from a Scottish regiment in the British army enjoying the good weather at Doolin in 1918. *Photo courtesy of Clare Library.*

Four of the most wanted men in Ireland. (Left to right) Seamus Robinson, Seán Treacy, Dan Breen and Michael Brennan O/C East Clare Brigade. This photo was probably taken while they were on the run in Clare. *Photo courtesy of Cork Public Museum.*

IRA volunteer Seán Breen. Killed in action during an attack on four RIC men at Kilmihil on Sunday, 18 April 1920. *Photo courtesy of Clare Museum.*

Members of G company Auxiliaries stationed at Killaloe. *Courtesy of Martin O'Dwyer, Cashel Folk Village.*

RIC auxiliaries bringing republican suspects for interrogation at Tralee Barracks, County Kerry. The 'Auxie' second from the right appears to be no more than fourteen or fifteen years old. *Photo courtesy of The Kerryman.*

General Lucas, centre, seated on chair, with his IRA captors in East Clare. (Back row) Patrick and Michael Brennan; (front row) Paddy Brennan and Joe Keane. *Photo courtesy of Cork Public Museum.*

Hunger striker being taken to hospital during the Mountjoy hunger strike, April 1920. *Photo courtesy of Kilmainham Jail Museum.*

Some of the republican prisoners who had taken part in the Mountjoy hunger strike. *Photo courtesy of Kilmainham Jail Museum.*

Mixed RIC and British army patrol. Photo taken in Clare 1920–1921. Appears to be a posed propaganda shot, rather than a photograph taken in the heat of battle. *Photo courtesy of The Imperial War Museum, London. Ref. Q107751.*

British army patrol at Killaloe. Dated St Patrick's Day 1921. The soldiers are members of the Oxford and Buckinghamshire Light Infantry. *Photo courtesy of the 'Soldiers of Oxfordshire trust'.*

Memorial card for the Loughnane Brothers, Patrick and Henry, who were murdered by British forces on 6 December 1920. *Photo courtesy of Clare Museum.*

Captain Patrick White, IRA, a native of Meelick. Shot dead by a British sentry at Spike Island internment camp on 1 June 1921. *Photo courtesy of Johnny White, Meelick, County Clare.*

Captain Christopher McCarthy, IRA, a native of Milltown Malbay, was captured and murdered by British soldiers from the Royal Scots regiment.

Lieutenant Richard C. Warren, MC, Oxford and Buckinghamshire Light Infantry. Fatally wounded during an IRA attack at Four Roads, Tulla on 12 June 1921. He died in Limerick Hospital on 28 June 1921. *Photo courtesy of the 'Soldiers of Oxfordshire trust'.*

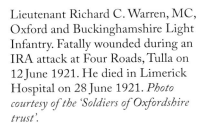

Mid Clare Brigade IRA: (front) Tom Gardiner, IRA; police officer, A. O'Donoghue; Bat. Comdt, P. Considine; Bat. Master, P. O'Brien; (back) Tom Liddy; Paddy Hehir; Joe Murphy; Jimmy Kelliher; Paddy Ward; James Lafferty; Mick Guthrie. *Photo courtesy of Clare Library.*

Mid Clare Brigade: (back) A. O'Donoghue, Michael Flanagan, P. Haran, Dan Clare, Mick O'Donohue, Thos Gallagher, Michael Maher, John Regan, Seamus Davenport; (front) Michael Long, Pat Finn, Sonny Hanrihan, Michael Vaughan, Peter Scales, Thos Liddy, John Davoren, Micko Laferty or Peter Williams. *Photo courtesy of Clare Library.*

Mid Clare Brigade officers. Probably taken during the Truce.
(Back, left to right) Andrew O'Donoghue, Seán MacNamara, J.J. Clohessey
and Seamus Hennessy. (Front, left to right) Frank Barrett, Peadar
O'Loughlin and Ignatius O'Neill. *Photo courtesy of Clare Library.*

Mid Clare Brigade 1921.
(Back, left to right) Pakie Kerin, Darragh; Pat Keane, Kilnamona; unknown.
(Seated centre) two unknowns. (Front, left to right) Vincent Barrett (in
uniform), Thomas Callaghan, Cloonanaha; Patrick McGough, Inagh.

Members of the Mid Clare Brigade of the IRA on parade at Kilfenora during the Truce period. *Photo courtesy of Pat Greene, Spanish Point, County Clare.*

Up Clare! IRA volunteers from Clare in Limerick city at the beginning of the Civil War. *Photo courtesy of Limerick Museum.*

IRA Volunteers John O'Gorman (left) and Patrick O'Dea (right). Taken at an IRA training camp during the Truce. Both men were killed in action fighting the Free State army: O'Dea at Ballyket, Kilrush on 15 July 1922 and O'Gorman, during an attack on Kildysart barracks on 11 August 1922. *Photo courtesy of Clare Library.*

IRA volunteer Martin 'Murt' Moloney was shot dead by a Free State army patrol searching his home in Cloontismara, Inagh on 9 April 1923.

Unarmed IRA volunteers march at the funeral of John McSweeney, September 1922. He was fatally wounded during an attack on Kildysart barracks the previous month. *Photo courtesy of Clare Library.*

IRA cycle unit at the funeral of John McSweeney, September 1922. *Photo courtesy of Clare Library.*

IRA firing party at John McSweeney's funeral. *Photo courtesy of Clare Library.*

Free State army on patrol in Clare. Note the rifles attached to their bicycles. *Photo courtesy of Clare Library.*

Free State troops stationed at Moyreisk House in Clare, September 1923. *Photo courtesy of Clare Library.*

Guardians of the Free State: men of the new National Army dispersing the crowds at Ennis, County Clare, who had gathered to hear de Valera address an anti-Treaty meeting. *Photo courtesy of Kilmainham Jail Museum.*

The arrest of de Valera at an anti-Treaty meeting in Ennis on 13 August 1923. *Photo courtesy of Kilmainham Jail Museum.*

'Was this the will of the people of Clare?' Competing Free State and republican posters in Ennis after the execution of five IRA Volunteers from Clare by the Free State army: Con McMahon, Patrick Hennessy, Patrick O'Mahony, Christopher Quinn and William O'Shaughnessy.

baffled our intelligence staff to find out the source of the leakage of such information.'

As the Mid Clare brigade was beginning to come to grips with the existence of a network of spies and informers in their brigade area, in October they were contacted by IRA headquarters who had discovered that British intelligence were about to mount a campaign of assassination against republicans in counties Clare and Limerick. In early November IRA headquarters contacted Austin Brennan, the acting commander of the East Clare brigade, and informed him that RIC Commissioner Smyth and members of the 'Cairo Gang', a group of British secret service men, would be travelling by train from Dublin to Limerick. Brennan was given detailed information about the their planned journey and in a joint operation with the Mid Limerick brigade he was ordered to hold up their train at Killonan station and assassinate Smyth and the British agents on board.

Joseph Honan from Tuamgraney was on the run in the Cratloe area, staying at Ballymaurice House with some of the other Volunteers who had been selected by Brennan to take part in the attack:

I think it was about the third day after the crowd left for Limerick that a British military plane made a forced landing in the Cratloe district. It came down in a field owned by Mr Punch. In the same field and about 200 yards away from where the plane came to a halt was a quarry, the top of which was about twenty or thirty feet above the level of the field. I did not actually witness the landing of the plane which took place about mid day, but soon afterwards I went to Hogans' house near at hand and got full details there of what had happened. One of the work-men, Ned O'Brien, was in the IRA and he told me that the pilot of the plane was unhurt because soon after landing he left the machine and went to the main road where he was able to send word of his position by some passer-by to the military at Limerick. I got a loan of a bike and with a young lad went off to investigate how matters stood, as the idea was forming in my head that there might be a machine gun in the plane which might be captured. We turned back as soon as we saw lorries coming from Limerick. On returning to Hogans' I discussed with Ned O'Brien the possibility of attacking the plane and the guard which we now knew would be placed over it for the night, and agreed that it was an opportunity which should not be missed. O'Brien went off to get the assistance of the local Volunteers. In a short while Jack McNamara, Moyhill, accompanied by Bill Lynch, two O'Halloran brothers and six others arrived at Hogan's. Two men were sent off to make observations as to what was happening at the plane while Ned O'Brien, Jack McNamara, the two O'Hallorans, myself and another man whose name I do not know went to Ballymaurice House and got the rifles. The scouts we had sent out came with the news that the military who had come out to guard the plane had built a fire in the field with a load of turf which they had commandeered from a man who was passing along the road and that they were amusing themselves around the fire at a game called share the ring, and were obviously not expecting an attack. O'Brien and myself took the party of riflemen through the fields on to the top of the quarry. It was then about 5.30 p.m. and quite dark. The fire lighted by the military gave us a splendid view of each soldier. We opened fire on them and kept up a hot fusillade for about twenty minutes of so. The military retaliated with heavy machine gun fire under which we retired to a wood at the rear of the quarry and from there we returned with our guns to Ballymaurice House. I never learned what casualties were inflicted in that engagement on the British forces, but after the first volley I'm positive two soldiers fell into the turf fire.

Private Alfred Spackman of the Oxfordshire regiment was killed in the attack. A second soldier, Private Maurice Robins, died of his wounds in a military hospital in Fermoy on 2 March. The British army responded to Private Spackman's death by staging a massive security operation in Cratloe and Meelick. Hundreds of soldiers searched the surrounding countryside for days afterwards and arrested every man and youth of military age they came across. A number of road blocks and checkpoints were set up in the district in an attempt to capture the Volunteers involved in the attack. By this time they had all gone back into hiding, but the members of Austin Brennan's party who were returning from Limerick had a narrow escape. The planned attack on the intelligence agents was abandoned when news reached the IRA that they were suddenly recalled to Dublin just before boarding the Limerick train. William McNamara was returning from Limerick with the other selected Volunteers on the Ennis Road when they encountered an army checkpoint that had been set up a few hundred yards from Punches' field where the republicans had mounted their attack on the soldiers a few days earlier:

All the Claremen were cycling along the main Ennis–Limerick road in pairs about twenty yards apart. Seán O'Halloran, Scariff, had been sent on in front of the party to scout the road. It was about nine or ten o'clock at night. Con O'Halloran and myself were in front and in the vicinity of Cratloe we were ordered to halt. At first we thought it might be IRA scouts along the road, but were not long left in doubt, as a burst of fire across the road quickly made us realise that we had run right into the enemy who were laying in ambush. The fire was heavy and concentrated and we were both knocked off our bikes. I managed to escape with an injured knee, probably caused in my fall from the bike. Fortunately the fence on the left hand side of the road was very low and the field inside it was a few feet below the level of the road. I clambered into the field and after a while made contact with Con O'Halloran and another of the Mid Clare crowd, Jack Hassett … Seán O'Halloran, the scout, cycled right into the ambushing party which consisted of military. He was fired on at point blank range and badly wounded. When the soldiers heard us coming they left him and jumped inside the road fence. Thinking that he was dead they left him lying on the roadside but he recovered consciousness, crawled along a road to a cottage where his wounds were dressed and from whence he was shifted on by some local Volunteers to a place of safety.

Though the British intelligence officers had escaped the planned IRA ambush at Killonan railway station, they were not to survive for long. Between 9 and 10 a.m. on Sunday 21 November (known afterwards as 'Bloody Sunday') members of the Squad, a group of Volunteers managed by Michael Collins and trained to assassinate leading members of the British forces, executed eleven British secret service agents working in Dublin and two members of the Auxiliaries in a coordinated operation which devastated the British intelligence network in Ireland. The Mid and East Clare brigades had supplied intelligence information to IRA headquarters which led to the execution of Captain Billy McLean and

Captain John Fitzgerald. McLean had been captured by the IRA in Ennistymon, interrogated and released on the undertaking that he would leave Ireland immediately. Captain John Fitzgerald had been stationed with the RIC in Clare, where he was captured and interrogated by the IRA, court-martialled and sentenced to death. He was taken to a field and placed against a wall for execution. At the last moment he attempted to escape and was shot. The Volunteers left him for dead but he escaped back to his barracks after they left. Volunteer Jim Slattery from Clare was a member of the Squad and led the group of gunmen who assassinated Lieutenant H. Angliss of the Royal Inniskilling Fusiliers on the morning of Bloody Sunday.

In revenge for the killing of their comrades, the Auxiliaries and army surrounded Croke Park later that evening, while a Gaelic football match was in progress between Dublin and Tipperary. They arrived in a large convoy of lorries protected by an armoured car and entered the grounds after thirty minutes of play, supposedly to search the crowd for armed Volunteers. The troops divided into four groups and occupied each corner of the playing field. When they were in position, a British army officer fired a revolver in the air as a signal. In immediate response a group of Auxiliaries stationed at the railway line at one end of the ground opened fire on the crowd with a machine gun. The crowd panicked and sparked a stampede in their desperate attempt to escape. By now the rest of the troops joined in, firing at random into the fleeing crowd.

Frank Doran witnessed what followed:

> We were horrified to see a row of Tans standing in extended order, rifles to the shoulder, firing into the crowd. There was immediate panic – people rushing everywhere. Men, women and children were knocked down and trampled on; others knelt or crouched in prayer … Mick Hogan, the Tipp full back, lay dead near the cinder track near Hill 16. Three or four Tans stood by, unconcernedly chatting. We had to step back to avoid treading on the body of a sixteen-year-old girl; she was lying on her back shot through the forehead, blood trickling slowly down her face. Further on, ambulance men were placing an elderly man on a stretcher. He was moaning in pain, shot through the stomach. Coats, hats, sticks

and umbrellas were strewn around and the new white football forgotten on the pitch held my interest. Outside, as we left, were Tans and more Tans, jibing and asking 'How did you enjoy the match?' The result of the British forces' bloody rampage was that fourteen unarmed civilians were killed and seventy wounded.

The British who committed the massacre claimed that they had been fired on first from Volunteers hiding in the crowd but Major Mills of the Middlesex regiment who had been in command of the Auxiliary company at Croke Park told Brigadier General Crozier, the commander of the auxiliary division, that this claim was nonsense and that the Auxiliaries had opened fire without provocation. Mills was furious:

> 'A ... rotten show ... the worst I've ever seen,' he said. 'The military surrounded the hurley [sic] ground according to plan,' he [Major Mills] went on to say, in reply to a question from me [Brigadier General Crozier], 'and were to warn the crowd by megaphone to file out of the gates where they would be searched for arms. A rotten idea anyhow, as, of course, if anyone had a gun he'd drop it like a red hot poker! Well, who would believe it, suddenly the Regular RIC from Phoenix Park – Black and Tans from England arrived up in lorries, opened fire into the crowd, over the fence without reason and killed about a dozen and wounded many more! I eventually stopped the firing. 'What d'you think of it?' [said Major Mills] 'Rotten,' I [Brigadier General Crozier] replied. 'Sit down here now, write out a report to me and I'll forward it to the Castle at once.' This was done ... No notice was taken whatsoever of Major Mills' report, though he gave truthful evidence at the inquest on the victims and was complemented by the coroner for stopping the firing and thus saving life, save that he was blacklisted by Dublin Castle and eventually discriminated against and got rid of.

Tragically, the British forces' desire to avenge their comrades shot that morning did not end with the massacre at Croke Park. Three more killings followed before the day ended. On Saturday night, only hours before the execution of the British agents, two Claremen, Peadar Clancy and Conor Clune, were arrested in Dublin. Clune worked as the head clerk at Raheen Rural Industries, was a fluent Irish speaker and member of the Gaelic League. He had no connection with either the IRA or Sinn Féin. Clune had gone to Dublin with his employer, Dr Edward McLysaght, for the business's annual tax audit; he also hoped to use the trip as an opportunity to meet his friend Seán O'Connell, a fellow Irish language enthusiast. They arrived in Dublin on Saturday morning and Clune went to Vaughans' hotel to meet O'Connell. At Vaughans' O'Connell introduced Clune to Piaras Béaslaí, who was there to meet Cathal Brugha, Dick McKee, Peadar Clancy and Michael Collins on IRA business. Clune was chatting in Irish with Béaslaí, Kavanagh and O'Connell when one of the hotel porters arrived with a warning for the IRA men that one of the hotel's guests, Mr Edwards, a suspected British spy, was acting suspiciously, making a number of phone calls and leaving the hotel after curfew. McKee, Clancy and the other IRA leaders immediately left the hotel.

A few minutes later a loud commotion was heard at the front of the hotel. O'Connell left Clune and Béaslaí in conversation and went to see what was happening. He looked out and shouted: 'Christ lads, it's the Auxiliaries!' before immediately taking off for the back door followed closely by Béaslaí. Both men escaped as a search party of soldiers and Auxiliaries rushed into the hotel. Clune was terrified and became very nervous and agitated. He was questioned by Captain Hardy, the intelligence officer with F company of the Auxiliaries. Clune panicked and told Captain Hardy that he was staying in the hotel, but his name was not on the register when checked, and when Hardy searched Clune he bellowed out: 'This bloody fellow hasn't even got a toothbrush on him' and arrested Clune. The Auxiliaries arrested two others before leaving Vaughans'; one of the 'prisoners' was Mr Edwards, an undercover Auxiliary that the hotel porter suspected of being a spy. A short time after Clune's arrest, members of the same raiding party arrived at Seán Fitzpatrick's house on Gloucester Street. Inside Dick McKee, the commander of the Dublin brigade, was staying there along with Peadar Clancy, the 1916 veteran from Cranny in west Clare who held the joint posts of vice-commandant of the Dublin brigade and IRA director of munitions. Both men had organised the assassination of British agents on Bloody

Sunday. When they heard the banging on the door downstairs they knew what was happening and began burning incriminating papers. This delayed both of them long enough to prevent their escape and they were arrested and taken to Dublin Castle for questioning, along with Conor Clune and ten others arrested that night. McKee and Clancy's location had been reported to the British forces by ex-British army soldier James Ryan, who was later shot dead by the IRA in Gloucester Place.

Two hours after their murderous rampage in Croke Park the Auxiliaries were again plotting revenge. At 5.30 that afternoon Captain Hardy and Captain King of F company ordered the transfer of prisoners to Beggars Bush barracks when McKee and Clancy were separated from the group and taken back to the guardroom. Both men had attempted to pass themselves off as anonymous prisoners in the larger group but were already identified. Ironically, the British forces still did not know that McKee was the IRA's Dublin brigadier or that he had organised that morning's assassinations. McKee was singled out because he had been captured with Clancy, who was well known to the British because of his leadership of that April's hunger strike in Mountjoy prison. One of the prisoners bound for Beggars Bush, Patrick Young, remembers that the Auxiliaries were scrutinising the group looking for a third man but there was some confusion when an Auxiliary eventually chose Conor Clune as the third wanted man:

> When they came to Clune and Fitzpatrick they were not sure what to do. One said 'That's him' ,and the other said 'No it's him.' My belief is that they were looking for Fitzpatrick as the others were arrested in his house. Both Fitzpatrick and Clune were similar in build and were wearing brown suits. In the end one of them said, 'Oh you'll do', sending Clune over to McKee and Clancy.

For the second time Clune was in the wrong place at the wrong time, but on this occasion it proved fatal. The three men were taken to the guardroom of Dublin Castle for interrogation by Brigadier General Ormonde Winter, the head of the British secret service in Ireland, and by Captains Hardy and King.

That night McKee, Clancy and Clune were shot dead while in custody in the guardroom at Dublin Castle. The Auxiliaries who murdered them and the British authorities claimed that the three were shot while trying to escape. However, Brigadier General Crozier remained unconvinced:

> Another incident – revenge no doubt, for the 'Bloody Sunday' murders – was the murder of three unarmed suspects in a police guardroom at Dublin Castle, in cold blood by the police, perpetrated while I was in hospital. The evidence before the military enquiry which enquired into these deaths was faked from beginning to end, evidence being given by the policemen that the unarmed and closely guarded men attempted to overpower the guard, in a guardroom inside the Castle which was itself closely guarded, in an attempt to escape. Anything did for a paper acquittal then because parliament accepted anything willingly as an explanation.

When the three men's bodies were released to their relatives their condition gives us the best indication of what really happened in the guardroom at Dublin Castle. Dick McKee's body had broken ribs, abrasions to his face, bayonet wounds to his liver and a number of bullet wounds. Conor Clune had been shot thirteen times in the chest and Peadar Clancy's remains showed several bullet wounds and signs of torture. These of course were extraordinary wounds for men who were supposed to have been shot while attempting to escape and their relatives and comrades believed that the men had been tortured to reveal the names of the Volunteers who had killed the eleven British agents earlier that morning, and murdered when McKee and Clancy refused to give information and Clune was unable to do so.

Kathleen Clarke, widow of the executed 1916 leader Thomas Clarke, knew both McKee and Clancy well and saw the three men's bodies lying in state in the pro-cathedral:

> I shall never forget the brutal murder of Peadar Clancy, Dick McKee and Conor Clune. I did not know Clune, but I did know Peadar Clancy and Dick McKee. Both men were of an outstanding type, and their death was a terrible loss to us. They were men who would have been

outstanding anywhere. The British were very discriminating in the men they sought to destroy. The bodies of the tree men were handed over to their relatives and lay in the mortuary chapel of the Pro Cathedral, Marlborough Street. I went in to see them and say a few prayers for them. While I was there Mick Collins came in; when he looked in the coffin of Peadar Clancy, tears rushed from his eyes and fell on Peadar. I did not wonder; all three men were horribly mutilated. One had a large hole in his forehead; it looked as if an explosive bullet had been used. All the faces had the look of tortured men, which even death had not washed away from the memory. What I saw in those coffins would bring tears to the most stony-hearted; Mick Collins had no need to be ashamed of those tears. He took great risks of being captured in coming to see them. We are asked to forgive and forget. How can we forget those things? Forgiveness can only be considered when the power behind the perpetrators of such deeds earn it by their complete removal from our thirty-two counties, leaving us in complete freedom.

9

Down into the Mire

They said I was ruthless, daring, savage, bloodthirsty, even heartless ...
the clergy called me and my comrades 'murderers'. But the British were
met with their own weapons. They had gone down in the mire to destroy us and our nation, and down after them we had to go.

Tom Barry

The British forces in Clare reacted swiftly to 'Bloody Sunday' by
mounting largescale raids for republicans and suspected Volunteers. Art
O'Donnell, the commandant of the West Clare brigade, was arrested
the following day, Monday 22 November at the courthouse in Ennis
while collecting rates paid to Dáil Éireann:

I was taken in a military lorry to the Home barracks. This barracks, in
which the British military were quartered, was originally a gaol ... A
number of prisoners were brought in that day as there had appeared
to have been a general round up. By evening upwards of fifty or sixty
prisoners were lodged in cells there, resembling the usual prison cells
but a lot more cheerless and dank smelling, as they evidently had not
been in use for many years ... I had been in the place for some days
when one night, almost outside my door, I heard two men being beaten
by the military police who were in charge of the prisoners. I found out
through a friendly military policeman on the following day that the
two men were brought in from the Feakle district and that their names
were Considine and Hennessy. I cannot actually recall his description of
the extent to which they were beaten, but he said at any rate they were
seriously hurt ... We were removed from the Home barracks about the
end of November to the ordinance barracks in Upper William Street
Limerick, and quartered in a stable from which horses had recently
been removed. The place was swept out and cleaned and military bunks

and blankets were installed. Prior to our leaving Ennis, as we were lined up outside, an officer, addressing the soldier escort, told them: 'In case of an ambush or attempted ambush shoot the prisoners.'

The order that the republicans should be shot if their army escort was ambushed was not a hollow threat. The British resorted to a policy of carrying hostages as a safe guard to prevent ambush. In addition these hostages could be killed as swift reprisal if ambushes did occur. The lives of republicans were of little worth to British soldiers and police, who could kill without fear of prosecution.

On the night of 8 December Thomas Tuohy was on the run, sleeping in a field near his father's house when he was captured by the RIC:

> After waking I had a look around and saw my father outside the house. He did not appear to be in any way excited, and taking it for granted that the coast was clear I headed towards my home to get a cup of tea. I had gone about 200 yards when I heard the shout 'Hands up!' I ran back, jumped into the river and waded up to my waist on the other side. Here I got onto a boreen, which gave me cover as far as Pat Minogue's house where I went into his yard. At this stage I saw two RIC men about 150 yards behind me. I ran across a field over 200 yards wide and was almost at the opposite fence when I was hit in the back by a bullet which passed through my groin. My leg became paralysed and I had to stay put with my hands up. Three RIC men came along and after searching me marched me back to my home. One of them helped me until I came to a deep trench, which I was made cross unaided. I could not do so and they pulled me across by the hair of my head. When I got as far as home my mother offered me a change of clothing, which the police refused to allow me to accept. Next I was brought as far as Pat Mooney's in Laccaroe where I was put in an outside car and driven to the ambush position at Feakle where I was closely questioned as to my part in it. I refused to admit having anything to do with the affair. I was then taken to the RIC barracks.

Tuohy was court-martialled and sentenced to two years' imprisonment with hard labour for possession of 'seditious documents'. When he arrived at Limerick jail he was stripped naked and given a prisoner's uniform to wear. Tuohy refused to wear a criminal's clothing and was left lying naked in his cell for four days before his civilian clothes were returned. He was moved to an area of the prison which housed a number of other republican political prisoners.

Following the burning of Ruan barracks, Joe Barrett and the Mid Clare brigade decided to increase the size of the brigade flying column:

> After Ruan, the armament of our brigade was substantially improved, and it enabled us to increase the strength of the brigade column by about fifteen men, making the total membership in the region of forty-five. It was deemed necessary that the column should undergo a special course of training, and orders were issued to the members of the column to report at Lickeen and Tullaha in the Kilfenora district about the second week in December 1920.

About sixty Volunteers from all six battalions in the Mid Clare brigade mobilised at Kilfenora vying for selection as part of the brigade's flying column. The brigade officers decided that the Volunteers should be given specialised training in extended order drill, skirmishing and advancing and retreating by section to avoid a repeat of the disorganised retreat under fire, which had followed the Rineen ambush. The mobilised Volunteers marched to Lickeen where they were billeted in farm sheds and safe houses in the district and trained in tactics and manoeuvres for the next six days.

Two ex-British soldiers, Ignatius O'Neill and Martin Slattery, trained the column. Though each Volunteer was allowed handle and fire a Lee Enfield rifle, the Mid Clare brigade still had not captured enough arms from the British to equip each man with a rifle. The remainder of the Volunteers were armed with shotguns, but to make these guns more effective candle wax was poured into the shotgun cartridges. This increased a shotgun's range greatly, making it a far more deadly weapon which could penetrate a quarter-inch plank at fifty yards. The Volunteers were also taught how to throw hand grenades using the Mills bombs captured from Ruan barracks.

Each night the Volunteers at the training camp took up ambush positions in the area in the hope of encountering a British transport patrol, and retired back to their billets after a few hours without any engagement taking place. During the last few days of the training camp the IRA received definite information that a mixed convoy of Black and Tans and soldiers travelled daily from Ennistymon to Ennis.

A faction within the brigade were anxious to increase the pressure on the enemy described by John Joe Neylon as 'a desperate wish among them to do something big, as big as what had been done in other counties, such as Ballinalee and Kilmichael'. Before dawn on 18 December, the Volunteers were woken early for the march to Monreal to ambush the convoy. The chosen ambush site was 200 yards north of the crossroads near Monanagh Bridge; it was not ideal for an ambush position but was regarded as the best location available. The ambush site was only two miles away from the workhouse near Ennistymon where a force of 100 British soldiers and Black and Tans were stationed. To prevent any interference from the British forces in Tulla, Volunteers armed with shotguns were posted as scouts in the surrounding area. The remaining men armed with rifles were divided into two sections of twenty. Section one was positioned on the western side of the road. The ground between the Cullinagh River and section one's position offered poor cover in case of a retreat. Peadar O'Loughlin took command of the Volunteers closer to the bend in the road to the north of the ambush site. They were hidden in a hollow and would not be able to see the British forces' lorries until they entered the ambush site. The riflemen further south, closer to the crossroads, were under the command of Frank Barrett. A small group of three Volunteers were in a flanking position behind Barrett's group covering the crossroads and the road leading to Monanagh Bridge.

Seán Casey was in charge of the Volunteers in section two, posted behind a loosely built stone wall running eastwards from the road straddling the rising ground. Volunteers armed with grenades were positioned where this wall met the road to attack the first British lorry. A large unroofed cattle shelter was attached to this wall twenty yards from the road. A gap in the rear wall of the shelter was cleared of obstacles to allow for a quick retreat back towards the crossroads if necessary.

The republicans expected the convoy to consist of two lorries with a mixed force of twelve to sixteen soldiers and Black and Tans. The republicans rested on the hard frost-covered ground for three hours before their scouts reported to Joe Barrett that the convoy was approaching:

> The approach of the enemy was not signalled until 9.15, when the IRA officers found to their concern that three lorries would have to be dealt with instead of the two for which they had prepared. They were travelling about 400 yards apart, which meant that the third lorry would still be outside the ambush position when the leading one was engaged, and that the enemy intelligence agents aboard it would be free to engage the IRA sections from outside the ambush position. That situation was bound to present the column with a serious problem, for the dispositions of the two sections had been made only with two lorries in mind, and the men in ambush would be fully occupied with the first and second lorries. There was the added factor that the enemy had an additional twenty fighters available, which gave him a substantial numerical advantage over the column.

As the first Crossley Tender approached, one of the Volunteers hidden behind the high stone wall to the east of the road accidentally fired a shot from his rifle as he attempted to get into a better firing position. This alerted the troops travelling in the first Crossley Tender driven by Corporal George Roberts:

> I was driving the first Tender which carried nine soldiers with myself; the second and third tenders carried all RIC and Black and Tans. The officer in charge of the convoy, Captain May, DSO Royal Scots regiment and son of the late Lord May, Irish Guards, sat beside me and in my lorry also was a Sergeant Clarke. As I was rounding the bend coming into Monreal crossroads, a single shot was fired and a bomb was then thrown which landed under the vehicle but failed to explode. Immediately a heavy volley of firing was opened. Captain May threw himself off the Tender and Sergeant Clarke shouted: 'Accelerate and pull up at the crossroads', where there was cover from fire. I did so. When

we got to the crossroads, Sergeant Clarke and Private Black, both also belonging to the Royal Scots, took a machine gun from the Tender and opened up on the attackers. I removed the wounded six privates and laid them on the grass margin on the side of the road.

At the other side of the ambush position, Andrew O'Donoghue and the IRA riflemen in the cattle shelter turned their fire onto the second and third lorries in the convoy:

The second lorry had rounded the bend and received a hot reception until it halted almost in front of a quarry on the roadside just beside the spot where the high wall from the shelter joined the road. The driver of this lorry had been hit, and his passengers were a mixed party of RIC and Black and Tans. They were quickly off the lorry and took shelter underneath it and also in the quarry. They were not long in getting into action, using rifle grenades with great effect, and of which we had our first experience. The survivors from the first lorry also were not slow in making their position felt as they brought a machine gun into action against our position. An attempt to dislodge the police from the quarry and from the vicinity of the second lorry was unsuccessful, as some hand grenades thrown by [Pat] Powell and O'Callaghan from the shelter did not explode. The rifle grenades used by the police began to prove effective. They concentrated on the corner of the shelter nearest them, and gradually began to batter down the wall. Flying shrapnel and splinters from the stones compelled our men to vacate that post. [Ignatius] O'Neill and myself were busily engaged in dealing with the machine gun and snipers firing from the direction of the crossroads ... I would say that, by this time the fighting was in progress for about a quarter of an hour. In the mean time, the occupants of the third lorry, which had pulled up before it reached the bend where it would have come under fire, had dismounted and began to advance from the road up the high ground on our right flank. This party had a machine gun also, but they were held in check by a few of our section who had left the shelter before O'Neill and myself, and who had retreated from the high wall coming up from the road. Our men had crossed this wall into a long field on the left, where there were a number of depressions in the ground that enabled them to move further away from the enemy by making short runs or crawling from one hollow to another ... Between myself and the by-road I knew that Paddy Devitt, Seán McNamara and Joe Griffey were pinned down by enemy fire. The trouble with them was that McNamara had been badly wounded in the thigh, and he had to be helped along. Gradually I made my way to the by-road and found the trio in a depression, Devitt firing an occasional shot whenever he saw a target. After joining them we decided that McNamara and Griffey should continue their way towards the by-road, while Devitt and myself covered their retreat. We opened fire, which was sufficiently effective to enable the retiring pair to reach their objective. I next went off while Devitt covered me. I too got clear, after which I was able to engage the enemy until Devitt made the journey. There was more shooting to our left as we got across the by-road, and we found that it was coming from O'Neill and a few others of the column who were with him. I sent off Griffey to tell them to wait as we needed assistance to carry McNamara who was after losing a lot of blood and was now in a weak condition. Devitt and myself helped him along for roughly a hundred yards when we made contact with O'Neill and the others … In view of the small size of our little force, nearly half of whom carried shotguns, we decided to continue the retreat as best we could through Cloona towards Lickeen.

To the west of the road section one began withdrawing across the Cullinagh River after the retreat eastwards by O'Donoghue and O'Neill's group. This allowed the British troops from the two Crossley Tenders that had entered the ambush position to turn their machine guns and rifles on the Volunteers retreating westwards. A number of the Volunteers had already crossed the river when the opening burst of machine gun fire wounded William McNamara and Bill Carroll. Paddy O'Loughlin was hit in the arm as he was running for cover; he dropped his rifle when he was wounded and the continuing hail of bullets forced him to take shelter, leaving his rifle behind. As the IRA continued their withdrawal back across the river Joe Barrett remained behind with Martin Slattery and John Minihan. They mounted a fresh attack on the army machine gun crew from the first lorry at the crossroads and the RIC and Black and Tans on the roadside from the second Crossley Tender. Their rifle fire forced the troops to hold their position as the other Volunteers retreated further still under fire from the British machine gunners across the road on the eastern side of the ambush position.

The IRA had safely withdrawn to the far side of the small hill that rises up from the west bank of the Cullinagh River where it was discovered that two of the men, Jack Hassett and Jim Kierse, were missing. Joe Barrett made the call for six Volunteers to return and search for the missing pair. It was a daunting task for men who had just undergone a difficult withdrawal under relentless pressure. For many of them it was their first experience of combat and they had never encountered machine gun and grenade fire before. But when the call was made every man present volunteered. On seeing the column men's display of loyalty to their two missing comrades, John Joe Neylon turned to Barrett and said: 'By heavens, Joe, but there are great men in Ireland still!' Joe Barrett then selected six of the most experienced men to return to the ambush site and search for Hassett and Kierse.

Jack Hassett and Jim Kierse were the last two Volunteers to attempt to retreat from the ambush site. While Joe Barrett, Martin Slattery and John Minihan attacked the soldiers and machine gun crew at the crossroads, Hassett and Kierse were still in position 100 yards further north keeping the RIC and Black and Tans from advancing. They held out for as long as possible against repeated machine gun, rifle and grenade attacks before deciding to withdraw. In their hurried retreat they had become confused about the column's planned escape route and were heading southwards towards Monreal Bridge. Hassett was wounded by machine gun fire in both legs. He was incapable of walking and Kierse attempted to carry him across the river but was unable. The two men managed to get as far as Monreal Bridge where they took shelter from the gunfire.

The troops had seen the pair and had pursued them from the cross-roads to the bridge when Joe Barrett and the IRA's search party located them:

Having sized up the situation, the section manoeuvred six men into a position from which they put down on the bridge a heavy fire that drove the British back to the crossroads. The British returned the IRA fire from the roadside, but, while these exchanges were taking place, column men, not engaged, succeeded in getting their wounded comrades from under the bridge and, having availed of the cover provided by surrounding fences, they conveyed them safely to the security of the far side of the hill. There the full section answered the roll call. The British made no attempt to follow the section beyond the bridge.

While section one were making their withdrawal northwards towards Sceach, Andrew O'Donoghue and the other IRA men in section two were still being pursued by soldiers when British reinforcements arrived at the scene of the ambush:

> As we were moving through Russa, reinforcements, comprised of RIC and Black and Tans from Ennistymon, approached the scene of the ambush. Seeing the figures on the high ground behind the cattle shelters vacated by us, they opened fire. The fire was promptly returned. The exchange of shots lasted for several minutes before the reinforcements realised they were firing on their own men, the military, who had advanced a short distance after us. There were some casualties, and it gave rise to a lot of bad feeling afterwards between the military and the police. Perhaps it was just as well for us that this incident occurred, as it may have been the cause of the enemy failing to press home his advantage, which he definitely had at that stage.

Five Volunteers were wounded in the attack, though none seriously, and they were all able to take up active duty again within a few months. Six British soldiers and one RIC constable were wounded. At the Monreal ambush the IRA failed to destroy the column – and thereby achieve 'something big' like the Kilmichael ambush – or capture weaponry from the British forces. However, the Monreal ambush was not a defeat for the Mid Clare brigade; the part-time Volunteers, many of whom had never been in combat before, had engaged superiorly armed and battle-hardened British troops and their reinforcements for over an hour, inflicting heavier casualties on their enemy and successfully escaping his attempts at encirclement without losing a single man. The Mid Clare brigade's fighting record at the Monreal ambush stands as quite an achievement for a military force with the limited weapons, training and resources then available to the IRA.

Patrick Devitt remembered that the British in the north Clare area were forced to further change their tactics after the Monreal ambush:

> From the date of the Monreal ambush to the truce it was very hard to get a chance in north or mid Clare to attack the enemy as they passed through the country without any hope of success. Their convoys were consistently strengthened and armoured vehicles were also brought into use. The best which could be done was to hamper their communications by road cutting, constructing roadblocks and destroying telephone lines. Long-distance sniping was also resorted to, but I'm not aware that such shooting ever inflicted a casualty.

The Mid Clare brigade's flying column went into action again a week after the Monreal ambush against another large convoy at Decamade, Lissycasey, seven miles to the west of Ennis. The flying column had called at Cahercon college to warn a Catholic priest with republican sympathies that a number of boats used by the college were about to be seized by the British. The IRA occasionally used these boats for transport and Joe Barrett was anxious to avoid their seizure by the enemy:

> As we were leaving the college in the morning, early, and crossing up to our own brigade area, we saw thirteen lorries leaving Kildysart and going towards Kilrush. The column, about twenty strong, marched to Lissycasey and there it was decided to ambush these lorries on their return to Ennis at Decamade, two miles away. The convoy returned about six o'clock that evening. The first and last vehicles were armoured cars and, in between, about 100 yards between each, were four lorries, all of them equipped with high wooded crates, covered on top with netting wire to prevent hand grenades from being thrown into them. The first two vehicles were allowed to pass without interference, and we concentrated our fire on the remaining four, apparently with good effect because we found a good deal of blood on the road afterwards. At the Ennis side of the ambush position, an old bog road ran from the main

road around the rear of our position. The fight had been in progress for about ten minutes when it struck me that the enemy might avail of the bog road to outflank us, so I took five men with me as far as a turn in the bog road, about 500 yards from the main road. On arriving there, we found the enemy troops had dismounted from the lorries and had actually begun advancing along the road towards us. We at once opened fire to which the enemy made but a brief reply, and then retreated back to their lorries and drove off to Ennis.

For three months since the shooting of Captain Lendrum, the British forces in West Clare had been seeking to avenge his death. Initially they had vented their anger through the reprisals that followed the Rineen ambush, but their efforts to mount further reprisals at Cooraclare, Doonbeg and Mullagh had been prevented by the actions of the IRA's West Clare brigade. Shortly after this, a British spy living in the area informed the forces that William Shanahan was in charge of the IRA unit that had shot Captain Lendrum and began giving them accurate intelligence information about his movements. Acting on fresh information provided by their spy, five lorries of Black and Tans raided a republican court being held at Craggaknock near Kilkee on 6 December. Republican scouts posted nearby managed to send warning of the approaching raiders moments before they arrived. William Shanahan, who was attending the court as a member of the republican police force, managed to escape just before the troops burst in. The Black and Tans became enraged upon discovering that Shanahan had escaped and they opened fire on the unarmed civilians attending the court, shooting dead Thomas Curtin.

The Black and Tans remained determined to capture Shanahan and his luck did not hold. On the morning of 18 December the Black and Tans surrounded Denis Reidy's house at Doonbeg and captured Shanahan and another IRA Volunteer, Michael McNamara asleep in their beds. They were taken to the RIC barracks at Kilrush where they were beaten, tortured and interrogated for five days. On 22 December Shanahan and McNamara were put aboard a Crossley Tender lorry and driven towards Ennis under armed guard. The British lorries halted on the roadside at Darragh between Kildysart and Ennis, and Michael McNamara was taken off the Crossley Tender he was travelling in and told he was free to go home, but was then shot dead. His dead body was bayoneted several times before it was chained on to the back of one of the Crossley Tenders and dragged behind it to Ennis.

At Ennis William Shanahan was taken to the jail, where his interrogation continued. During a break in his interrogation when he was being taken to the toilet, Shanahan was shot in the head at point blank range by Provost Sergeant David Finlay. Shanahan's body was found the next day in the county infirmary. At Ennis jail Shanahan appears to have suffered the most brutal treatment. When his body was returned to his family a few days later almost every bone in it had been broken and a number of his finger and toe nails had been torn out.

As 1921 began, the Mid Clare brigade were planning another ambush to keep up the pressure they had mounted on the British in their brigade area. On 9 January they went into action at Caherea. Members of the IRA had kept surveillance on a British convoy usually made up of four lorries carrying a mixed force of Black and Tans and British soldiers sometimes accompanied by two armoured cars which travelled regularly from Ennis to Kilrush. The brigade officers decided to attack the convoy at Caherea, eight miles from Ennis. On 8 January twenty of the most experienced Volunteers from the 1st battalion assembled after dark at Barefield and marched the eight miles to Slaveen where they were billeted with another thirty Volunteers from the 3rd and 4th battalions. The next morning they travelled to Caherea where twenty men and officers from the 2nd battalion were already waiting for them. At 8 a.m. the seventy-strong flying column marched to the ambush site near Caherea national school where they were divided into four attacking sections.

The IRA's attacking parties were stationed at each side of the school. The IRA hoped to trap the convoy on a long straight stretch of road between two bends. The convoy was expected to travel from Ennis and enter the ambush around a sharp bend in the road 250 yards to the east of Caherea school. The IRA had dug a series of deep trenches in the road the previous night. These trenches had been carefully camouflaged so that a heavy vehicle passing over them would collapse their covers and fall into them immobilised. The republicans hoped that the leading vehicle into the ambush position would become stuck in these trenches and block the road, trapping the following vehicles between it and the sharp bend to the east of Caherea school.

The first section comprised the main attacking party; about forty riflemen under the direction of Frank Barrett and Seán O'Keefe were spread out for 300 yards along a by-road on rising ground running from the school into the bog. Seán Casey was in command of the second section of fourteen Volunteers armed with rifles and shotguns, positioned behind the walls of the school yard. Frank Barrett commanded the seven riflemen in the third section in the fields to the south-east of the school 200 yards from the road. The last section of ten riflemen under William McNamara's leadership were placed at the roadside on the outside of the sharp bend where the British convoy would enter the ambush. Their task was to hold the British vehicles inside the ambush position and cut off their line of retreat. A dozen scouts armed with shotguns had been posted watching the road for the approach of the convoy.

The scouts finally signalled its approach late in the afternoon to Joe Barrett:

> About three o'clock in the evening scouts reported that lorries were coming from the Ennis direction. This was a late hour for them to come, and we had just been wondering if the enemy might have received information that an ambush might have been prepared for him. In view of the subsequent behaviour of the enemy, I became convinced that he had been warned of our presence, and as a result of later enquiries, made by us, I'm satisfied that this happened through loose talk on the part of certain parties in the Caherea district. Shortly after hearing from the scouts, they sent a further report that the enemy troops were dismounting from the lorries, about three-quarters of a mile from the ambush position, and that they were moving towards us through the fields in two parties, one on the north side of the road and one on the south side, with the obvious intention of trying to outflank us. While this movement was proceeding, an armoured car and two caged lorries of troops advanced as far as the Fergus View school, almost into the centre of our

position. This was clearly a manoeuvre designed to entice us into a fight while the out-flanking operation was in progress. For fear of our men falling into this trap, I sent a message across the road to our main party warning them of the enemy's plans and urging them to withdraw in a northerly direction, which would leave them outside the right wing of the encircling forces ... My advice was promptly put into operation and, though the men came under heavy fire in the process, they sustained no casualties in attaining their objective though they had to fall back for half a mile.

As the battle commenced between Joe Barrett's riflemen and the Black and Tans attempting to encircle them, the main section of the IRA's attacking party opened fire on the troops for about ten minutes before Frank Barrett and Seán O'Keefe gave orders not to engage the armoured car and two Crossley Tenders which had entered the ambush site in order to escape the British attempt at luring them into a fight and encircling them. William McNamara's section could hear the gunfire of the continuing battle but were unaware of what was happening because the bend in the road cut off their view of the Crossley Tenders where the Black and Tans had dismounted 500 yards away. When he saw the main force of the IRA, led by Frank Barrett, withdrawing up the hillside he followed suit and joined them near the hilltop where both groups halted and again opened fire on the Black and Tans in an attempt to draw them into battle on the hillside. Upon seeing the main body of the IRA withdrawing, the members of the convoy who had entered the ambush position dismounted from their transport and attempted to pursue Joe Barrett's group. They used the by-road running south and about 150 yards to our left. Simultaneously fire was opened on us from the armoured car at the school. I detailed two men to engage the troops advancing along the by-road, while myself and the others opened up on the armoured car and the troops in the second lorry. Soon I found we were confronted with a fresh threat. The soldiers, who had earlier dismounted from the lorries and gone into the fields at the south side of the road, were now closing in on our rear from the east. Our fire was now directed to them while, at the same time, we withdrew gradually towards the south and also to higher ground. Only a field shaped like an isosceles triangle, about fifty yards at the base and with sides about a hundred yards, now separated us from the forces, who constituted this new danger. My immediate objective was to get to the top or apex of the field before them as whoever got there first was certain to be victorious. I detailed two of the five men I had left to make their way, as quickly as they could, to the top of the field. From there they could command both sides of the field and, with well directed enfilade, beat off the enemy's threat sufficiently long to enable the rest of us to get outside his enveloping movement. During the fighting on the sides of this triangular field I know that we hit some of our opponents. At times we were only twenty yards apart and every man I had with me was a sharp shooter. I caught a Black and Tan crossing a gap at twenty-five yards' range and 'knocked him kicking'. This casualty slowed up the advance of the enemy towards the top of the field. It happened at a crucial stage of the fighting, because it helped in allowing the two men I had sent off to try to reach the top to get there first. They held on to that position until the rest of us arrived there, and once this happened we were not long in forcing our opponents to retreat back to the main road. The first two men who had been detailed to pin down the enemy advance along the by-road did their job well, and they retired in the same direction we did, meeting us later that night.

On seeing their comrades escape, the main IRA force also withdrew and the two parts of the column regrouped at Kilmaley. It was obvious from their action that someone in the area had supplied the British forces with detailed information about the IRA's presence at Caherea. Suspicion centred on an attendant working at the Ennis mental hospital who had been returning from a short holiday when he cycled through the ambush position. He was later shot at in the grounds of the hospital but was not injured.

As a result of the ambush the Mid Clare brigade staff re-examined the suitability of one large flying column with upwards of fifty Volunteers. The main brigade flying column was re-formed with between thirty and forty Volunteers from the 1st, 2nd and 3rd battalions. The 4th, 5th and 6th battalions each formed their own smaller battalion flying columns with about fifteen riflemen and fifteen shotgun men in each. A week after this reorganisation Joe Barrett, and the other staff officers arranged a training course for the brigade's new flying columns.

The East Clare brigade were anxious to mount fresh ambushes on British transport convoys in an attempt to further wear down the morale of the British and relieve the enemy pressure on their comrades in the Mid Clare brigade. Jack Egan, one of the Mid Clare brigade's intelligence officers, had uncovered detailed information and schedules for weekly RIC motorised patrols between Broadford and Sixmilebridge. The IRA planned to ambush one of these patrols as it passed through Castlelake on 6 January but an inspection of the area showed that it was an unsuitable place to mount an ambush. The operation was indefinitely postponed and the IRA organised a second ambush at Oatfield on 11 January. Having waited in ambush for several hours the republicans withdrew when the RIC patrol failed to travel through the ambush position. On the same day General Neville Macready placed County Clare under martial law. The IRA's response was to carry on their business as usual, and that morning raided the GPO in Ennis, taking letters to check them for intelligence information. About the same time reports reached Michael Brennan that RIC Crossley Tenders regularly travelled from Limerick to Ennis along the Redgate to Cratloe road because republican road-blocking operations had rendered sections of the main Ennis Road impassable. RIC convoys travelling from Ennis were usually transferring prisoners to Limerick prison or carrying hostages on board and the IRA intended that only Crossley Tenders travelling towards Ennis from Limerick would be attacked. The date selected for the attack was 13 January.

The republicans had selected an ambush site between two bends in the road, on farmland owned by the McInerney family, a short distance to the east of Cratloe railway station. A group of sixteen Volunteers armed with rifles and shotguns moved into position before dawn. The IRA were divided into three sections under Michael Brennan, his brother Austin Brennan and Joseph Clancy. The main section of the attacking party under Michael Brennan's command occupied a large derelict house about twenty yards to the north of the roadside which gave the republicans inside a clear line of fire across the ambush site. Although Michael Brennan had not fully recovered from the wound he received in the attack on the RIC at O'Brien's Bridge the previous September and still did not have the use of his right arm, he still planned to take part in the attack using his automatic pistol. Joseph Clancy and four other Volunteers were positioned in a small farmyard shed on the same side of the road a short distance away. The third group directed by Austin Brennan was stationed across the road covering the other side of the ambush position.

A number of republican scouts were placed along the road in both directions to give warning of any approaching patrols. The ambushers' objective was to attack RIC Crossley Tenders expected to travel from Limerick. Michael Brennan issued orders that RIC lorries travelling from Ennis were not to be attacked for fear of killing or injuring prisoners and hostages being carried in them. If lorries approached the ambush from the Ennis direction the Volunteers were to remain hidden and allow them to pass unchallenged to prevent the RIC discovering the ambush and calling reinforcements from Limerick.

Shortly before 10 a.m. the IRA's scouts reported that an RIC Crossley Tender was approaching from Ennis and Michael Brennan gave the order 'heads down' and the Volunteers scrambled into hiding. As the lorry entered the ambush position one of the riflemen in Austin Brennan's section accidentally fired a shot, revealing the IRA's presence to the RIC who immediately opened a blind fire on both sides of the road. Michael Brennan shouted orders to return fire and all three sections opened a hurried attack on the RIC men in the lorry as it turned the first bend in the road. The RIC's driver was uninjured and drove at speed towards the next bend to get clear of the ambush position. As the lorry drove through a hail of heavy rifle and shotgun fire from the IRA, RIC Sergeant Jeremiah Curtin and two constables were wounded. The commander of the patrol, Sergeant Stephen Carthy, was shot dead and fell out of the vehicle onto the road. The Crossley Tender sped out of the ambush position and drove straight to Limerick without stopping. Sergeant Curtin had died of his wounds by the time the survivors of the patrol reached Limerick.

After the Crossley Tender escaped from the ambush, the IRA moved quickly onto the roadside and collected Sergeant McCarthy's revolver and a rifle dropped by a member of the patrol. The republicans were now in a dangerous position. The survivors of the patrol would reach Limerick within a few minutes and a large force of troops would start flooding into the area now that the IRA's presence was known. One of the Volunteers, Matty McGrath, was accidentally shot in the leg by one of his comrades during the attack and Michael Brennan needed to take swift action to get him medical attention and prevent the capture of the rest of the men under his command. They immediately moved northwards across Woodcock Hill and narrowly avoided encirclement by a very large military force sent from Limerick to search the area. Frustrated by their lack of success and angered by the killing of two of their men, the British troops searched and then burned a number of houses in revenge before withdrawing. These were the first 'official reprisals' to take place in Clare. The policy had been proposed by Winston Churchill, that houses in the immediate area of an ambush would be burned by the British forces acting under government orders if their occupants did not give them information about the IRA. Of course the beginning of official reprisals in January 1921 did not mean that unofficial reprisals and murders stopped.

That night the republicans moved through the Windy Gap and on towards Oatfield where the column dispersed. A few days later they reassembled when mobilisation orders were sent to all six battalions of the Mid Clare brigade asking all available Volunteers to assemble at Parkers' house, Belvoir Cross on the morning of 20 January. The officers of the Mid Clare brigade had decided to make a second attempt to ambush the RIC patrol travelling from Broadford to Sixmilebridge. An intricate network of roads and junctions offered the patrol a wide choice of routes between the two towns, and the IRA could not be certain that the RIC would travel. To further complicate matters the British forces had become particularly wary of ambushes and often returned to their barracks by a different route to their outward journey. A fair was due to be held in Kilkishen on 20 January and the IRA were confident they could predict the route chosen by the patrol that day.

Thirty-seven Volunteers reported for duty in the fading twilight at Parkers' house. Half carried rifles while the remainder were armed with shotguns and revolvers. A number who had arrived unarmed volunteered as scouts. Michael Brennan inspected his troops, checked their arms and equipment and divided them into different sections, explaining the plan of attack. Originally Brennan decided to attack the RIC patrol in the vicinity of Parkers' but Joseph Clancy pointed out that if the patrol travelled from Sixmilebridge through Kilkishen towards Broadford it would bypass the chosen ambush position. Clancy suggested an alternative location for the attack at the rear entrance to Glenwood House. Michael Brennan accepted his advice and at the last moment the IRA column marched to Glenwood occupying their new positions shortly after 7 a.m.

At Glenwood the republican scouts were posted along the road a short distance in both directions from the IRA's new position. The thirty or so remaining Volunteers were dived into three sections under the command of Michael Brennan, his brother Austin Brennan and Tom McGrath. The men in Michael Brennan's section were all armed with rifles and positioned along a high stone wall just north of the gate to Glenwood House. Michael Brennan himself was armed with a revolver and stood a few yards behind the men in his group positioned along this wall. Joseph Clancy was hidden behind a large holly bush on top of the wall keeping watch along the road as the other Volunteers remained hidden. Austin Brennan's group, equipped with rifles and shotguns, was placed fifty yards further north behind another stone wall. The remaining men under Tom McGrath's command were located along the edge of a field 100 yards to the south of the gate armed with revolvers. The ambushers were to hold their fire until riflemen under Michael Brennan's command attacked the lorry.

The intelligence information gathered by Jack Egan showed that the RIC patrol was due to travel through the area at 11 a.m. One of the republican scouts was despatched to Kilkishen to see if he could get any news of the patrol's location. He returned with the report that the patrol had not passed through the village before he began his return at noon. By 3.30 the IRA officers at Glenwood came to the conclusion that the patrol had travelled by a different route, and began to recall their scouts when they reported that a lorry was approaching from Kilkishen. A few moments later Volunteers waiting in ambush heard the roar of the vehicle's engine. With a number of the scouts already withdrawn, the IRA still did not know whether or not it was the RIC patrol, as a number of civilian lorries had passed during the day. After their long wait the IRA officers were anxious that the column men would not repeat the mistake of the Cratloe operation and alert the RIC by firing an accidental shot. As the lorry approached, Joseph Clancy climbed on top of the wall behind which Michael Brennan's section was positioned and kept watch to check if it was the expected RIC patrol. Clancy made repeated appeals to John Ryan and the other riflemen to hold their fire until the lorry came into view; he then entered the ambush position, shouted 'police' and dropped down into his position.

As the patrol entered the ambush position the IRA still did not know its strength or whether there was a second or possibly even a third Crossley Tender following. Because of this uncertainty Michael Brennan did not give the order to fire until the Tender had almost drawn level with his section's position:

> There was no time to get the outposts posted, but as it sounded like only one lorry, it seemed to be a fair chance … The whistle brought a burst of fire from front and side. My party all aimed at the driver, but though they knocked off his cap and hit nearly everyone else on the lorry, he was unscathed. His steering column was broken though and the lorry went out of control, rolling in against the wall where we were standing.

While the lorry was slowing to a halt, Dan Lenehan threw a Mills bomb grenade into the back of the Tender but it failed to explode. As the IRA continued firing on the lorry its driver, a wounded Black and Tan named Selve, jumped clear across the bonnet of the vehicle and ran for cover, throwing aside his belt, revolver, ammunition and coat in an effort to escape. Under fire from all three sections Selve managed to leave the roadway and disappeared into Belvoir woods. A second RIC man, Sergeant Egan, who had been wounded, left the rear of the Tender and escaped while the republicans had turned their attention from the lorry onto its fleeing driver.

Within two minutes the ambush ended and Michael Brennan ordered a ceasefire. The IRA's initial attack had been so effective that the entire

RIC patrol was either killed or wounded and the troops inside were unable to return fire. Most were killed instantly, while the others, who were mortally wounded, were carried to the roadside and one member of the flying column was sent to Sixmilebridge to summon spiritual aid for them from Fr Daly and Fr O'Dea. The Volunteers searching the dead and wounded recovered eight rifles, seven .45 revolvers and almost 1,000 rounds of ammunition. Knowing that the sound of gunfire would have been heard and reported to the British, the IRA withdrew southwards towards Oatfield after setting fire to the Crossley Tender. Three Black and Tans, Michael Moran from Castlebar in Mayo, Frank Morris from London and William Smith from Kent, were killed in the ambush alongside two regular RIC men, Sergeant Molloy from Mayo and John Doogue from Laois. The sixth British casualty was the commander of the patrol and the local district inspector, DI William Clarke from Armagh, who had recently been promoted from the Auxiliaries to the regular RIC.

As the remainder of the IRA flying column crossed the hills towards the south, they saw the first houses burning as the British forces began another night of terrorism and reprisals in revenge for the ambush. Lorry loads of Black and Tans and RIC from Sixmilebridge and Broadford converged on Kilkishen firing their weapons at random into houses along the roadside as they travelled to the area. Having raided a number of pubs for drink they began to fire wildly at the inhabitants of the village as they made their way towards Joseph Clancy's home. When the Black and Tans arrived and found the house empty, they began a 'police search' of the house and reduced its entire contents to pieces. By now word of the ambush had reached the Auxiliaries stationed at the Lakeside Hotel in Killaloe, who set off to join in the reprisals at Kilkishen. They stopped on their journey to burn the Bridgetown creamery and various houses along the way. Their next stop was at Cloneconry, where they torched Hayeses' and Ryans' before continuing on their way, stopping at Lissane, Ballykelly, Annaghclare, Belvoir, Knockatureen and Sixmilebridge, marking their progress with a trail of burning farmhouses. Upon reaching Kilkishen they set alight a number of farm buildings and haystacks belonging to the Dwyer family. When they eventually arrived in the centre of the village they joined the Black and Tans in looting and burning more houses before they all got so drunk and out of control that their officers had to disarm a number of them that were shooting their rifles and revolvers so freely that they were a danger to themselves and the other members of the RIC. By morning the Black and Tans and Auxiliaries had reduced twenty-one houses to ashes, but the British reprisals had still not ended. They returned early the next morning with some soldiers who assisted them in ransacking houses, burning them and questioning or beating up their occupants.

Twenty-two local people were arrested and interned without trial. Reprisals were not limited to revenge for IRA attacks; a few days after the reprisals at Kilkishen, a group of Black and Tans from Kilkee arrived at the home of Thomas Shannon, a farmer and magistrate in the republican courts, at Moyasta and shot him dead when he answered his door.

The IRA's successes in both Mid and East Clare forced the British forces of occupation to remain within their barracks and restricted most of their activity within the county's heavily garrisoned towns and villages. This was a partial victory as the British had essentially abandoned the territory outside of these towns to the republicans, as they could only enter the countryside in force with three or more Crossley Tenders packed with a large numbers of troops often accompanied by one or more armoured cars. This produced a temporary stalemate as the IRA was unable to attack these patrols with any chance of success and they needed to find another way to keep up the pressure and show that they remained undefeated. Initially they resorted to the tactics they had used early in the war in 1919 when they entered towns and villages garrisoned by the enemy forces mounting a series of small-scale sniping attacks on troops and their barracks.

The Mid Clare brigade began this new campaign with an attack on the RIC stationed in Ennistymon in January. While the police refused to be drawn out into the countryside to fight the IRA except with the advantage of force, their men could not remain holed up safe within their large fortified barracks all the time and so still patrolled the town on foot and left barracks to attend religious and social functions and to buy additional supplies. In Ennistymon the Catholic members of the garrison still attended mass at the local church every Sunday morning, with eight armed RIC men leaving their barracks briefly to walk the short distance to the service and back again afterwards. Peadar O'Loughlin, the vice-O/C of the brigade, entered Ennistymon before daybreak one Sunday morning with fifteen Volunteers from the 5th battalion of the Mid Clare brigade intending to attack the RIC as they returned from mass. Armed with rifles, they took up an ambush position hidden behind the walls of the monastery grounds about 400 yards from the barracks. Pádraig Ó Fathaigh from Galway, a member of the 5th battalion, describes the attack:

> Commandant O'Loughlin sent eight men to attack the enemy coming from church and took four others to cover the retreat. I happened to be in the latter group. The eight men rushed across a paddock and fired on the enemy in the street. Then the five [in the covering party] kept firing on the barracks to allow the eight to get back and check the pursuit. Running back we soon saw the eight men in front of us and at length came up with them ... as we reached Cahersherkin, Paddy O'Loughlin looked back and said 'The Tans are on us.' We jumped over a moat and took up a bad position on the exposed side of the moat. It happened that we tore up a culvert on the road beside our position the previous night and we could hear the despairing cries of the Black and Tans as their lorry went into the trench. We were about fifty yards from the moat and awaited an attack. Then a scout was sent out who informed us that the Tans had made for the nearby Cahersherkin Cottage which they occupied expecting an attack.

The IRA withdrew from the area without being pursued any further by the Black and Tans.

In February the British forces scored a number of successes against the Mid Clare brigade, capturing several leading Volunteers and a small number of the brigade's weapons. William McNamara and twenty other members of the newly formed 1st battalion flying column had mobilised for active service at Kearneys' castle. A small number of the men who had reported for duty were unarmed and McNamara and James Corry decided to collect a number of rifles from the brigade's arms dump to equip these men. The next morning they called to Kearneys' house near the castle, which served as the headquarters of the 1st battalion, before leaving to collect the rifles:

> Just as we reached the door at Kearneys' house we saw two lorries of Tans pulling up at the gate 300 yards off. We ran around to the back of the house, being under fire as we did so. We then made off through the fields at the rear. Jack Hassett and a [Fianna Éireann] boy scout from Ennis named Coote joined us during the retreat and we all reached the top of a hill where the country stretched out into a big open bog. At this point Corry hid in some bushes while we continued into the bog. Unknown to us, more soldiers and Tans had taken up positions in the bog and we found ourselves surrounded. At this stage fire was being directed at us from all angles but fortunately none of us was hit. I was still trying to evade capture when I found myself only ten yards away from an RIC officer. He was firing from an automatic pistol while he shouted to me to put up my hands. I then had no option but to do so, but he continued firing until he came close when he hit me on the head with the pistol. My comrades were also captured, except Jim Corry who was not found … The house and a large area was thoroughly searched during the course of which a few rifles, single-barrel shotguns and hand grenades were discovered. This material had been brought to the place a couple of days previously along with other weapons, but it had been condemned as not being fit for use. A serviceable rifle and revolver hidden away elsewhere were also captured … Before our captors left they set fire to the house and also to whatever hay and straw Mr Kearney had. He was also arrested. We were taken into Ennis as prisoners.

The British garrison in Clare was by now strengthened with the addition of a second force of Auxiliaries posted to Corofin. Given the IRA's previous successes in turning RIC men to provide intelligence information and capturing the police barracks at Newmarket and Ruan, members of the Auxiliaries were approached by Michael Hehir and an ex-RIC sergeant named Harrison while drinking in the town and sounded as to their readiness to sell arms and ammunition. Both men were arrested shortly afterwards.

Further disaster followed on 7 February when Patrick Falsey was accidentally shot dead by the IRA. He was filling in a trench cut across a road in Cooraclare with a group of local men. The trench had been dug by the IRA to stop British patrols entering the area and when they discovered the group filling in the trench they fired a few shots in the air to scare them off; one of these wounded Falsey, who died that evening.

The same day the British forces scored another success with the capture of three leading members of the Mid Clare brigade – John Joe Neylon, Tom McDonough and Joe Murphy – at Kilfenora. As part of the Dáil's programme of republican government Neylon and McDonough seized the rate books from the local collection agent. The three IRA members were late in delivering the rate money because of a strong military presence in the area and continued on towards O'Deas' house where Tom McDonough planned to leave the money for collection:

Nearing O'Deas' place we stopped and Murphy got off the car to go make enquires. He was not gone twenty yards when two lorries of RIC and Black and Tans in charge of DI Hilliard and Sergeant Larkin arrived. We were unarmed at the time. 'Tosser' [John Joe Neylon] slipped off the car and started to walk up a by-road, where before being captured he threw the money into a drain. Murphy was also captured. Sergeant Larkin came over to me where I was seated on the sidecar and asked me what I was doing. And I replied that I was just out for a drive. He then looked into the well of the car and saw the rate books ... The police had meantime found the money which Neylon had thrown into the drain. District Inspector Hilliard announced that he had no intention of bringing us in and he proposed to shoot us there and then. He placed the three of us standing on the grass margin on one side of the road and fell in with a firing party of six at the opposite side – two men aiming at each of us. Sergeant Larkin pleaded with him and, referring to Neylon, said he was no ordinary prisoner as his uncle was a general in the British army. That was quite true, for 'Tosser' was a nephew of General Sir Daniel Neylon who had been knighted after the 1914–18

Great War. This, however, seemed to cut no ice with Hilliard who said: 'Little good that would do you if this so-and-so got you from behind a ditch.' He pulled Larkin out of the way and ordered the party into the firing position. While we waited the order to fire, the thought entered my mind that I would not hear the shot that killed me. Then the unexpected happened. A woman cyclist who came along cycled between us and the firing party. Then she appeared suddenly to realise what was happening. She screamed, fell off the bicycle and became hysterical. That caused a diversion and we were ordered to get up into one of the lorries. We were brought to the RIC barracks in Ennistymon where we were interrogated and given a few kicks and bashes. We were then removed to the military post in Ennistymon where we were interrogated in a gentlemanly manner by a British officer. A few days later we were removed to Ennis military barracks. There we were savagely attacked by a party of military led by a provost sergeant named David Finlay. Finlay was a native of Scotland and he had earned a notorious name for himself in Ennis for his cruelty and for the third degree methods he used on prisoners. When Finlay and his gang were finished with us I would say that Neylon was the worst hurt. He was covered with cuts and bruises; he was bleeding from the scalp and his fingers were damaged when, with his hands, he tried to ward off kicks.

A week later Neylon, McDonough and Murphy were transferred to Limerick prison and court-martialled under the Defence of the Realm Act for armed robbery. Neylon refused to recognise the court. Despite James Hynes' denials that he was one of the men who had taken the rate books and the fact that the three men were unarmed, Neylon was sentenced to seven years' imprisonment for armed robbery. McDonough was sentenced to six months' hard labour and Murphy to three months.

Four members of the East Clare brigade's flying column – Michael Brennan, John Ryan, Peter Flannery and Jim Tuohy – had a close escape from the British. During the second week of February a combined operation between the Mid and East Clare brigades was arranged to attack a large British army convoy on the road between Ennis and Tulla, but when they arrived at the rendezvous point a messenger told them that the convoy was not travelling and the operation was cancelled.

Brennan dismissed the members of the column and continued with the three others to McDonnells' at Rossaroe near Sixmilebridge.

Gilligan, the captain of the local IRA company, thought that his house was likely to be searched and arranged accommodation for them in McDonnells' barn a short distance away. The four men were called for breakfast at nine the next morning by one of the Gilligan girls. The four were slow to rise and when the girl returned in a few minutes telling them to get out of bed at once because the Black and Tans were raiding the area, the men thought this was a ruse to get them up in time for breakfast. Michael Brennan went to the door and saw a group of Black and Tans dismounting from two Crossley Tenders on the roadside 100 yards away. He called to the others to get up immediately as the Black and Tans began crossing the fields towards them. The barn was attached to the family home and the Black and Tans walked straight past the barn to begin searching the house.

Brennan ordered Ryan to walk slowly across the farmyard to the edge of the field and cover the Black and Tans as Peter Flannery and Jim Tuohy made their way to join him. When the other three made it successfully into the field Brennan moved to follow them:

> I had seen the Black and Tans leaning on their rifles watching the others, but by the time the fourth man appeared they had probably started wondering where the devil all these men were coming from. I tried to keep my tell-tale sling and bandage covered with a raincoat draped over my shoulder while I managed my Mauser pistol and stock plus a Webley revolver I had found under one of the pillows in a last check around in the left hand which was the side away from the lorries. The distance to the wall around the field was about thirty yards or so and I was ordered to halt when I had gone about half way. I pretended not to hear and I walked on without any appearance of hurry. The challenge was repeated several times but I reached the wall safely and climbed up on it with some difficulty. The police opened fire as I reached the top and then the loose stones slipped from under me and the wall and I arrived in the field somewhat mixed up. A cheer went up from the Black and Tans, apparently under the impression that I was hit.

John Ryan had seen Brennan fall and also thought that he had been shot. He was about to return fire when Brennan sprang to his feet and shouted: 'Don't fire; they'll burn the house'. Brennan's bandaged arm had identified him to the search party and as the four IRA men crawled along under the cover of the stone wall the RIC and Black and Tans entered the field in pursuit. Brennan told Ryan to fire one shot at their pursuers but not to kill, as he was still fearful both farms would be burned in reprisal. According to Ryan his shot had the desired effect: 'The shot sent clay splattering around the feet of the leading policeman, whereupon, along with the others, he beat a quick retreat to the lorry which immediately drove off, leaving us to proceed on our way without any further interference.'

It was obvious for some time that Michael Brennan's movements were being reported by a local British spy, and Brennan narrowly escaped capture again while staying at Gleesons' in Bodyke:

> When tea was half way through one of the Gleesons rushed in to say he thought he heard the squeak of brakes coming down the hill. He said he heard no sound of engines and he was sent back for a further report. Almost immediately he returned and shouted 'Auxiliaries'. We jumped from our seats and ran for the back door just as a terrific hammering started at the front door. We crossed the yard in minus a second and just as I got through a fence I saw the 'Auxies' swarming over the road wall into the yard ... We stayed quietly in the field and when the raiders left we came back to inquire into the extraordinary silence of their approach. We found that engines and lights had been switched off at the top of the hill outside the village and the lorries had coasted silently down to the very gate of Gleesons' house. It was one of the first appearances of Auxiliaries in east Clare and they had announced that they had made a bet of a case of champagne with the Tulla officers' mess that they would get me within a week. Their first attempt had gone near enough.

In February of 1921 the IRA captured Private McPhearson and a second soldier, Private Robinson, in the Connolly district. Both claimed to have deserted from the British army but refused to give their names. Suspecting that they had captured McPhearson, who was responsible for the murder of Charles Lynch, the IRA sent for Ned Lynch to identify the soldiers:

> I recognised McPhearson straight away. The local IRA company held the prisoners with a warning from me to watch McPhearson as he was a dangerous man possessed of a quick mind and devoid of scruples. I made contact with the battalion commandant and returned to Connolly. McPhearson had escaped after tricking his guard, Volunteer Hehir, a giant of a man athletically built but much too innocent for the character with whom he was dealing. Hehir was loading a .45 British revolver under the eye of the prisoner, who commented Hehir did not have the proper technique. He offered to demonstrate this and Hehir handed the loaded weapon to the prisoner, who escaped. The only consolation which resulted from his capture was that the £10 which he had stolen from my neighbour was found on him and restored to its lawful owner … McPhearson made his way back to the military post at Miltown and guided the army to the houses he had been held in in the Connolly area.

The second soldier, Private Robinson, was executed at Eustaces' house in Lisroe, after McPhearson's escape. This soldier was buried secretly at an area of bog land near Connolly, specifically chosen because it was owned by the Totenhams, a prominent unionist family, and was not likely to be searched by the British. A second soldier disappeared from Miltown Malbay at about the same time, a young private who regularly left his barracks after dark to court a local girl. When this was brought to the IRA's attention they abducted the soldier, executed him and buried him secretly at the edge of some boggy land in the Moy area.

On Sunday 20 February a mixed force of British military, RIC and Auxiliaries shot at a group of boys during a search operation at Blackwater Mill in Clonlara, killing brothers Cecil and Aidan O'Donovan. The boys had been searching the area for birds' nests with a third brother, Thomas, and one of their cousins. The British claimed that they had mistaken the boys for an IRA detachment and had called upon them to halt before opening fire. On 19 February members of the East Clare brigade arrested three Englishmen wearing civilian clothing who were wandering about the countryside north of Feakle. The three, Privates D.J. Williams, W.S. Walker and H. Morgan of the Oxford and Buckinghamshire Light Infantry, claimed that they were deserters from the British army. The three were court-martialled as spies and executed. Their bodies were discovered three days later near Woodford on the Clare and Galway county border bearing the placards 'Spies. Executed by the IRA.' On 25 February Brigadier General Crozier resigned as head of the auxiliary division saying he 'could not go on leading a drunken and insubordinate body of men'.

With February 1921 a disastrous month for the IRA in Clare, their fortunes changed in March. On 12 March members of the East Clare brigade, under the command of Joseph Clancy, captured and executed Daniel Murphy, a Black and Tan intelligence officer from Cork who was on an intelligence mission in the Sixmilebridge area:

> It was noticed by the local Volunteers that an RIC man named Murphy had started to make visits to houses around Oatfield, Belvoir and Broadford dressed as an agricultural labourer, and that in the same disguise he frequently took despatches between the RIC barracks in Broadford and in Sixmilebridge. During the course of his visits to houses in the locality he was always asking questions about the IRA. Two of the IRA men 'on the run', Martin McNamara and John Curley, were told about Constable Murphy's movements and decided to waylay him in the vicinity of the scene of the Glenwood ambush. He came cycling from Broadford in the middle of the day … and was held up. On being searched he was found to be unarmed and, as far as I now can recollect, the only things of interest found were a number of snapshots of police in Broadford barracks, including himself. He was taken to Enagh wood and shot that night by McNamara and Curley. His body was buried in the vicinity.

On 13 March Thomas Shanahan was shot dead by British forces at Moyasta. Three days later an accidental shooting led to the death of IRA Volunteer Patrick Hassett, a native of Killimer. The Sinn Féin court at Kilkee made a ruling against Mr Rickman-Gore, a landlord accused of rack renting by his tenants. Rickman-Gore ignored the ruling and a group of ten armed Volunteers from the West Clare brigade went to his home at Kilmore House to force him to comply with the court's ruling. As the IRA approached the house they challenged Mr Martin, a land agent working for Rickman-Gore, who opened fire on the Volunteers with a revolver. During the gun battle one member of the IRA accidentally shot Hassett at close range. The IRA retreated with their wounded comrade. Though wounded, Martin survived the attack and left Clare shortly afterwards. Hassett died at St John's hospital in Limerick on 21 March.

With a number of their leading Volunteers captured and their attempts to mount ambushes repeatedly foiled by the strength and tactics of British motorised patrols, the Mid Clare brigade continued with sniping attacks on barracks and small-scale urban ambushes to assassinate British troops out of barracks. In mid-March the brigade headquarters staff issued orders to each battalion to mount attacks on RIC patrols or any enemy troops outside of barracks on the night of the 31 March. This date was chosen for the attacks because it was pay night for the RIC and it was thought that groups of RIC men, Auxiliaries and Black and Tans would be out of barracks drinking in local pubs. However, the IRA's plans were foiled when most of the RIC garrisons remained confined to barracks for the night. Thirty members of the 5th battalion under the command of Andrew O'Donoghue mobilised at Kilcorney when Seán Healy and another local man came to warn them that the RIC and British army knew of the attack and had taken up ambush positions on the outskirts of the town. The 6th battalion's planned attack on the RIC at Lisdoonvarna was also cancelled. When they were only half a mile away from the town they were told that a prominent local businessman had reported their mobilisation to the RIC.

The 4th battalion managed to mount one successful attack at Miltown Malbay under the command of Ignatius O'Neill when a number of Black and Tans ventured out of their barracks to go drinking. John Jones, the battalion's intelligence officer, arranged the plan of attack:

> I met the attacking party on the Ballard road just outside the town about nine o'clock and led them into the town through Hills' Lane into

the ruins of the O'Neills' old home which had been burned about six months earlier as a reprisal for the Rineen ambush. In these ruins the party took up positions waiting for the Tans to leave Wilsons' pub, and I had arranged with the party to withhold their fire until the Tans had left Wilsons' and were passing a demolished house formerly owned by a family named Roche. At half past nine the Tans came to the door accompanied by Mr Wilson, where they remained in conversation for a few minutes and they moved off. No sooner had they done so than someone in our party fired. This started a fusillade from the guns of the others. Both Tans fell and were presumed dead, but it later transpired that only one, Constable Moore, was killed and that the other, Constable Hersey, was wounded.

The dead Black and Tan, RIC Constable Stanley Moore, was a thirty-one-year-old single man from Glamorgan and had been a dentist and soldier before joining the Black and Tans.

The seemingly endless round of reprisals against republican sympathisers and Irish civilians began again a few days after his death. The RIC and British army rounded up almost the entire adult population of the town, at gun and bayonet point, and forced them to watch as John Sullivan's drapery shop on Main Street and the home of Morgan Hayes, both republican supporters, were destroyed by explosives.

10

Freedom?

We know only one definition of freedom; It is Tone's definition, it is
Mitchel's definition, it is Rossa's definition. Let no man blaspheme the
cause for which the dead generations of Ireland served by giving it any
other name or definition than their name and definition.

Patrick Pearse

April 1921 began with another narrow escape from capture for Michael
Brennan and the men of the East Clare brigade's flying column. On
the night of 3 April members of the flying column were sleeping in
a number of farmhouses at Bohatch, just outside Mountshannon, in
preparation for an attack on the British forces. At 3 a.m. they were
woken when local Volunteers arrived with news that they had seen
the lights of several lorries in the distance approaching from Tulla.
The IRA assembled at a prearranged meeting point before beginning
a march straight towards the safe haven of the mountains between
Mountshannon and the Galway border. After a short time they saw
the light from torches 1,000 yards away as a party of British soldiers
dismounted, crossing the fields straight towards them.

Day was now beginning to dawn and Joseph Clancy called for the
soldiers to be allowed advance without resistance so the column could
draw them deeper into the hills, cut them off from any reinforcements
and get an accurate idea of the size of the force following them. He also
feared that if the raiding party included an armoured car it could drive
up a by-road behind them and cut off their retreat. However, Brennan
favoured fighting the British to slow their advance and ordered the
riflemen under his command, including Clancy, to open fire:

While getting to this point a number of our men were observed and came under machine gun fire from the enemy, who were now coming through the fields in an encircling movement and were about three-quarters of a mile from us. Myself and three or four others returned the fire as we gradually retreated into the hills towards the rest of the party, who under Michael Brennan's direction were falling back into mountainous country free from roads over which the enemy could not run vehicles if they attempted an outflanking movement. The enemy kept advancing after us, the section below us being led by an RIC sergeant named Norton. He was coming over a turf bank well exposed but at a distance of about 800 yards when I fired at him. He rolled back into a bog hole. In the course of the exchange of shot another police constable called Kelly was also wounded. As soon as the sergeant was put out of action this halted the enemy. The few men and I who were covering the retreat now assumed that the rest of our party were well clear of any threat of encirclement and we accordingly fell back and joined the others.

The column successfully escaped the British encircling movement without any casualties but one of the two RIC men wounded in the skirmish had his leg amputated as a result of his wounds.

With the British forces on the defensive and almost completely con-fined to large, well-fortified barracks inside towns and villages except to venture out in very large raiding parties, the IRA in Clare was finding it increasingly difficult to keep mounting successful attacks on the enemy and prevent a stalemate from developing. As the RIC and army abandoned the battlefields of the Clare countryside and began a long-term strategy of refusing to engage the IRA on their own terms of guerrilla warfare, the republicans were forced into a campaign of assassination against troops who ventured outside of the barracks and suspected British spies.

On 16 April Peadar O'Loughlin and Volunteers from the 1st battalion of the Mid Clare brigade mounted an attack on off-duty army officers and their unionist collaborators in the town:

While the Black and Tan war was raging, very few of the loyalist supporters carried their colours on their sleeves and of those who did, two families made themselves particularly objectionable to the IRA. One was Shaughnessys, who kept a pub in Market Street, and the other was Mills, who resided in Mill View. Mr Mills was an Orangeman and a bigot. He detested the Sinn Féin movement and everyone belonging to it ... It was suspected that he was involved in the attempted burning of the bishop's palace, while he openly assisted in the supervision of the destruction of T.V. Honan's premises ... At O'Shaughnessy's, though all the publicans were warned against serving drinks to the enemy forces or at least letting them know that they were welcome, the Black and Tan members of the Ennis garrison were received with a 'céad míle fáilte' and also their friends and especially the ladies ... At about 10 p.m. on the night of 16 April 1921 a party of eight or nine men under Paddy Con McMahon and including Éamonn Barron, Jim Quinn, Frank Butler, Joe Frawley, Jack D'Arcy and myself all armed with revolvers called at O'Shaughnessy's pub. The door was shut at the time but was opened in answer to Paddy Con's knock, who stepped back a few paces after knocking. As soon as the door opened he hurled a Mills grenade into the bar and the rest of us fired into the place with revolvers. Inside were Sergeant Rue [Sergeant Rew, Royal Scots], who was killed outright, Constable Vanerburgh, Mrs Danagher and Miss O'Shaughnessy, who were all wounded.

In reprisal for the attack, the shop of T.V. Honan, a leading member of the Ennis Sinn Féin club, was set on fire by the army, who then demolished the burned out shell of the building with explosives. The home of Patrick Considine and the Old Ground Hotel were also burned before the Clare Hotel was raided and all its furniture made into a bonfire. The following day the IRA raided Mill View House and burned it to the ground as a warning to the British forces and local unionists against further reprisals.

The military situation in the West Clare brigade area was still relatively quiet as the Mid and East Clare brigades bore the brunt of the fighting. Michael Brennan accepted a request from Seán Liddy, the commandant of the West Clare brigade, to help him mount an attack on the British stationed in the area. At that time the West Clare brigade's flying column were in a weak military position, having only a handful of rifles. In addition their military efforts were constantly frustrated by the activities of the Black and Tans and Auxiliaries stationed in the area. Due to the distance involved and the chance of meeting a strong mobile British patrol it was decided that Volunteers from the East Clare brigade's flying column would travel to west Clare across the estuary of the River Fergus by boat from Rineanna to Kildysart on the night of 18 April.

Before departing for the West Clare brigade area, Michael Brennan gave an order to Pat Reidy, the adjutant of the 1st battalion of the East Clare brigade, to execute John Reilly, an ex-British soldier living in Newmarket on Fergus. Reilly drank a good deal and had ignored repeated warnings from the IRA to stop associating with Black and Tans and the RIC in local pubs. He came to the IRA's attention again after the murder of Volunteers Henry and Patrick Loughnane in Gort, County Galway on 6 December 1920. Both the murdered men's father and the IRA strongly suspected that Reilly had supplied the British with information that led to their capture and murder. This was confirmed when a letter bearing Reilly's name was found addressed to the British giving information about the IRA during a raid on the Limerick to Ennis train at Cratloe station.

The day after receiving Michael Brennan's order to execute Reilly, Pat Reidy notified fifteen local IRA Volunteers to report for duty outside Newmarket at 9 p.m. and had Reilly's movements monitored during the day. James Quinn was one of the Volunteers who arrested John Reilly at 11 p.m:

He was then taken under guard about a mile out the Ballycar road and led into a by-road which runs to Monafola. About 300 yards or so down this by-road Fr William Kennedy, CC Newmarket on Fergus, was waiting to hear our prisoner's confession. Guards were posted around the spot while he was receiving spiritual attention, which lasted fifteen or twenty minutes. When this was over a bandage was placed over the prisoner's eyes and he was ordered on his knees. The firing party, which, so far as I can remember, were all armed with revolvers, consisted of Jack Brennan – Clonmoney, Florence O'Neill – Rathfoland and myself. We stood about three yards away from our target and on orders from Paddy

Maher, I think, we fired about three rounds per man. Reilly fell back dead and he was then anointed by the priest who witnessed the execution. A label bearing the words 'Spy. Executed by the IRA' was then tied on his body which was left on the spot where he was shot until it was removed next day by the RIC and Tans.

Having arrived in the West Clare brigade's area, the East Clare brigade flying column was joined by John Flanagan and the members of the local flying column on the night of 20 April to attack the RIC at Kildysart. Michael Brennan attempted to lure the police out of the barracks by sending two members of his flying column to act drunk in the middle of the street and cause a ruckus by bawling out republican slogans and rebel songs at the top of their voices. Frustrated by the lack of response, the pair began throwing stones at the barracks and broke several of its windows but even this failed to draw any reaction from the garrison inside. In the end John Flanagan watched as Brennan approached the barracks: 'Brennan himself went up to the door of the police barracks and, knocking loudly, challenged the police to come out. The challenge was not accepted and the IRA party then set off for Tullycrine and Knockerra where I had arranged billets for them.'

Having failed to engage the forces in Kildysart the officers of the column decided to mount an attack in Kilrush which was occupied by a strong British garrison and where Michael Brennan and the other IRA officers felt sure they would be able to find a target. The town was occupied by three separate British forces – a detachment of 100 soldiers were stationed in the workhouse, a mixed force of fifty Black and Tans and regular RIC held the barracks on Toler Street in the centre of the town and a group of Royal Marines manned the former coastguard station at Cappagh a mile outside the town. The town was patrolled most nights by a foot patrol of sixteen RIC men and Black and Tans from the barracks. The IRA planned to enter the town, attack the patrol and disarm any troops who were off duty drinking.

The RIC station and British army's temporary barracks at the old workhouse were too well defended for the IRA to attack, and the coastguard station was located on the river and was too difficult to raid. The

IRA's plan centred on ambushing the RIC foot patrol in the streets of Kilrush; when the shooting from the ambush was heard in the military and police barracks in the town it was hoped that more troops could be contained within their barracks or ambushed as they came to the patrol's aid.

On the evening of 22 April the flying column set out from their billets in Tullycrine for Kilrush, reaching the outskirts of the town at 8 p.m. Here the members of the column were broken up into four groups. A dozen volunteers under Michael Brennan and Tom McGrath's command formed the ambushing party to attack the RIC foot patrol. The patrol was to be ambushed as it passed down Moore Street, and the men in this group were positioned at the junctions of Moore Street and Ball Alley Lane, and Malt House Lane and Stewart Street. The second group, commanded by Stephen Madigan from the West Clare brigade, were positioned in the convent field covering the entrance to the police barracks. Four members of this group formed a bombing party armed with hand grenades to attack the RIC patrol as they retreated towards their barracks after the ambush. Liam Haugh, the adjutant of the West Clare brigade, was in charge of the third group of eight column men covering the front entrance to the temporary British military barracks at the workhouse, ready to attack the soldiers and prevent them from reaching the town centre. A smaller section under Seán Liddy's command were posted at the rear of this building. Six Volunteers led by Michael McMahon were waiting at Cappagh to prevent the Royal Marines from the coastguard station from reaching Kilrush. Local members of the IRA were on protection duty at various points in the town and acting as guides, messengers and scouts for the four groups.

At 9 p.m. the republican scouts reported that the RIC patrol left the barracks and began following their usual route. Then, unexpectedly, the RIC ended their patrol upon reaching the square and went directly back to their barracks for the night without entering the ambush position on Moore Street. John Flanagan later discovered the reason why the patrol abandoned its usual route. During the evening the RIC district inspector, Captain May, got very drunk in one of the local hotels. The sergeant in charge of that night's patrol, Sergeant Foley, decided to finish for the night and take the patrol back to the barracks without going through Moore Street since DI Captain May was in no condition to inspect them that night.

Having waited in ambush for two hours Michael Brennan, Tom McGrath, Joseph Clancy and Matt Bermingham left their positions along Moore Street and went in search of the patrol. On reaching the square they saw two men, Sergeant McFadden and Constable Hopkins, a Black and Tan, who had left the barracks to go for a drink. As they approached, Michael Brennan challenged them:

> I heard steps coming down this street again on the shadowy side and I saw two figures coming towards me. When I challenged them they replied, 'It's alright' and came on. I was standing in the moonlight and I repeated my order peremptorily. One of them snapped back, 'It's all right, police!', at the same time stepping out into the light … as the stranger's arm reached the moonlight I saw it was clothed in black with the Vs of an RIC sergeant on the sleeve and with a revolver gripped in the hand … I fired and he dropped, the other turning and darting away. I called to Tom McGrath and Joe Clancy to get this man's revolver and papers and I set off after the second man but lost him … Even as I ran I realised that I must have been mistaken for an Auxiliary and that my shot had given them a much worse shock than they had given me.

At the same time as Constable Hopkins reached the barracks, the IRA bombing party outside had just captured an unarmed soldier passing the barracks and took him prisoner. Just then the commanding officer of the Royal Highland Light Infantry came down the street dressed in civilian clothing. When the republicans challenged him he opened fire and was wounded but managed to escape, as did the captured soldier in the confusion of the firefight. The RIC and Black and Tans inside the barracks immediately opened rifle and machine gun fire on the four IRA men in the square and Seán Madigan's section. Having taken cover, Brennan and the others were joined by the ambushing party from Moore Street and moved into another firing position where they began sniping the barracks with Madigan's group. The RIC and Black and Tans kept up a barrage of fire against the republicans and sent up flares to call for reinforcements.

The sound of gunfire in Kilrush was the signal to the Volunteers stationed at the coastguard station in Cappagh to go into action. They had already captured two marines who were outside the station courting local girls. The Royal Marines inside did not attempt to leave the building after the republicans opened fire; they returned the IRA's fire with a machine gun and sent up flares to signal for assistance. Back in Kilrush the soldiers of the Royal Highland Light Infantry mobilised. As they left their barracks at the workhouse through a small wicket gate Liam Haugh and his riflemen were watching 100 yards away. The soldiers began making their way towards the barracks in groups of four and Haugh's men were under strict orders not to fire until the soldiers came within fifteen yards and Haugh gave the signal in order to maximise enemy casualties.

One nervous Volunteer under Haugh's command opened fire, scattering the soldiers before they were in place for the attack. On hearing this shot, Seán Moroney and the other men armed with rifles in the section opened fire:

> [We] opened fire on them at close range. The military retreated immediately after firing a few shots, leaving their dead and wounded comrades where they fell. They had to enter the barrack through the small wicket gate, which caused crowding and made them an easy target for us. A fierce barrage was opened up on us from the barrack.

Since most of the soldiers had escaped the ambush, Liam Haugh decided to make the best of a bad situation and snipe at the barracks for the next hour to keep the military confined inside:

> All nine rifles now opened on the post itself. The crash of glass and splintering slating mingled with the hum and lightning of ricocheting bullets. Two Verey lights [flares] were sent up; one fell short, the other fell directly on the attacking party. Wild firing from rifles and machine

guns opened from all posts and, in the midst of the confusion, the retreat signal sounded.

Seeing no point in continuing a fight against a well entrenched enemy,
Michael Brennan gave the order to call off their attacks. The members
of the flying column led by Michael McMahon continued sniping at the
coastguard station until 5 a.m. when they returned to Kilrush taking the
two captured Royal Marines as prisoners. They reached Canny's house
in Derra, joining the other Volunteers who had withdrawn only half
an hour earlier having patrolled the streets in the hope that the British
forces might move outside their barracks. British machine gun and rifle
fire could still be heard from Kilrush when the IRA finally left the town.
At 10 p.m. the following night the members of the East Clare brigade
boarded boats and returned to their own brigade area.

The British admitted the death of an RIC sergeant and the wounding
of a constable and three soldiers. The IRA suffered no casualties during
the attack. The sergeant who was killed at Kilrush was John McFadden
from Derry (one of the RIC patrol that was ambushed at Feakle post
office). In revenge for his killing members of the Highland Light
Infantry and a number of Black and Tans stationed at Kilrush raided
Liam Haugh's family home at Monmore. Army engineers placed strong
explosive charges in the house and farm buildings, and they were doused
in petrol while armed sentries held back members of the Haugh family.
The excessive amount of explosives and petrol used seems to have been
for morale as the explosion threw one British soldier head first from
the Crossley Tender from where he was watching. Another soldier was
knocked unconscious having been hit by a splinter of flying stone from
the explosion and died of his injury later that week.

After the East Clare brigade's flying column returned from Kilrush
the active service unit of the 6th battalion under the command of Michael
McGrath attacked a large force of soldiers heading out on manoeuvres
from their temporary barracks in Tulla on 12 June. The British soldiers
were marching in two sections, 200 yards apart, when they were attacked
at Four Roads, a mile outside the town. The opening volley from the IRA

killed Lance Corporal M. Hudson and fatally wounded First Lieutenant Richard Warren, who died of his wounds a few weeks later on 28 June. The soldiers, thinking that they were under attack from an equally large republican force, immediately broke ranks and took cover. Some returned fire while the IRA withdrew.

With the RIC and army having abandoned their posts in Bally-vaughan, Seán McNamara, the O/C of the 6th battalion, was busy devising new schemes to draw the Royal Marines at the coastguard station into the open. After the IRA raided the mail in Ballyvaughan post office in May the Royal Marines had begun to travel to the village to collect their post. Several mornings each week a group of twelve marines led by a corporal left the coastguard station at 10 a.m. and travelled the mile to the post office. A local woman, Mollie Grant, who worked in the post office, agreed to send notice to Seán McNamara when the marines were due to collect their mail. A local IRA Volunteer waited outside the post office each day with a bicycle to report to the IRA. McNamara contacted the 5th battalion of the Mid Clare brigade for assistance in ambushing the patrol. In response, Andrew O'Donoghue mobilised twelve Volunteers armed with rifles and shotguns on 19 May at Corkscrew Hill, who marched to Ballyvaughan. Having waited in ambush until evening the IRA withdrew when the marines failed to show. The republicans marched back to Corkscrew Hill where they had billets for the night at the house of Mrs Lyne, a member of Cumann na mBan.

While the Volunteers were at Mrs Lyne's home, Kathleen McNamara, another member of Cumann na mBan from Carron, arrived. She reported to Seán McNamara that she had met an off-duty member of the Royal Marine garrison at Ballyvaughan drinking in Kerins' hotel and overheard him saying that the marines would be in Ballyvaughan the next morning. At 5 a.m. on 20 April, McNamara set out for Ballyvaughan. A number of republican scouts were already in position near the coastguard station. On reaching Ballyvaughan, McNamara posted four riflemen – Michael Burns, Austin McNamara, Paddy Ward and Pat Kilkelly – inside the post office. Other small groups of armed

Volunteers were posted in a laneway off the main road and behind a low stone wall lining the marines' route. McNamara commanded the operation from a ruined house sixty yards from the post office. By 1 p.m. the scouts reported that the marines had not left the coastguard station and McNamara had begun withdrawing his men when Martin Keane reported to McNamara that the marines were approaching:

> I rushed the party back to the positions they had left. When the marines came in sight I was disappointed to see that they had changed their formation. Instead of coming in marching four deep, they were in a staggered formation about twenty paces apart in the files and twelve yards or so diagonally. The leading man was the corporal – Bolton by name – and as soon as he came opposite me I fired at him. This was the signal shot and all the rest of the attackers opened up simultaneously. The corporal was killed outright and also another marine named Chandler. The others rushed for cover and engaged us. A hot interchange of shooting lasting about fifteen minutes then ensued, during which two other of the enemy were wounded, one opposite the hotel and the other at Linnane's gate. Another of them had his rifle broken in his hands, after which he tried to seize one of the wounded men's rifles. As he was doing so his tin hat was shot off by Joe McNamara and this caused him to run away with his own broken gun. The fight was brought to a close when Michael Burns, Paddy Kilkelly and my brother Austin left the post office and began advancing along the open street towards our opponents, who on seeing this movement beat a quick retreat to the coastguard station. We immediately collected the arms and equipment, which was left behind – four rifles, four tin helmets, four sets of web equipment and a small quantity of .303 ammunition.

When the remainder of the marines reached the coastguard station they sent up flares appealing for reinforcements and began firing their weapons in all directions. The rifles and ammunition captured during the ambush meant that the Mid Clare brigade now had enough weapons to arm an active unit within the 6th battalion based in Ballyvaughan under McNamara's command.

De Valera had returned from his year in America, spent canvassing for the support of American politicians for the Irish Republic on Christmas Eve 1920. He immediately accepted the role of armchair general and complained to Richard Mulcahy that the IRA's military campaign was not being fought properly: 'This odd shooting of a policeman here and there is having a very bad effect from a propaganda view on us in America. What we want is one good battle about once a month with about five hundred men on each side.' A few weeks later de Valera again dismissed the propaganda value of the IRA's guerrilla campaign and proposed that the tactics should be dictated by headline-grabbing spectaculars. He proposed the capture of Beggars Bush barracks or the destruction of the Custom House, which housed the British government's inland revenue service in Ireland. De Valera's proposal was grudgingly accepted and the IRA went into action on the morning of 25 May. The Customs House was destroyed by fire but the operation came at a disastrous cost to the IRA – five Volunteers were killed and eighty-three others were captured, including almost all the members of the Squad. Volunteer Jim Slattery from Feakle, a member of the Squad, was badly wounded in the attack.

The following day the West Clare brigade surprised two Black and Tans, Constable Edgar Budd and Constable Irvine, who were travelling between Ennis and Kildysart. The pair were in plain clothes but were recognised by the Volunteers who ambushed them at Cooga. Constable Budd was killed instantly but Irvine managed to escape. Budd was from Hampshire and had been a soldier before joining the Black and Tans. In reaction to the shooting, a large force of RIC and Auxiliaries were mobilised in Ennis and despatched to Kildysart to search for Constable Budd's killers. On 29 May they marched to Kilmihil and surprised Michael Killoughery, a Volunteer from Clonakilla. Killoughery opened fire on the Auxiliaries and escaped.

The Auxiliary column moved east the next day. Part of the West Clare brigade flying column was stationed at the Barrett family home in Barnageeha when word reached them that the Auxiliaries were close by, travelling on bicycle. At short notice Frank and Joseph Barrett decided to attack them at Darragh Cross six miles from Ennis, and managed to assemble twenty of the column men. On reaching Darragh Cross at 2 p.m. the IRA only had twenty minutes before the expected arrival of the Auxiliaries and so quickly divided into three groups. The main attacking section was placed in the fields about 350 yards from the road. Three riflemen positioned in a by-road half a mile away, protected this group along with a second flanking party of two men placed further to the left of the main force.

Joseph Barrett was checking the final arrangements for the ambush when the Auxiliaries cycled into view:

> They were much stronger than we had expected, numbering about eighty men, and they were extended along the road for a mile … It was roughly half past two in the evening and just as the rear of the Auxiliaries had passed Darragh Cross we opened fire. After the opening volley, the enemy quietly took cover and for the next quarter of an hour the firing was of a desultory nature. The enemy started to advance on our main position through the fields. He had little cover and the accuracy of our fire began to tell. Five Auxiliaries were wounded, and the remainder were halted for a while. They were in very extended formation and, finding that there was less opposition coming from our right flank, they were quick to exploit this weakness. A number of them advanced to a position 600 yards from our main party and using a machine gun started to rake us with enfilade fire. At this stage our two left flankers proved useful. The machine gunner was shot through the shoulder by my brother, Bernard, and after that he and his companion succeeded in holding the enemy in check. The advance against our main position was resumed but after half an hour's fighting, the enemy could not come nearer to us than 200 yards. Now he began to probe our right flank and met with some success. Realising that danger now threatened the main party, I sent off a section of seven men to occupy an old fort, 400 yards to our rear. This fort was on an eminence which commanded the ground over which the enemy was trying to advance, and from it the section which had retired were able to pin him down while I and the remainder of the party were retreating to the fort. The three men on our right flank fell back also, more or less parallel with the men who had gone to the fort … My brother, Bernard and his companion on our left fought a rearguard action on their own for a while but eventually they joined us beyond the Rathkerry River … Ultimately our main party had crossed the Rathkerry River at the point where it touches

the Ennis–Kilmaley road. The enemy broke off the engagement, retiring back to Darragh Cross; he resumed his way to Ennis.

The East Clare brigade of the IRA suffered a serious blow when Patrick White was shot dead in Spike Island prison. White was a member of the IRB and a captain in the Meelick company of the IRA. He had been captured by the British forces, with Thomas Ringrose, after the Glenwood ambush and interned in Spike Island prison in Cork. A few days later White was shot dead, allegedly while trying to escape:

On the particular day of White's death I had got the loan of a newspaper, a fortnight old, on the condition that I would have it back within a quarter of an hour. I sat on my bed to read and White came over and said: 'What about our walk?' I said wait, I have to give this paper back very soon. White then did something he never did. He looked around the hut and saw a hurley, picked it up and said: 'I will go out and hurl, come out after with the news.' I said: 'Right.' A few moments later, I heard a shot and on looking through the window I saw somebody throw up their hands and fall back. I dashed out, hoping it was not White, but indeed it was. I held him until he died. The only words he spoke were: 'What will my poor people do?' The circumstances were the hurling ball went near the wire and the players shouted to hit back the ball into play as he was nearest to it. The sentinel, a Scottish soldier, was evidently out to have a go and let him have it.

Prisoners who had taken part in the hurling match with White claimed that he had called out to the sentry to return the ball. The sentry replied 'Come here and get it' and shot White dead when he followed this order.

On 15 June the Meelick company of the IRA suffered double loss with the death of Captain Patrick Gleeson in action against the Royal Scots at Burton Hill in Meelick and the murder of Captain Christopher McCarthy by soldiers after the ambush. Christopher McCarthy, a native of Miltown Malbay, was a member of the 4th battalion of the West Clare brigade of the IRA who had transferred to the East Clare brigade. On the morning of the Meelick ambush a small group of Volunteers including Gleeson and McCarthy went to Burton Hill early in the morning to raid the Limerick to Ennis train for mail to check for intelligence information. A low stone barricade had been built across the railway track a short distance before the Cratloe railway station. One Volunteer was travelling on the train ready to signal to the IRA in case there were British forces on board.

As the train approached the barricade after 10 a.m. the Volunteer on board began signalling frantically to his comrades that soldiers were on board by waving a handkerchief out the window of one of the leading carriages. However, his signal was not seen by the raiding party, who held their positions. The soldiers travelling on board saw them and a brief fight ensued, during which the soldiers forced the train driver to drive the train through the stone barricade to Cratloe station. On reaching Cratloe the soldiers forced the other passengers off the train and ordered the crew to reverse the train back along the track to Burton Hill. As the train approached the bend where the IRA were, the engine driver repeatedly blew the steam whistle to warn the republicans that the British soldiers were returning, until an officer with the Royal Scots drew his revolver and threatened to kill him.

Most of the Volunteers were still in the fields to the north of the track waiting for their comrades who had climbed telegraph poles attempting to disrupt British communications when the soldiers halted the train and dismounted, firing their rifles and machine guns at the Volunteers retreating towards the tree line at the top of the hill. Patrick Gleeson was mortally wounded by the opening volley of machine gun fire and fell to the ground, unable to continue. As McCarthy was withdrawing with the others he noticed Gleeson was missing and returned to rescue him. The soldiers began advancing up the hillside from the railway track. McCarthy opened fire on the advancing soldiers and attempted to drag Gleeson to safety. The pair were surrounded and captured after McCarthy ran out of ammunition. By this time Gleeson was already dead. Having captured McCarthy the soldiers of the Royal Scots murdered him by cutting his throat and shooting him a number of times at point blank range. The rest of the IRA party had already escaped to Woodcock Hill.

The British soldiers went to the farm of the Burtons, a local unionist

family, and forced a number of the farm labourers there to help them
remove the two bodies. Michael Doherty was carrying McCarthy's
body with another man when he lifted back the covering the British
soldiers had placed over it and saw that McCarthy's throat had been cut
and his chest was riddled with bullet wounds. Immediately he received
a blow of a rifle butt from one of the Royal Scots, who replaced the
covers on McCarthy's body. Both bodies were taken to the house of the
Collins family, where the soldiers guarded them until reinforcements
arrived and took them to Limerick. To cover up their crime the military
did not release the bodies of Gleeson and McCarthy to their relatives
for burial for over two months, until after the truce. Their bodies were
eventually exchanged with the IRA in return for the body of Daniel
Murphy, the Black and Tan intelligence officer from Cork who was
executed by members of the East Clare brigade at Glenwood on 12
March. Gleeson and McCarthy were buried in the republican plot in
Meelick churchyard alongside Patrick White.

Seán Moroney was still on the run in East Clare with Patrick Houlihan
after the attack on the British military at Tulla. Early in June he returned
to his home in Feakle to help in burning a local hunting lodge which
had recently been occupied by the Auxiliaries to prevent them from
reoccupying it.

> We were armed with service rifles and had about sixty rounds of am-
> munition each. Two Volunteers – my brother, Denis Moroney, and
> Volunteer Patrick O'Brien – went in front as scouts on bicycles. Four
> other Volunteers accompanied us on foot, carrying tins of paraffin oil
> to burn the house. When about half a mile from the lodge, on an open
> mountain road, we heard in front of us several voices shouting to halt.
> This was followed by a volley of shots. Captain [Patrick] Houlihan or-
> dered the four Volunteers who were with us to get back as quickly as
> they could. He and I then lay down on the side of the road and could
> make out the forms of a large force of mounted soldiers – Lancers –
> coming over the top of a hill about 300 yards away. They were on an old
> road that was impassable for horses except after a long period of dry
> weather. We opened fire on them and they dismounted and returned
> the fire. We knew after a very short time that it was a large force we

had run into. They spread out on both sides as if to encircle us and kept up a very heavy rifle and grenade fire. We changed our positions several times and kept them at bay for over an hour. During a lull in the firing we slipped away into a ravine where a small river runs and were out of their view.

Other Volunteers caught within the British forces' encirclement were not as fortunate. Michael Gleeson was captured at Coolreagh bog near Feakle along with James Rochford, Ned Doyle, Jack Considine, Michael Tuohy and Paddy Tuohy. Gleeson and the other republicans suffered brutal treatment at the hands of their captors:

At first I was questioned about the IRA and when I refused to give any information I was led away under guard and ordered to a part of the field on which the troops were encamped. One of my legs was tied to a stake driven deeply into the ground. I was compelled to put my two arms straight past my head. The other prisoners were similarly treated. Darkness had by this time set in and sentries were mounted over us. Throughout the night these sentries kept walking hither and thither using our chests as stepping-stones. According as the mood struck them they kicked us or beat us with their rifle butts. Frequently too, a soldier would bend down and commence twisting our necks from side to side. At dawn some of these troops collected cow dung from a neighbouring field and rubbed it into our hair. Then a firing party came along and we were informed that we were all going to be shot. At this stage a cavalry officer arrived and when he saw our condition he said to some other officers that were about: 'It's a good job the press has not got hold of what's going on here.' I turned my head to get a look at this man but as soon as I did so I received a blow of a rifle on the head, which rendered me unconscious ... After about a week we were sent on to the Curragh where I was interned in Rath Camp.

Since the brutal deaths of William Shanahan and Michael McNamara by British forces the previous December, it was obvious to the IRA that a spy was operating in the West Clare brigade area. Further confirmation came in May when the IRA captured intelligence documents from a Royal Air Force plane that crashed in Limerick. These documents included a number of reports from a spy in west Clare, giving accurate information of the location of republican dugouts and the movements of Volunteers. The IRA unit in Limerick immediately made contact with Liam Haugh and passed on copies of these reports to him. However, the intelligence officers in the West Clare brigade were unable to identify the culprit until a British army officer from the Kilrush garrison was overheard revealing the man's name during a slip in conversation.

The man concerned was Patrick Darcy, a native of Cooraclare, who worked as a teacher in Doonbeg. Two of his brothers were Volunteers; one of them, Michael, had drowned following an IRA attack on the RIC at Cooraclare in January 1920. Because of his family's involvement in the republican struggle he was on friendly terms with members of the local IRA units. However, during 1920 it was noticed that Darcy began drinking heavily and frequenting a pub in Kilrush owned by a retired ex-RIC man named Sheehan, in the company of British soldiers and Black and Tans. According to Michael Russell the possibility that Darcy was a spy had long been mentioned by local republicans in the area:

> As the year 1921 wore on Darcy's name was a byword among all the IRA in West Clare as a British spy. He continued to frequent Sheehan's public house and to mix in the company of the enemy forces. Every decent person in west Clare strongly condemned the Shanahan and McNamara murders and even people who were not in sympathy with the Sinn Féin movement shunned the company of the British garrison in Kilrush after these happenings. But Darcy was seen to come into frequent contact with the enemy as time went on. He also drank more.

On 21 June the IRA in West Clare moved against Patrick Darcy and Sheehan, the retired RIC man and publican who was also believed to be guilty of spying. Sheehan was visiting a farm he owned in Kilmihil when he was held up at gunpoint and arrested by Seán Liddy, the commandant of the West Clare brigade, Michael Russell and four other Volunteers. He was taken into one of his farm buildings, interrogated and accused of spying. He strongly protested his innocence, denying that he had ever given the British forces any information. Michael Russell was detained outside the building on some other task and arrived inside in time to witness the end of Sheehan's interrogation:

> On being threatened with execution by the brigade O/C Sheehan began to cry and said: 'It was not me who gave the information about Shanahan and McNamara, but it was Patrick Darcy who gave it to the police in my house.' The brigade O/C then released him and Sheehan proceeded home in his pony and trap, which he had brought with him from Kilrush. I have a very distinct recollection of having heard Sheehan make this accusation against Darcy.

Later that night Russell received orders to arrest Darcy and he led five Volunteers to Darcy's house at Cooraclare. Darcy was not home and the arresting party left and reported his absence to Seán Liddy. It was discovered that Darcy had not heard of Sheehan's arrest and was in Ennis to visit his brother, a Volunteer in the town, and would be returning to West Clare on the late train that evening. Darcy was arrested by Michael Russell after returning home that evening.

> [John] Cunningham and myself cycled on to Darcy's house and as we entered it we saw him leaving by the back door. We followed and overtook him in the yard. I told him that Bill Haugh wished to interview him. His reply was: 'What would Bill Haugh or any one else want with me?' I told him to come along and that Haugh was only a short distance away. He did so and, meeting Haugh about 600 yards from Cooraclare, we delivered the prisoner to him. Addressing me, Haugh said: 'You take my bike, Micky,' and turning to Darcy he said: 'You come with me. I want to have a few words with you.' The two of them went across the fields towards Cree, while John Cunningham and myself cycled on to that village. In Cree we learned that the brigade staff were holding a court-martial on Darcy in an outhouse owned by Tim O'Donnell. There was a guard of IRA men thrown around the village. Cunningham and myself waited outside O'Donnell's place. Half an hour later Darcy and the members of the court, which comprised of the brigade O/C, Seán Liddy, Bill Haugh, Conor Whelan, Tom Marrinan and Tom Martin, came out of the building. Darcy sat on a seat and called John

Cunningham, with whom he had a brief conversation. The latter then returned to me and said: 'Darcy is after telling me that he is going to be shot and he asked me to intercede on his behalf with Seán Liddy.' We both went to Liddy and suggested that before doing anything with Darcy the latter should be confronted with S, the Kilrush publican. Candidly, I felt that Sheehan was as much guilty as Darcy and that the latter, when faced with the former, might be able to incriminate him also, and that between the pair of them a lot of useful information might be obtained. We volunteered to go right into Kilrush and arrest Sheehan. Liddy told us that he was now finished with the case and Darcy was in the hands of Bill Haugh.

Russell witnessed Darcy's execution:

After being blindfolded and bound, he was shot by a firing party comprised of two members of the brigade staff – Bill Haugh and Tom Marrinan. I was standing near Darcy as he was being blindfolded and I distinctly heard him say: 'I forgive ye boys. Ye are shooting me in the wrong.' After being shot, a label was pinned to the dead man's breast bearing the words 'Spies beware'. His body was left on the street, where it remained until the next day when British troops from Kilrush removed it in a lorry to the barracks in that town. Widespread raids throughout west Clare were made by British forces following the execution of this man.

On 24 June two Volunteers from Kilnamona, Frank Keane and Patrick O'Keefe, attempted to disarm two Black and Tans on duty outside Duggans' shoe shop in Ennis. Their attempt failed and a running firefight broke out as the Volunteers rushed through the streets into a dead end. Trapped, they continued to fight until they were wounded and taken prisoner by the troops chasing them. Six-year-old Patrick Morrissey was killed in the crossfire.

A few days later the East Clare brigade went into action at Carrigoran outside Newmarket on Fergus. The Newmarket RIC garrison in the town sent a daily patrol of regular RIC men and Black and Tans from the village through the woods around Carrigoran House. The patrol usually entered by the back and continued their journey out through the front gates. A column of twenty Volunteers commanded by Jim Hannon travelled into the area at the beginning of July to ambush the patrol as it approached the front entrance of Carrigoran House. On the day of the ambush a number of local Volunteers acting as scouts mistakenly crossed the path of the patrol as it approached the ambush position and came under fire from the RIC Crossley Tenders. When the republican scouts reached a safe position the IRA ambushers returned the RIC fire and a brief fight ensued before the patrol reversed out of the ambush position and drove off unhindered in the direction they had come.

The IRA immediately withdrew from their positions and were marching through Craighalough where they were overtaken by a lorry of Black and Tans from Sixmilebridge who had received a telegram from the RIC barracks at Newmarket ordering them to try and intercept the IRA column. The Volunteers took up hasty fighting positions in the fields around Enrights' farm on the left side of the road facing Sixmilebridge. From here they fought a rearguard action through the fields until one Black and Tan was wounded and the rest broke off the engagement and returned to their lorry. During the course of the fighting one of the Volunteers, Tom Healy, collapsed and died of a heart attack. Healy was an ex-member of the RIC from Duagh in Kerry who had supplied the IRA with important intelligence information while serving as the clerk for the district inspector of the RIC in Ennis. When suspicion fell on Healy he resigned from the police and joined the IRA.

At Elmvale, three miles from Corofin, the Mid Clare brigade was presented with another chance to ambush the Auxiliaries stationed in Corofin. The IRA had laid an ambush for them at Toonagh that May, but it was abandoned when the Auxiliaries' patrol did not travel their usual route. The Auxiliaries began travelling to the farm of a local unionist named Patterson to collect a supply of water for their barracks a few times every week. A force of almost sixty Volunteers armed with rifles and shotguns were mobilised and moved into their attacking positions near Pattersons' farm at 9.30.

The Auxiliaries' luck held as they were called out to take part in raids on a number of republican homes on the opposite side of Corofin that morning. By the time they travelled to Elmvale at 4.30 p.m. Andrew O'Donoghue had decided that they were not going to come and had already dismissed the majority of the IRA force. The handful that remained were gathered on a piece of high ground when two of the Auxiliaries' Crossley Tenders were sighted. The lorry drove out of the remaining IRA men's view and into Pattersons' yard to collect the water unchallenged. Patterson and his workers warned them about the presence of the IRA column in the area and, unknown to the IRA, the Auxiliaries dismounted from their transport and quickly climbed into firing positions behind the wall of the avenue while their lorries sped back to Corofin to summon reinforcements and to make it appear to the IRA that the water had been collected and the Auxiliaries' were proceeding as usual.

Once their lorries had left the scene the Auxiliaries opened fire on Andrew O'Donoghue and his comrades, taking them completely by surprise:

> When the lorries got into the avenue the occupants jumped off and at once opened fire. We were in an exposed position at the time, and the heavy growth of bushes and briars into which we had to retreat for cover considerably hampered us. Anyway none of the IRA party was hit. The Auxiliaries made no attempt to leave the avenue but sent a lorry back into Corofin for reinforcements. This move was counteracted by the action of a few men whom I had placed on the Corofin side of the crossroads who had orders to erect a barricade as soon as the lorries had gone down the avenue. These men had carried out their job alright. A position of stalemate had more or less then arisen; the enemy would make no move without reinforcements and owing to exposed ground surrounding the avenue we could not advance to where we hoped to inflict losses. In the avenue the Auxiliaries had splendid cover and could easily hold out until nightfall. After some return fire by our men I decided to send them off in sections towards Kilmore where they dispersed.

Andrew O'Donoghue's description of this operation accurately surmises the general military situation in the struggle between the IRA and British forces in July 1921. 'A position of stalemate had more or less

then arisen; the enemy could make no move without reinforcements ...
we could not advance to where we hoped to inflict losses.'

The IRA and the Dáil still enjoyed the unflinching support of a large
majority of the Irish people and as such had the upper hand over the
British forces and the British government, whose conduct in Ireland
and failure to defeat the IRA had lost the support of the British people
for the continuing war. By spring 1921 Lloyd George, the British prime
minister, was under pressure to begin talking to the Irish rebels. The
IRA's continued resistance to British rule had shown the world that
they were still an effective fighting force despite Lloyd George's claims
to have the Irish 'murder gangs' by the throat. The atrocities, war crimes
and murders committed by the British during the war had received
international attention and were increasing diplomatic pressure on the
British government to negotiate. The atrocities carried out by British
troops had also shocked the British people and press, who had begun
calling for an end to the war.

On 8 July de Valera met General Neville Macready, commander of
the British forces in Ireland, and they agreed to a ceasefire in which each
army would retain its arms. All attacks, reprisals and counter-attacks
would cease. The truce would come into effect at noon on 11 July. A
number of IRA units throughout the country were eager to mount
pressure on the British government right up to the moment of the truce.
On 10 July the Mid Clare brigade assassinated Alfred Needham, a
twenty-one-year-old Black and Tan from London, on O'Connell Street,
Ennis. He had married a young woman in the town that morning. At
2 p.m. that day two motorcycle despatch riders from the 2nd battalion
Royal Welch Fusiliers were crossing Bunratty Bridge from the Limerick
direction when part of the structure, sabotaged by the IRA the previous
night, collapsed. Private R.W. Williams was plunged into the river
below and drowned. His body was swept away and was not recovered
until weeks later when it was washed up on the eastern bank of the river;
he was buried by a local farmer who had witnessed the incident.

Seán Moroney and the members of the East Clare brigade were in
action right up to the moment that the truce came into effect:

On 11 July 1921 I was one of the battalion active service unit who took up ambush positions about one mile outside Gort, County Galway to ambush a military or police patrol. We remained in positions until the Angelus rang at noon without any patrol coming our way, as the truce was then on. We disbanded and returned to our homes.

A few minutes later Michael Brennan entered Ennis with a small group of IRA men and witnessed the celebrations marking the truce:

> Just after midday on 11 July I went into Ennis with some comrades and when our car stopped at the Clare hotel we were surrounded by an almost hysterical crowd. One of the most excited was a British sergeant, named Doyle I think, wearing the ribbon of the Victoria Cross on his tunic. We were of course fully armed and equipped and our appearance was tangible proof that 'the Terror' was ended.

But Michael Brennan was wrong – 'the Terror' was not ended. Peace had not yet come to Ireland and a far more horrific terror was about to be unleashed. When the terms of the truce were published, they enraged the hard-line unionists led by Edward Carson, and the next day widespread rioting lasting a week broke out in Belfast. It was sparked by unionist mobs attacking republican areas with the help of the newly formed British police force, the Ulster Special Constabulary. Sixteen republicans and seven unionists were killed in the sectarian-inspired violence. The terror had not ended.

11

All Our Efforts Have Been in Vain

If you remove the English army tomorrow and hoist the green flag over Dublin Castle, unless you set about the organisation of the Socialist Republic all your efforts will be in vain. England would still rule you. She would rule you through her capitalists, through her landlords, through her financiers, through the whole array of commercial and individualist institutions she has planted in this country.

James Connolly

Douglas Duff, a Black and Tan stationed in Galway, witnessed one of the last IRA sniping attacks on the coastguard station at Ballyvaughan on 9 July and was taking the wounded marines from Ballyvaughan to hospital when he first heard of the truce:

We could not believe it, we knew only two well that the 'Shinner' resistance was almost finished, we had broken the back of armed rebellion, and that the desperate and defeated fugitives in the wild bogs and mountains of the west were ready to surrender in their hundreds, if their lives and liberties were promised to them. Of course we argued this talk of truce is all moonshine; not even Lloyd George would be fool enough to stop when victory is within his grasp.

Duff was of the opinion that the British forces had defeated the republicans. But were the IRA really desperate, defeated and ready to surrender by July 1921?

At the time of the truce the British government had 80,000 troops in Ireland, mostly British army soldiers. This number included a combined force of 12,000 Black and Tans, 3,000 regular RIC, 1,500 Auxiliaries, 3,000 members of the Ulster Special Constabulary supported by the

Dublin Metropolitan Police, the British secret service, Royal Marines, the Royal Air Force and the Royal Navy. But only 15,000 of these troops were considered capable of taking offensive action against the IRA by July 1921 and British generals estimated that they needed another 100,000 troops to defeat the republicans. All of these troops were well armed with Lee Enfield rifles, Lewes and Vickers machine guns, trench mortars, tanks, armoured cars, artillery and aircraft.

No more than 15,000 Volunteers took an active part in the military struggle. Only about 3,000 could be mobilised for action at any time. The IRA were supported by 3,000 members of Cumann na mBan and about 4,000 members of Na Fianna Éireann, the republican scout movement. Some 4,500 Volunteers had been interned throughout Ireland. Another 1,000 Volunteers and forty Cumann na mBan members had been imprisoned in Britain and in Irish jails. The IRA were armed with approximately 3,000 rifles, fifty machine guns and a few thousand shotguns, revolvers and automatic pistols. They did not have any of the military resources available to the British forces, having no pay, barracks, motor transport, artillery or aircraft. Instead they lived off the generosity of the Irish people and relied completely on them for accommodation, clothing, food and information.

Between January 1919 and July 1921 the IRA killed 140 British soldiers and Royal Marines, 428 members of the RIC including members of the Auxiliaries, the Black and Tans and Ulster Special Constabulary, and destroyed over 500 RIC barracks. About 100 suspected British spies were executed by the IRA The British forces had killed about 350 Volunteers; twenty-four had been executed and many others may have been killed immediately after capture instead of being taken prisoner. Approximately 150 other Volunteers and 600 civilians were killed in British reprisals for republican ambushes. The rate of attrition in the war was slowly increasing in favour of the IRA; 235 members of the RIC were killed between January and July 1921, fifty-seven more than for the whole of 1920. May 1921 saw the highest number of casualties inflicted on the British forces in the entire war with fifty-six RIC killed by the IRA that month alone.

Although the West Clare brigade had never been as strong or active as the Mid and East Clare brigades, the IRA were in a strong position throughout the county. At the time of the truce fourteen units of the British army were stationed in Clare with 1,510 soldiers, but less than 900 were considered capable of taking action. During the war the IRA killed forty-one members of the British forces including nineteen RIC, nine Black and Tans, eleven British soldiers and two Royal Marines. Another eight members of the British forces died in Clare either in accidents or by suicide. The IRA also executed three suspected British spies. Between 1913 and 1921 the British government established fifteen new RIC barracks in Clare; in the same period the IRA burned and destroyed twenty-eight barracks and IRA attacks led to evacuation of twenty-six others across the county.

By contrast, the British forces killed fifteen members of the IRA in Clare and one member of Na Fianna Éireann; six were killed in action while on IRA duty and ten were killed in British reprisals or murdered after capture. Another five Volunteers died by accident or on active service of natural causes. Twenty-seven civilians were killed in Clare during the war, the vast majority by the British forces in reprisals.

To compare these figures in their most crude terms, the IRA in Clare inflicted more than twice as many fatal casualties on the British forces as they did on the IRA, and forced fifty-four barracks to close throughout the county. The IRA in Clare also captured large supplies of arms and ammunition from the British stationed in county, including fifty-eight Lee Enfield .303 rifles, 6,800 rounds of .303 ammunition, eighteen RIC carbine rifles, 31 Webley and Scott revolvers and a number of Mills bomb hand grenades. The Clare IRA's weaponry also included another sixty rifles of various makes, almost 400 shotguns, 180 revolvers and automatic pistols, fifty hand grenades and a small quantity of explosives.

Eight branches of Cumann na mBan were organised in the county and eight slughta (companies) of Na Fianna Éireann were active there. Both organisations and the local civilian population were an integral part of the republican resistance and without them the IRA could never have functioned as an effective army. Michael Brennan paid tribute to the important work carried out by Cumann na mBan in Clare 'Those girls stood by us and at the height of the terror we found that the more dangerous the work the more willing they were to do it.'

The truce came as a shock to most of the IRA's rank and file, who believed they were winning the war and that it was only a temporary agreement lasting for a few weeks giving the IRA time to regroup and train their Volunteers before hostilities recommenced. A group of IRA commanders including Michael Collins, Richard Mulcahy and Piaras Béaslaí had supported the truce, arguing that the IRA did not have the military strength to continue fighting. This was strongly disputed by the local IRA commanders who felt that they were winning the war and could continue fighting for some time.

There was confusion among those who had proposed the truce as to the outcome of the war. Arthur Griffith, who initially supported the truce because he believed that the IRA were defeated, hailed Michael Collins only a few months later as 'the man who won the war'. At the end of June Michael Collins told the cabinet of Dáil Éireann that the IRA could only continue their military campaign for another two to three weeks. Richard Mulcahy, the Minister for Defence and commander in chief of the IRA, claimed: 'We have suffered a defeat'. He agreed with Collins' assessment that the IRA could not continue the military campaign, and argued that in the fighting up to the truce the IRA had failed to drive the British troops from even one fairly good sized barracks.

When Tom Barry travelled to IRA headquarters a month before the truce he reported that the 3rd West Cork brigade and the other IRA units in the county could continue the fight against the British forces for another three years:

Excluding naval personnel approximately 12,600 armed British troops, Auxiliaries and Black and Tans occupied the county of Cork seven weeks before the truce between Ireland and Britain. Standing against this field force was that of the Irish Republican Army, never at any time exceeding 310 riflemen in the whole of the county of Cork, for the very excellent reason that this was the total of rifles held by the three Cork brigades. The only other IRA arms within the county were five machine guns and some 350 automatics and revolvers ... Those figures showing the Irish Republican Army outnumbered by over forty to one in armed men and to a far greater ratio in fire power before the truce may just cause one to wonder why the British did not succeed in exterminating the small Irish field force in 1920 and 1921. The answer of course is that in the last analysis the struggle was never one between the British army and a small Irish force of flying columns and active service units. Had this been so the few flying columns operating would not have existed for a month no matter how bravely and skilfully they fought. This was a war between the British army and the Irish people, and the problem for the British from mid-1920 was not how to smash the flying columns but how to destroy the resistance of a people who, for as sure as day follows night, if a flying column were wiped out in any area another would arise to continue the attacks and the resistance to alien rulers. The Irish people had a weapon which the British lacked: their belief in the righteousness of their cause, their determination to be free, their political structure as declared in the general election of December 1918, and a strong militant of youth who, though as yet unarmed, were a potential army of great possibilities ... It is true that the British did not take all this lying down, and they made our people pay. The shops and public houses where service had been refused were looted, broken up and sometimes burned, old men felt the butts of rifles and old women, girls and children were assaulted and insulted. But those reprisals did not stop the expressions of hate and contempt and the isolation of the British grew as the boycott intensified. This was only part of the people's contribution to the fight for freedom. Nearing the truce, unmasked and unorganised, nine out of ten of the adult civilian population were watching and reporting to us on the movements of the British troops or on the activities of any suspected British agent ... Who can fully estimate the value of men and women like those in a nation's fight against alien rule? Their spirit and faith in the justice of their cause did not allow of defeat at the hands of imperialist mercenaries. British guns were not able to cow them, British money could not buy them, nor could British guile and duplicity wean them from their support of the Irish Republican Army for indeed they were as truly soldiers of the resistance movement as any Volunteer of the flying column.

Tom Barry felt that the truce had a devastating effect on the IRA as a military force. Because the IRA were an army of Volunteers they were unable to maintain their military strength in peace time. Most IRA Volunteers had family and work responsibilities and since the republican army could not afford to keep them as fully paid regular soldiers most of them left active service and returned to their civilian lives during the truce. In the same period the British government could maintain their forces in a state of readiness. As military tensions eased during the truce the IRA's efficiency and discipline slackened and Barry estimated that this caused a 30 per cent drop in the effectiveness of the republican army's morale, organisation and structure. In the type of guerrilla campaign the IRA had been fighting, a truce was much more harmful to their capabilities than it was to the professional British forces. Key figures in the secretive war now became exposed, the high-strung tension upon which the morale of guerrilla fighters depended eased, and a population overwhelmed by the relief from violence automatically became unwilling to resume the war.

Tom Barry was not the only IRA commander who thought the truce was a mistake. Liam Deasy also felt that the IRA were holding a strong military position against the British and was shocked when he heard about the truce:

> We who, so to speak, had manned the front line and had fought imbued with the full Republican ideal and with greater hopes of success than at any other time in our history felt we could settle for nothing but an Irish Republic. In the light of what followed this may seem to have been a vain hope, but it was not without solid foundation. My own knowledge and experience of the military efficiency of our brigade as well as the achievements and successes of other Cork brigades assured me that we were decisively winning the war. Nor was this belief confined to County Cork. It was also true of the Kerry, Limerick, Tipperary and Waterford brigades. Since 1916 the three Clare brigades had been at the forefront of the struggle, indeed relatively more families in Clare than in any other county in the thick of the fight, with the Brennans and the Barretts being the leaders in that great county which never failed in a national challenge ... We believed that England was once

again at her old game of compromise, a role too familiar to Irishmen and a role that bred suspicion rather than hope or trust in the heart of any Republican.

Ernie O'Malley held the rank of staff captain commanding the IRA in east Limerick, south Tipperary and Kilkenny as part of the 2nd Southern division. As an organiser for Michael Collins and a member of the IRA executive, O'Malley was in a good position to assess the IRA's strength at the time of the truce:

Our area was improving daily, the people were becoming more staunch in their allegiance to the Republic, and the British as a government no longer functioned ... Some areas were week, that was true, and there the enemy had attempted to cow the spirit by showing their strength and might as brutally as they well knew how. In general the IRA companies made or marred the morale of the people. If the officers were keen and daring, if the organisation was good, if the flying column had been established, and if the people had become accustomed to seeing our men bearing arms openly the resistance was stiffened. When the fighting took place the people entered into the spirit of the fight even if they were not republican; their emotions were stirred, and the little spark of nationality which is borne by everyone who lives in Ireland was fanned and given expression to in one of many ways. The enemy controlled the cities and the larger towns but English departments of government did not function as before ... The enemy ... had suffered in morale during the past two years, particularly in the last eight months. Their very campaign of terrorism had defeated itself. It had affected the discipline of their police force and of their army. Cooperation between the forces of oppression was anything but happy. The Auxiliaries did as they liked. The Black and Tans followed suit. The old members of the Royal Irish Constabulary resented the intruders and their tactics ... One evening in July 1921 a despatch rider asked to see me. He was shown into the kitchen of Mrs Quirke's in Donohill, in south County Tipperary. The despatch was from general headquarters and stated that all hostilities would cease after forty-eight hours, by twelve noon on 11 July ... We had not time to plan an attack on any of the local posts as we would have wished, and the day of the truce dawned, leaving us in a state of uncertainty ... Why had the truce been ordered? We were gaining ground, each day strengthened us and weakened our enemy; why then was it necessary to put a stop to hostilities?

Jeremiah Murphy, an IRA Volunteer in Kerry, also felt that the republicans had not been defeated:

> Both sides had reached an impasse but not their limit. In spite of all the oppression by the British, the IRA had become immensely stronger and the people had cultivated a will to resist which was the ingredient with the greatest effect. People who had grown up in the 1880s and 1890s and were scared by a few RIC men had rendered that force impotent and caused the complete breakdown of all government agencies. They had replaced them with a brand of their own and watched the British army make fools of themselves. It made the Irish feel important for the first time since Davitt and Parnell pulled them out of the mud and hopelessness of peasant farming.

Clearly there was a huge difference in the analysis of the military situation by the two groups of IRA commanders. The group who supported the truce were mostly members of the IRA general headquarters staff based in Dublin and were probably focusing on the military situation there, where the IRA were under severe enemy pressure and close to breaking point. Counties Cork, Kerry, Limerick, Tipperary, Clare, Galway, Mayo and Dublin had been the strongest republican military areas during the war but IRA units in Leinster and parts of Ulster had few arms, were disorganised and had not inflicted heavy casualties on the enemy. The thick of the fighting and the largest concentrations of British troops were based in the stronger republican areas where the IRA leaders were opposed to the truce.

Field Marshal Sir Henry Wilson, chief of the imperial general staff, saw the situation in desperate terms by that May: 'If we don't reinforce Ireland by every available man, horse, gun, aeroplane that we have got in the world we would lose Ireland at the end of the summer and with Ireland the Empire.' A number of other British army commanders knew that they could not defeat the IRA and were losing the propaganda war in the British and international media. Military commitments throughout the British empire had already placed severe demands on the resources of the army. As well as fighting the war in Ireland which was costing £20 million a year, the British were also in occupying Iraq and Germany, at war with Afghanistan, attempting to suppress other rebellions in India and Egypt, fighting for the White Russians in the Russian Civil War and facing a potential war with Turkey.

On 7 April 1921 Basil Thompson, the head of the British police special branch's Irish division, wrote to Lloyd George warning him:

> It cannot be conscientiously said that any headway has been made against the Irish Republican Army and there is a feeling among the people that Sinn Féin will win. This feeling is due to the increased prestige gained by Sinn Féin owing to its success in guerrilla warfare especially in the martial law areas ... They are beginning to be proud of the Irish heroes who have gained such victories over the Crown Forces in spite of all the restrictions imposed by martial law.

Major General Douglas Wimberley of the Cameron Highlanders knew that any widespread suppression of the IRA's military campaign would only be a temporary victory and would not destroy the republican revolution:

> At last the British government in July 1921 decided to treat and compromise with the rebel leaders. To my mind this was the only course open to them, for though no doubt we, in the army, given the powers of life and death and [an] official policy of ruthlessness, could easily have quelled the actual active Sinn Féin revolt by means of really stern measures backed by the British government, I feel certain the discontent would merely have smouldered underground. It would have burst into flames as soon as we withdrew. The really brutal measures which Cumberland and his army took in Scotland in 1745, finally to crush the rising there, would never have been tolerated by public opinion in Britain in 1921!

Major Bernard Law Montgomery commanded the 17th infantry brigade of the British army in Ireland during the war and was equally as enthusiastic as Major General Wimberley for a further series of reprisals against the Irish people, in an attempt to break their spirit of resistance and support for the IRA. He detailed this in writing during the civil war a year later:

> Personally, my whole attention was given to defeating the rebels and it never bothered me a bit how many houses were burnt. I think I regarded all civilians as 'Shinners' ... My own view is that to win a war of this sort you need to be ruthless. Oliver Cromwell or the Germans would have settled it in a very short time. Nowadays public opinion precludes such methods, the nation would never allow it and the politicians would lose their job if they sanctioned it. That being so I considered that Lloyd George was really right in what he did; if we had gone on we could probably have squashed the rebellion as a temporary measure, but it would have broken out again like an ulcer the moment we removed the troops. I think the rebels would probably have refused battles, and hidden away their arms etc. until we had gone. The only way therefore was to give them some form of self government and let them squash the rebellion themselves. They were the only people who could really stamp it out, and they [the Irish Free State government and army] are still trying to do so and as far as one can tell they seem to be having a fair amount of success.

Morale among the British forces was severely weakened by 1921, not just among the ordinary troops but among their commanding officers. Sir John Anderson, a member of the British secret service, warned his superiors: 'We could not have won the great war under those conditions'. Though not stationed in Ireland, Colonel Sir Hugh Ellis, commandant of the Royal Tank Corps, visited Ireland on 13–14 May 1921 and was shocked by what he saw:

> Officers must move not only armoured and in bodies but with their revolvers very handy; in motor cars they carry them actually in their hands. Troops sleep in defended barracks – behind barbed wire. Communication is becoming increasingly difficult. To go from Dublin to Cork one may fly or one may go very slowly – by armed train.

This is a curious situation for a force whose *raison d'être* in the country is to maintain order.

Another great pressure on Lloyd George was the implementation timetable for the Government of Ireland Act. Unless a southern Irish parliament was functioning in Dublin under the terms of the act by 14 July, the British viceroy would have to dissolve it and the British government would have to implement crown colony government rule for the twenty-six counties of southern Ireland and impose universal martial law for the whole island. General Macready drafted proposals to be effected on 14 July. All motor transport was to be seized, all ports closed, compulsory ID cards introduced, membership of the Dáil, the IRA or IRB was treason punishable by death and anyone caught using arms against the British forces was to be executed on the spot. As many as 100 republicans a week might have to be executed:

> Anything short of these extreme measures the present situation might go on for such time that political pressures or political change will cause us to abandon the country and we shall be beaten.

But Macready also warned that these conditions were not a guarantee of victory and might 'land this country deeper in the mire'.

By the time of the truce the British were little closer to defeating the IRA than they had been a year earlier. In effect the IRA were winning the war because, to them, their survival meant success. To repeat Tom Barry's words: 'The very existence of such a column of armed men, even if it never struck a blow, was a continuous challenge to the enemy.' As long as the IRA existed, the British government's administration could not function in Ireland. The British forces in Ireland were quickly losing the war because their mission was to restore peaceful conditions in Ireland under British rule. This was only possible through the complete destruction of the IRA, a goal which the British had failed in after two and a half years of conflict. The republicans had won the war but were about to lose the peace.

While the British forces appeared to be losing the war of attrition their numerical strength in Ireland meant that they had always had the capacity to absorb the losses inflicted on them by the IRA, but as long as the war continued and British casualties mounted so did British public opposition to the conflict and the occupation of Ireland. Rabidly unionist and conservative newspapers such as *The Times* and *Daily Express* were questioning the British policy in Ireland and voicing opposition to the war by 1921. Public criticism from opposition politicians, leading clergymen and trade unionists increased the pressure on the British government to reach a settlement with Dáil Éireann and the IRA. The prospect of continuing a long and costly war with the republicans and facing a major political embarrassment on both the domestic and international fronts eventually brought the British government to a position where they were forced to open negotiations.

Éamon de Valera travelled to London immediately after the truce in July, as president of the Irish Republic, to open negotiations with Lloyd George, the British prime minister. The British government suggested that an Irish delegation should travel to Britain to continue official negotiations.

The Irish cabinet select a five-man negotiation team. It was assumed that de Valera would lead the Irish team but he stunned the Dáil by announcing his intention not to go to London; de Valera argued that he was needed in Ireland to keep the hard-line republicans in check and maintain the truce. He claimed that this would strengthen the Irish delegates' position as negotiators, giving them time for serious consideration on crucial points and ensure that any final decisions would have the approval of the unified Irish cabinet. It was more likely that after his meetings with Lloyd George de Valera knew that the British government would never concede an Irish Republic and that the negotiations were doomed. By remaining in Ireland de Valera would be able to blame the Irish delegates in London for failing to secure British recognition for the Irish Republic.

Arthur Griffith, the Republic's vice-president, was selected instead to lead the delegation. Griffith was a strange choice of negotiator in any attempt to secure British recognition for an Irish Republic. Griffith was a committed monarchist, not a republican, and described himself as 'a King, Lords and Commons man'. His politics were those of a conservative, right-wing, Irish nationalist and supporter of home rule, making him one of the more 'moderate' voices in the Dáil who was prepared to settle for far less than a republic. De Valera insisted that Michael Collins go to London, to which Collins agreed, reluctantly, out of a sense of duty. Another republican, Robert Barton, was chosen as a delegate. Barton was a former British soldier who had resigned and converted to republicanism after the 1916 Rising and was elected Sinn Féin TD for Kildare–Wicklow. The Irish team was completed with the addition of two lawyers, George Gavan Duffy and Éamon Duggan. Erskine Childers was appointed as the non-voting secretary to the delegation. As an English Protestant, ex-member of the British army and former clerk in the House of Commons, he would be able to give the other members of the Irish negotiating team an inside perspective on the British mindset during the talks.

The Irish delegation's two main aims were to secure recognition for an Irish Republic and reverse the partition of Ireland introduced by the Government of Ireland Act. (The great irony is that the north-east of Ireland which had opposed Home Rule so strenuously for fifty years was the only part of the country to get it. And when they did they misused it in exactly the same way they had feared that the southern nationalists would: to implement sectarian discrimination and oppression.) The Irish delegates were under instruction to refer every agreed point during the negotiations back to the Dáil for ratification and were not to sign anything without prior approval. Before they left for London each Irish plenipotentiary was given a specific set of instructions. Article 2 read:

> It is understood, however, that before decisions are finally reached on the main questions that a despatch notifying the intention of making these decisions will be sent to the members of the cabinet in Dublin, and that a reply will be awaited by the Plenipotentiaries before the final decision is made.

The Irish delegation which left for London only contained some committed republicans, including Barton and Childers. Griffith had a strong personal dislike of Childers and regarded him as de Valera's spy. The political and personal divisions within the Irish delegation coupled with their limited experience as politicians put them at an immediate disadvantage. The British government's delegation was far more unified and experienced by comparison. The British delegation was headed by Lloyd George and included Winston Churchill, Minister for War, Austen Chamberlain and Lord Birkenhead, two leading members of the Conservative party. Negotiations began on 11 October 1921, the same day that de Valera was busy reviewing the Limerick and Clare brigades of the IRA and warning them about the possible breakdown of talks and resumption of war. The British held the advantage of knowing that if negotiations broke down it was the Irish people who would suffer the most.

With the truce in effect, the British forces and the IRA began meeting in the open for the first time. Because both sides believed that the truce was only a temporary ceasefire there was a tense and uneasy atmosphere in Clare, remembered by Michael Brennan:

> Meeting Black and Tans and Auxiliaries also armed was at first a rather nervy business and we circled rather than walked past each other, both parties becoming adept at watching sideways and over their shoulders and keeping a right hand ready to pull a gun. Near Lisdoonvarna about fifteen Auxiliaries ran into three of us unexpectedly. Guns were drawn on both sides, but nobody fired and after a tense few seconds they started their lorry and drove on.

This situation made it inevitable that a low level of hostilities would resume as both sides sought to settle old scores. The truce allowed combatants in hiding to reappear in public; RIC Constable William Carroll surfaced, having surrendered Ruan RIC barracks to the IRA and faking his capture to join the Mid Clare brigade flying column. When word of Carroll's deception and involvement with the IRA spread, a group of Black and Tans attempted to shoot Carroll at a race meeting in Kildysart but were stopped when a number of IRA Volunteers challenged them.

This same desire for revenge among Volunteers led to the first British casualty of the truce in Clare. A few months after Thomas McDonough was released from Limerick prison in August 1921 he was confronted by Sergeant David Finlay, William Shanahan's killer and the man responsible for the torture of other republican prisoners held in Ennis jail:

> I chanced to be in the Queen's hotel in Ennis one day when Finlay came in. He was in civilian clothes and I am sure that I would scarcely have recognised him were it not for the fact that he approached me and, wagging his finger at me, said: 'I know you; you are a so-and-so and you are one of the Shinners'. I learned that he was then a regular visitor to the hotel bar. I passed this information on and that night, when Finlay left the hotel, he was met by some of our boys in Ennis who took him down a laneway and administered him such a dose of his own medicine that he died from its effects the following day.

The Irish and British delegations met in conference several times between 11 and 24 October. At these initial meetings Griffith agreed that stenographers would not be used and as a result no official record of what was said at the negotiations was recorded. On 24 October the British negotiators sought private meetings with Griffith and Collins at which the three other Irish delegates to the conference would be excluded. Griffith and Collins agreed to this proposal, much to the annoyance of the others, and from this point onwards the Irish delegation failed to act as a united team. These private meetings quickly became the standard form of negotiation and Barton, Duffy and Duggan were no longer able to express their opinions on important aspects of the talks. Griffith and Collins met with Lloyd George and Birkenhead in private one-to-one sessions to discuss the key issues while the other delegates dealt with less important areas. During the negotiations the Irish delegates called for the people of each of the nine counties of Ulster to be allowed decide for themselves whether they wanted to remain under British rule or be part of the new Irish state. The British rejected this and instead offered that the six counties ruled by the newly established Northern

Ireland parliament would be ruled by the new Irish state's government in Dublin provided that Ireland remained inside the British Empire.

During one of the first private sessions on 24 October, Griffith said he would agree to recognition of the king as head of the new Irish state as long as all other points were agreed and the unity of Ireland was guaranteed. When de Valera received the minutes of this meeting he sent Griffith a sharp reply outlining the position of the Dáil:

> We are all here at one that there can be no question of our asking the Irish people to enter an arrangement which would make them subject to the Crown, or demand of their allegiance to the British King. If war is the alternative, we can only face it, and I think the sooner the other side realise that the better.

However, Griffith was determined to support this idea, which tied in well with his outdated ideas of home rule for Ireland under dual monarchy based on the Hungarian model for independence. There was now a serious political rift between Griffith and Dublin.

On 2 November the unionist MPs in the House of Commons put forward a motion condemning the negotiations. To ensure its defeat Lloyd George asked Griffith to write a letter, which he could show to wavering Conservative MPs to secure their opposition to the motion. In his letter Griffith promised that if the British government guaranteed essential Irish unity he would support Irish membership of the British Empire and recognition of the king as head of the Irish state. In return Lloyd George promised he could get Craig to agree to bring the six counties under the control of an all-Ireland parliament. But despite Lloyd George's promises and assurances, Craig refused to even consider the idea.

On 8 November Lloyd George told Griffith and Collins of Craig's refusal and instead put forward the idea of a boundary commission to redraw the border between 'northern' and 'southern' Ireland. The commission was to conduct a detailed survey within the six counties asking which state the local population wanted to be part of and redrawing the border accordingly. Craig travelled to London two days later and again completely rejected the British government's proposals and ruled out any unionist cooperation with a government for the rest of Ireland. On 13 November Lloyd George met with Griffith again. Even though he already knew that the unionists would never agree to the proposal, Lloyd George persuaded Griffith to accept the idea of a boundary commission, and in turn Griffith agreed not to use the issue of partition to break off the negotiations. Both Collins and Griffith believed that the boundary commission would give the Irish government in Dublin control of counties Tyrone and Fermanagh as well as south Armagh and Derry city. They believed that this would make the unionist state of Northern Ireland so small it would be unworkable and put pressure on the unionist government at Stormont to reunite with the rest of Ireland. But by accepting this proposal they had conceded the idea of a partitioned Ireland.

The truce was beginning to have a negative impact on IRA units in Clare. With the war on hold, some Volunteers experienced a loss of direction and purpose, and splits started to emerge in the republican army's unity. Colonel Tottenham, the unionist landlord whose house had previously been raided for arms by the IRA, dismissed two of his cattle herders in November and reduced the rest of his workers' wages by two shillings and six pence per week with the result that all but two of his workmen went on strike. The colonel struck a deal with a local IRA leader who used the Volunteers under his command to crush the strike and the colonel was able to reduce his employees' wages without any further difficulty. The action of the IRA commander in supporting Colonel Tottenham during the strike caused great bitterness among the Volunteers in the Mid Clare brigade as it became clear that sections of the republican army were ready to support the rich and powerful in return for favours granted by them.

Rumours began circulating among ordinary Volunteers in the Mid Clare brigade that Ignatius O'Neill, the commandant of the brigade's 4th battalion and leader of the Rineen ambush, was about to be assassinated by G company of the Auxiliaries, the same men who had tortured and killed

McMahon, Egan, Rodgers and Gildea at Killaloe. Volunteer Pádraig Ó Fathaigh was sent to Carmodys' hotel in Ennis to check on O'Neill and was shocked by what he found:

> It was reported that Ignatius O'Neill and Pat Powell (alias Cahill) had been drinking since the truce with two Auxiliaries and fears were entertained for their safety. That night to our astonishment there arrived Ignatius, Pat Cahill [Powell] and two Auxiliaries. One of the Auxies just sat down and drank; the other man, the notorious 'Splendid', kept singing, drinking and falling. His oft repeated song was 'I know my love'. He felt very delighted and honoured to be in the company of Sinn Féiners who were fine soldiers and fine gentlemen. 'If there had to be a fight again it would be a fight between gentlemen, twenty Auxiliaries, or thirty-five, or a hundred, pitted against an equal number of Sinn Féiners. I'll let my decision rest with that. 'What about the arms?' said Mr Carmody. 'An equal number of rifles or revolvers,' said Splendid. O'Neill had apparently lost sight of the republican ideals he had been fighting for in a mist of alcohol, allowing him to partake in Splendid's nonsensical fantasies. The Auxiliaries' campaign of terrorism, torture, murder and arson was already being forgotten.

Back in London, since the British considered that the issue of partition was settled, negotiations continued with a focus on the other contentious question – that of the measure of independence from Britain that would be given to the new Irish state. While the Irish delegation continued to insist on complete independence as a republic for the new Irish state, the British refused to be moved in their demand that Ireland would remain part of the empire. The Irish delegation put de Valera's idea of external association forward as a solution whereby the Irish Republic would leave the empire but retain some of its formal connections with Britain. Again the British refused to accept the idea, insisting that the Irish state would only be granted dominion status. The negotiations entered their final stages in the last week of November, during which time the British softened slightly in the measure of political independence they were willing to grant to the Irish people. However, the British government were unflinching in their demands that Ireland would have to remain inside the British empire with the king as head of state and that members of the 'southern' Irish parliament would have to swear an oath of allegiance to him. They presented a draft treaty to the Irish containing these proposals. The British ploy at this stage in the negotiations was to give the Irish people a republic in name only. At the time Sinn Féin were using the archaic Irish language term 'saor stát', literally 'free state', as their translation for the English word 'republic' instead of the word 'poblacht', a more modern Irish translation. The British negotiators seized on this trivial point of linguistics, and proposed 'saor stát' or 'Irish free state' as the name for the new Irish state. This term might appease the Irish delegation through the argument that they had received an Irish Republic in name; at the same time it avoided use of the word 'republic' in English, which would be more acceptable to British conservative and unionist sentiment.

On 3 December the Irish delegation brought the draft treaty back to Dublin for approval by the Irish cabinet, who rejected the idea of dominion status for Ireland and instructed them to return to London to renegotiate for external association. This issue became the central point for discussion by the cabinet to the extent that little attention was paid to the British proposals for partitioning Ireland. The Irish representatives were immediately sent back to London with strict instructions not to sign anything but to refer all British proposals for a settlement back to the Dáil for approval. When the delegation arrived back in London on 4 December, Griffith and Collins at first refused to go to Downing Street to continue negotiations and insisted that the two republicans, Barton and Duffy, should demand external association for Ireland and use the issue to break off the talks; however, after much argument Griffith, Collins and Duffy finally agreed to go. During this meeting Griffith deliberately attempted to avoid the question of Irish allegiance to the king and Ireland's membership of the British empire, hoping that if the negotiations were to break down it would be over the issue of partition instead. Gavan Duffy was not aware of Griffith's stance, having been excluded from the key issues of the negotiations for over a month, and attempted to broaden the talks by raising the question of Ireland's membership of the empire. Austen Chamberlain, realising that this gave the British delegates the chance to show that the talks broke down over the issue of the British crown and empire, jumped to his feet and shouted: 'That ends it!' The meeting immediately fell apart in disagreement.

The British were keen to build on their position of strength and the next morning Lloyd George contacted Griffith, Collins and Barton and persuaded them to return to Downing Street for further discussions. Lloyd George softened his approach, offering the Irish a minor change to the oath of allegiance whereby Irish TDs would first swear an oath to the new Irish constitution and allegiance to the king afterwards. Lloyd George also offered the right to protect Irish goods by placing taxes on British imports, a particularly important issue to Griffith as an economist. Next he told them that the unionist parliament of Northern Ireland was due to meet the next day and he had promised to let Craig know its fate before then and needed to know if the Irish would accept the British proposal for a boundary commission and sign a finalised treaty. The Irish replied that they needed to know Craig's attitude on the issue first but Lloyd George refused to accept any further delay, producing Griffith's undertaking of 13 November, and demanded to know if Griffith was ready to break his promise not to repudiate the boundary commission. By now it was impossible for the Irish to break off the talks by using partition as an excuse. Griffith said he would not go back on his word and agreed to sign the treaty.

Lloyd George then insisted that this was as much as he could possibly offer the Irish people and asked Barton and Collins to sign. The two men protested that they needed the Dáil's approval to sign anything, but Lloyd George claimed they must sign at once. Lloyd George then played his final card and threatened Barton and Collins that they must sign or face immediate and terrible war. The two men withdrew to discuss their position. Collins and Duggan agreed to sign. Barton and Duffy both refused to sign, but after several hours of heated argument and debate Duffy relented. Erskine Childers desperately attempted to convince them not to sign but was unsuccessful. At 2.10 a.m. on the morning of

6 December 1921 the Irish delegation returned to Downing Street and signed the treaty.

The final draft of the treaty contained eighteen articles. Articles 1 and 2 gave the twenty-six counties of the Irish Free State the same constitutional status as Canada, Australia and the other dominion states. Under Article 3, the king would be represented in Ireland by a governor general appointed in the same way as the Canadian governor general. Article 4 set out the oath of allegiance to be taken by all members of the Irish parliament. Article 5 covered the amount of the British war debt that would be paid by the Free State. Article 6 dealt with defence and under its provisions the British military would have permanent naval bases at Cobh, Berehaven and Lough Swilly. Article 10 ensured that the Free State would pay compensation to former British civil servants stationed in Ireland and pay for the pensions of the RIC. Articles 11 to 15 detailed the position of Northern Ireland. In theory the Free State was to take over the functions of the British government for ruling the six counties under the Government of Ireland Act unless the unionist parliament at Stormont voted to remain within the United Kingdom. In such an event the border between 'northern' and 'southern' Ireland would be redrawn by a boundary commission. Article 16 forbade either the Free State or Northern Irish governments to give special treatment to any religion. Finally the British government would hand over control of the twenty-six counties of southern Ireland to a provisional government made up of existing Irish MPs.

In reality what the treaty meant was that Ireland was still not free and that the Irish people were still subject to foreign rule from Britain. The treaty ensured that the king remained the head of state for Ireland and that all of Ireland remained part of the British empire. While in theory Northern Ireland could re-integrate with the rest of Ireland under the terms of the treaty, the selection of the six Ulster counties with the highest unionist majority and the exclusion of large republican populations in Counties Donegal, Cavan and Monaghan ensured that gerrymandering was engrained in Northern Ireland for years to come and that a unionist government would always be returned which was certain to reject any plans for Irish reunification. The boundary commission, by redrawing the border between 'northern' and 'southern' Ireland, would only reinforce the artificial social and political make-up of Northern Ireland by ensuring that the proposed redrawing of the border would increase the number of unionists north of the border and at the same time take republican areas south, further compounding the artificial unionist make-up of the state. Despite Article 16 of the Treaty, which prevented either the Free State or Northern Ireland from favouring any one religion, the unionist government at Stormont was declared 'A Protestant parliament for a Protestant people'. The Catholic population in the north were treated as second-class citizens in their own country, subjected to continued sectarian attack from the Royal Ulster Constabulary (RUC) and B-Specials, and excluded from almost all well paying jobs and positions in an effort to keep them downtrodden.

Even though the Irish Free State was to have its own parliament in Dublin, it was not independent, having little more than a glorified form of home rule. Its members would have to swear an oath of allegiance to the king and the laws it passed would still need the approval of the British government to become law. Supporters of the treaty claimed that the oath was merely a formality and a very weak form of oath at that, but Lloyd George contradicted this by telling the British cabinet: 'The terms of the oath to be taken by members of the parliament of the Irish Free State are remarkable and are better in many respects than the terms of the oath of allegiance ordinarily required in Great Britain.'

The ordinary people in the Free State would not be citizens of an independent state but subjects of a king. The treaty would also place a financial burden on the Irish people. Even though the British government had exacted over £18 million a year through corrupt taxation from the Irish people, they would still be expected to pay land annuities to the government for lands which had been stolen from them during the British plantations. In addition, under Article 5 of the treaty, they would have to pay part of Britain's war debt for the First World War, despite the fact that 49,000 Irishmen were slaughtered in a war that had nothing to do with them.

For fourteen months the Black and Tans and Auxiliaries had terrorised the Irish people, stolen from them, burned their homes and murdered their friends and relations. For decades before this the RIC had kept the Irish people in oppression, evicted them in times of poverty, beat them back into the poverty of the gutter when they went on strike for a fair wage and constantly reported their movements and political aspirations at the behest of a foreign government. Now because of Article 10 of the treaty the Irish people were expected to pay the pensions of these same RIC men and Black and Tans.

The British union flag would be taken down and replaced with the Irish tricolour; the British army would be withdrawn and replaced with the new Free State army and a provisional government with limited legislative powers would rule the twenty-six counties from Dublin instead of British politicians ruling from London. But it was all as superficial as the imperial red British post boxes which were painted nationalist green throughout southern Ireland on the orders of the Free State. Symbols changed and everything was given a thin veneer of nationalist independence, but the substance of the corrupt core remained intact just beneath the surface. Ireland remained a British colony subject to the whims of a foreign king and government, partition was strengthened and the Irish people divided. Now it became obvious that many of the supposed converts from home rule to republicanism had never changed their conservative politics:

We did not realise it at the time but what happened was not that Sinn Féin had captured Ireland, but that the politicians in Ireland and those who made them, all the elements which had sniffed at Sinn Féin and libelled it, which had upheld corruption and jobbery, had realised that Sinn Féin were going to win and had come over to it en masse … In their hearts they remained still corrupt, still just politicians.

The career politicians' hold on Sinn Féin had grown even stronger as the young men and women in movement left to join the IRA and Cumann na mBan when the war began, leaving the party organisation in the control of middle-aged conservative former home rulers who sided with the social elite, the Catholic Church and big business in any local dispute using the guise of republicanism to bring them to power. Now that a settlement had been reached with the British government these men came to the fore eager to secure jobs and powerful political positions which asserted their claim as the rulers of the new Irish state.

The real effect of the treaty was made clear by Lord Birkenhead, who said the purpose of the treaty was 'to hold Ireland for England with an economy of British lives'. James Connolly had warned against this prospect of Ireland achieving a sham measure of independence under which Irish people would live under the illusion of freedom while the British government still influenced Irish domestic and economic affairs from behind the scenes and using the Irish establishment to their own ends.

12

Our Dreams Like Rags About Us

We were flattened. We felt the Irish public had forgotten us. The tinted trappings of our fight were hanging like rags about us.

Sheila Humphries

When the details of the treaty were published the Irish cabinet met to discuss it. The majority of the cabinet were outraged that Griffith and Collins and the other Irish delegates had signed despite very specific written orders not to, without approval from Dublin. De Valera was ready to sack Griffith and Collins from the cabinet and for the Dáil to issue a proclamation at once repudiating the treaty. However, William Cosgrave came to their defence, appealing for the treaty's signatories to be allowed to state their case for signing and to postpone any statements until they had been heard. Once this initiative was lost it was never recovered. A telegram was despatched for the Irish delegation to return and state their case. On 8 December the full cabinet met in session and de Valera, Brugha and Stack called for an immediate rejection of the treaty but the three Irish delegates demanded that it should be put before the Dáil for a full debate. Cosgrave cast his deciding vote in favour of this proposal and the treaty had to be put to the Dáil before it could be rejected or approved.

On 10 December Michael Collins arranged a meeting of the supreme council of the IRB. The organisation's membership was split on the issue and because of the IRB's nature as a secret society we will probably never know how many of its rank and file were opposed to the treaty but a majority of its leaders in the supreme council were prepared to accept the treaty with Liam Lynch as the sole opponent. Immediately the IRB issued orders instructing ordinary members to support the treaty. The same orders made it clear that TDs who were members of the organisation were free to vote on the treaty according to their consciences. Further support for the treaty also came from the Irish middle- and upper-classes that had remained neutral, eager to protect their business interests during the war against the British. They came out from behind the walls of their large country houses and businesses in whose shelter they had spent the War of Independence and bawled out support for the treaty, not for the limited freedoms it gave but for the fetters it imposed.

The majority of the press who had utterly condemned the republicans immediately swung around to back those IRA and Sinn Féin members who were now prepared to support the treaty, with only one newspaper supporting the republicans. Editorials and articles in the so-called independent Irish press, which were frequently owned by larger British newspapers or conservatives like William Martin Murphy, attempted to pressure the public into supporting the treaty by using simplistic scare-mongering headlines such as 'Rejection and Chaos' or 'Ratification or Ruin'.

The Irish Labour Party held a vision drastically different to James Connolly's dream of a socialist workers' republic and supported the treaty. The Communist Party of Ireland, however, still upheld Connolly's ideal of a workers' republic and rejected the treaty as 'a shameful betrayal': 'The so-called Free State will bring neither freedom nor peace. Instead civil war and social hell will be loosed if it is accepted.' Their stand against the treaty was supported by the Irish Citizen Army, who had cooperated with the IRA during the war and carried out their own independent actions against the British forces in Dublin.

On 14 December the Dáil met to discuss the treaty. On the same day the Catholic bishops played their hand again in support of the rich, the powerful and the status quo against the Republic when the *Irish Independent* published a manifesto from fifteen leading members of the Catholic Church supporting the treaty. According to Dan Breen: 'The Hierarchy went out and attacked the Republic, threw bell, book and candle at it in nearly every pulpit in the country.'

Dáil Éireann's debate began with a private session during which de Valera called on the Dáil to reject the treaty and replace it with an alternate treaty he proposed, known as Document No. 2. Document No. 2 was based on the treaty that the Irish delegation had signed in London except that the king would not be head of the Irish state and there would be no oath of allegiance, no British-appointed governor general and Ireland would only be informally linked to the British empire through external association. De Valera wanted this document to be given to the British government as the minimum demand for independence that the twenty-six county state could accept. De Valera hoped that this compromise would keep the Dáil united, but Document No. 2 was rejected by republicans and supporters of the treaty and de Valera was forced to withdraw it. The republicans still refused to accept anything less than a fully independent Irish Republic and felt that Document No.2 was little better than the treaty. The supporters of the treaty argued that the British government had already rejected these demands.

Five days later the Dáil met in public to debate the treaty. The IRB's influence over its members in the treaty debates should not be under-estimated. When TDs who were members of the IRB arrived for the debate they were met by groups of Michael Collins followers in the IRB who put pressure on them to support the treaty and told them that each member of the brotherhood would have to make a speech publicly declaring their position.

The republicans completely rejected the treaty as a betrayal of every-thing they had fought for, suffered for and seen their comrades die for. They argued that the Irish Republic had been declared in 1916 and confirmed by the results of the 1918 general election, the establishment of Dáil Éireann and its passing of the Declaration of Independence in 1919. To them the republic already existed and no treaty or government assembly could ever abolish the established right of the Irish people to the complete independence it entailed. They had sworn allegiance to the republic and were prepared to die to defend it. The republicans viewed those who were ready to abolish the Irish Republic by accepting the treaty as traitors who had broken the solemn oath they swore to defend the republic and the rights of the Irish people. If the only alternative to the treaty was to return to war then they urged the Dáil to choose war.

A second group, led by de Valera, also opposed the treaty out of pragmatism rather than belief in republican ideology. They believed that a compromise far short of an Irish Republic would have to be reached with the British government, but still maintained that the treaty did not go far enough towards this. Their main objection to the treaty was the position of the King George V as head of the Irish state and the oath of allegiance to him.

The TDs in favour of the treaty were equally as divided in their motives. While a few 'advanced home rulers' like Arthur Griffith and Eoin McNeill, who had switched their allegiance to Sinn Féin after 1916, genuinely supported the treaty, many more only supported it because they saw no alternative other than continuing the military struggle, which many of them had not taken part in; they did not have a good understanding of the military situation throughout the country and felt that the IRA could not win. Their action in supporting the truce strengthened their claim by weakening the IRA's discipline as a fighting force and by drawing out the period of conflict which made the IRA's support base among the ordinary Irish people more unstable and made their supporters more unwilling to return to war. Michael Collins and his supporters in the IRB argued for support for the treaty as the first step in achieving a completely independent Irish Republic.

Collins' popularity was a major factor in mustering support for the treaty. Only a year before, Collins had warned the Irish people:

At the moment there is a very grave danger that the country may be stampeded on false promises and foolish ill-timed actions. We must stand up against that danger. My advice to the people is hold fast and that everyone in Ireland has reason to be profoundly distrustful of British politicians of all schools ...'

Many of the same people followed Collins' example blindly. Rather than heeding his warning and examining the treaty in detail and forming their own opinions, they simply repeated the mantra: 'what's good enough for Mick Collins is good enough for me'. Another group of treaty supporters traded their previous ideology during the war for pragmatism and political gain and saw advantages to dominion status for the Irish Free State as a part of the British empire. They claimed that British dominions were gaining an increasing level of independence within the empire and that other dominions like Canada and Australia would act as a safeguard to ensure that the British government would not interfere too deeply in the affairs of the Irish Free State.

Arthur Griffith introduced the motion that 'Dáil Éireann approves of the treaty between Great Britain and Ireland signed in London on December 6, 1921'. Seán MacEoin seconded the motion. The first speakers in the debate attempted to stick to the issues involved but towards the end of the debate deep political and personal bitterness took over. Many of the pro-treaty TDs strayed from the point of the debate and kept raising de Valera's proposed Document No. 2 which had never been passed by the Dáil and was outside the confines of the debate. When one of the signatories of the treaty, Robert Barton, spoke he made a short speech during which he never discussed the content of the treaty and instead confessed that he was opposed to it and that he had only broken his oath to the Irish Republic under severe duress but still had to regard his signature on the treaty as personally binding.

Pro-treaty TDs claimed in their speeches that the republicans executed in 1916 would have solidly supported the treaty, and the name and spirit of Patrick Pearse was invoked frequently despite the fact that Pearse had declared:

> The man who in the name of Ireland accepts as a final settlement anything less than one fraction of an iota than separation from England … is guilty of so immense an infidelity, so immense a crime against the Irish nation that one can only say of him that it would be better for that man, as it were certainly for his country, that he had not been born.

After pro-treaty TDs made speeches claiming that the men executed in 1916 would have supported the treaty, Kathleen Clarke spoke, claiming that her executed husband Tom Clarke would never have supported the treaty and neither could she:

> It is to me the simple question of right or wrong. To my mind it is a surrender of all our national ideals. … If this treaty is ratified, the result will be a divided people … I too can go back to 1916. Between one and two o'clock on the morning of the 3rd of May, I, a prisoner in Dublin Castle, was roused from my rest on the floor and taken under armed guard to Kilmainham jail to see my husband for the last time. I saw him not alone but surrounded by British soldiers. He informed me he was to be shot at dawn. Was he in despair like the man who spoke of him on Tuesday? Not he. His head was up, his eyes flashing, his years seemed to have slipped from him. Victory was in every line of him. 'Tell the Irish people,' he said, 'that I and my comrades believe we have saved the soul of Ireland. We believe she will never lie down again until she has gained absolute freedom' … I never visioned a settlement which would mean complete separation from England at that stage of our struggle. I knew England was still too powerful to agree to such. I knew there would be some halfway house for a period even though I could not agree to its acceptance, but the last thing I thought would happen was the agreement to partition.

As the names of republican martyrs were repeatedly used by pro-treaty TDs to make their case, the widows and relatives of these men, such as Mary MacSwiney, Kate O'Callaghan and Margaret Pearse came forward to denounce the distortion of their loved ones' beliefs and their memory to aid the pro-treaty cause. Each of these female TDs then called for a rejection of the treaty. In response the pro-treaty TD for Sligo, Alex McCabe, claimed that the female TDs only opposed the treaty because they were left deranged and mentally unbalanced because of their suffering during the war. He claimed Mary MacSwiney's 'mind and outlook were distorted by the terrible experience she had passed through'.

Because she had no dead martyrs to be thrown in her teeth Constance Markievicz's speech rejecting the treaty met with equally bitter and stern resistance of a different nature. Markievicz used her speech rejecting the treaty to highlight the need for social reform and workers' rights because she could see in the treaty the 'deliberate attempt to set up a privileged class' and asserted that she still stood for the workers' republic that she, James Connolly and the Irish Citizen Army had fought for in 1916. She was interrupted by abusive roars of 'Soviet republic!' from the pro-treaty TDs who were eager to rewrite the history of the revolution and erase from the record any memory of James Connolly's socialist ideals. Despite the interruption Markievicz continued in her speech:

> A state run by the Irish people for the people. That means a government that looks after the rights of the people before the rights of property … My idea is the workers' republic for which Connolly died. And I say that this is one of the things that England wishes to prevent. She would sooner give us home rule than a democratic republic. It is the capitalists' interests in England and Ireland that are pushing this treaty to block the march of the working people in Ireland and England … While Ireland is not free I remain a rebel, unconverted and inconvertible … I have seen the stars and I am not going to follow a flickering will o' the wisp.

The debate dragged on painfully long and the crucial vote was postponed until after the Dáil's Christmas recess. If the vote had been taken before the recess it is likely that the Dáil would have voted to reject the treaty. On 7 December fifteen Catholic bishops voiced their support for the treaty and over the Dáil's recess the bishops and parish priests worked hard delivering pastorals and sermons supporting the treaty and urged wavering TDs to vote in support. According to Todd Andrews, a member of the IRA headquarters staff, the actions of the Church and press destroyed any hope of unity:

> Unity might have been achieved if it had not been for the violent, some-times vile propaganda of the newspapers. The bishops fully supported the treaty, thus adding to the difficulties of re-establishing unity either in the movement or the country generally. Every conservative force – landlords, businessmen, gombeen men, large farmers all the traditional opponents of separatism – came out to shriek their approval.

The Dáil session and the treaty debate continued after the Christmas recess until 7 January when the Dáil voted by sixty-four votes to fifty-seven in favour of the treaty. After the vote de Valera resigned as president and was replaced by Arthur Griffith. Griffith appointed a new cabinet with Michael Collins as Minister for Finance, Richard Mulcahy as Minister for Defence, William Cosgrave as Minister for Local Government and Kevin O'Higgins as Minister for Economic Affairs. The republican TDs withdrew from the assembly in protest. Under the terms of the treaty the Irish Free State was to come into existence on 6 December 1922, the anniversary of the signing of the treaty. Until the Free State was established the British government would hand over power in stages to a provisional government elected by the parliament of 'southern Ireland' under the terms of the Government of Ireland Act. In reality the 'southern' parliament consisted of the members of the Dáil, including the four unionist TDs representing Trinity College Dublin who had refused to attend the Dáil. The provisional government met for the first and only time on 14 January 1922 and elected Michael Collins as its leader. Collins then appointed Cosgrave and O'Higgins to the cabinet. So to confuse the issue there were now three government bodies in Ireland – the unionist puppet government of Northern Ireland, the republican members of the Dáil whose anti-treaty TDs claimed that it was the only legitimate government for all of Ireland and the provisional government, which only met once and had almost exactly the same membership as the pro-treaty former members of the Dáil.

Following the narrow vote in favour of the treaty, Cumann na mBan were the first republican organisation to debate the treaty and overwhelmingly rejected it. Sinn Féin split on the issue, while Na Fianna Éireann voted unanimously to reject it. With the Dáil and the other republican organisations tearing themselves apart over the treaty, the most urgent task, to prevent civil war, was to stop the IRA from splitting. The majority of the IRA's headquarters staff based in Dublin supported the treaty. Two members of the staff, Liam Mellows and Rory O'Connor, led the majority of the ordinary Volunteers throughout the country who rejected the treaty. Control of the IRA was vital to both the republicans and the treaty's supporters, now known as the 'Free Staters'. On 12 January the leading officers in the IRA called on Richard Mulcahy to organise an army convention to discuss the treaty. Despite protests from Griffith and O'Higgins he agreed to their demand and this unified the IRA by postponing the inevitable split. In Clare both the West and Mid Clare brigades opposed the treaty and only Michael Brennan's men in East Clare supported it.

With the formation of the Provisional Government on 7 January 1922, the British army began withdrawing from their barracks throughout the twenty-six counties and either returned to Britain or were transferred to the north. As the forces withdrew, their former barracks were taken over by both pro-treaty and anti-treaty units of the IRA. The first to be evacuated was Beggars Bush barracks in Dublin, which was taken over by pro-treaty members of the Dublin brigade IRA. The provisional government wanted to make sure that they looked well for the occasion and sent their pro-treaty troops to the Co-op tailors in Abbey Street to be fitted for new green uniforms. Now the political split between the pro-treaty and anti-treaty IRA units became clearly visible, with the pro-treaty former IRA Volunteers wearing their new green Free State army uniforms.

There were mixed emotions as the British troops evacuated the twenty-six counties. As the first departing soldiers marched along the Dublin quays to their transport, a small crowd of local unionists arrived to cheer them and wave British flags. When the Devonshire regiment pulled out from the quay at Waterford, Major Reginald Graham heard one of his soldiers approving of the British government's decision to withdraw from the Free State and remain in occupation of Northern Ireland: 'One soldier said: "They should have pulled the bloody plug years ago"; because Southern Ireland was poor, there wasn't the industry there that existed in Ulster.' This soldier was sharp enough to recognise the real reason many republicans believed to be behind the British government's withdrawal from the Free State. It would allow them to sacrifice most of Ireland as an unprofitable and troublesome colony and at the same time exact land annuities, war debt payments and other taxation from the Free State without any further cost and still keep control of the six most profitable counties of north-eastern Ulster where the textile and shipping industries were based.

In Clare the scenes of British withdrawal were far more bitter. On 31 January the British government authorised the evacuation of RIC barracks throughout the Free State. The next day as the RIC garrison in Ennistymon were loading their possessions and equipment onto lorries, preparing to withdraw from their barracks, RIC Constable Francis Cosgrave threw a Mills bomb hand grenade at a crowd of children returning from the local school who taunted the RIC by shouting 'Up Rineen' and 'Up the IRA'. Six of the children and two adults were wounded in the attack, four of them seriously. Retaliation was swift and within an hour the RIC were under attack from snipers. Fearful of their safety the RIC garrison made a speedy withdrawal from the village that evening. The local Volunteers mounted an ambush for the RIC on the Ennis Road but they travelled by a different route and the IRA were forced to abandon their plans for the time being. Constable Cosgrave was charged with the attack and remanded in custody at Ennis by the RIC for a week.

On 3 February two Black and Tans, William Gourlay from Lanark and Frank Kershaw from Lancashire, were having a drink with a regular RIC man, Constable Cahill, in Greenes' pub in Lisdoonvarna. As Gourlay and Kershaw left the pub to return to barracks they were shot dead. It is likely that the attack was ordered by the local IRA company to take revenge in the genuine belief that Gourlay and Kershaw were responsible for the attack on the children; more likely, Joe and Frank Barrett and the leadership of the Mid Clare brigade had decided to use the RIC's attack at Ennistymon as a reason to restart the war against the British and prevent the split within the IRA growing and leading to civil war.

Tensions and armed clashes between the IRA and the new Free State army grew as both jostled to gain the military advantage. Both armies began raiding arms dumps to capture rifles and ammunition belonging to the other. The competition to take over barracks as the British army and RIC withdrew became part of this struggle. Liam Forde, commanding the Mid Limerick brigade of the IRA, took over two of the four military barracks in Limerick, the New barracks and the Ordinance barracks in William Street. The New barracks, which had held 600 British soldiers, was now guarded by a handful of IRA Volunteers as the Mid Limerick brigade had neither the numbers, money nor food supplies to post a stronger force there on a full-time basis. For the same reason the Strand and Castle barracks were only briefly occupied by the IRA and were eventually left without an IRA garrison because they held less strategic military value than the New and Ordinance barracks. On 18 February the Mid Limerick brigade issued a proclamation denouncing the treaty and repudiating the authority of the IRA's headquarters staff in Dublin who supported the treaty and declared their brigade independent of headquarters control and loyal to the Irish Republic.

Officially the Provisional Government's policy was that the local force was to take all evacuated army barracks in their brigade area regardless of whether they were IRA or the Free State army. However, Limerick city was regarded as a key military position; it had always been strongly garrisoned by the British forces who had used it as a base during the war to dominate large parts of Counties Clare, Limerick and Tipperary. Its position spanning the Shannon meant that it linked control of Munster and the western coast. If the IRA took military control of the city Seán Mac Eoin and Michael Brennan's Free State troops in Clare, Galway and the midlands would be surrounded by IRA brigades, leaving them dangerously isolated from the rest of the Free State forces. In response Richard Mulcahy broke from the provisional government's policy and ordered Michael Brennan and the Free State troops in the 1st Western division to move from Clare into Limerick city, with reinforcements from Free State units in Dublin, and take over the two unmanned military barracks.

This was the first time during the British withdrawal that one army division had been ordered into another's divisional area and the tension between Michael Brennan's Free State troops and the local IRA created a powder keg in Limerick, ready to explode and ignite civil war. Captain Hurley, the quartermaster of the IRA's Mid Limerick brigade, organised his own republican force using Volunteers under his command to attack Michael Brennan's Free State troops and reclaim the areas of the city they had occupied. Limerick city was part of the area controlled by the 2nd Western division under Ernie O'Malley's command. As soon as the Mid Limerick brigade discovered that Michael Brennan's Free State troops had occupied the two barracks, they sent a courier with word to O'Malley to come and take control of the situation.

O'Malley went to Dublin and requested a team of IRA engineers with explosives to be sent to Limerick for an attack on the castle barracks but Rory O'Connor denied his request in an attempt to halt the slide into civil war. O'Malley protested that if the IRA did not act in Limerick the Free State army would occupy all the important military barracks in Dublin, Athlone and Limerick and would have the military advantage; in short the Free State army would have won the war before it even began. But without O'Connor's approval, engineers and explosives, O'Malley's attack on the Free State-held barracks in Limerick would be bound to fail and he returned to Limerick to await developments.

Neither Michael Brennan's nor Ernie O'Malley's forces were prepared to concede control of the city and as the situation grew more fraught the outbreak of war in Limerick seemed inevitable. The situation escalated as both the IRA and Free State troops continued to commandeer hotels and other large buildings in the city as barracks. A small force of British troops – mainly RIC and Black and Tans – still remained in four of the city's RIC barracks awaiting the order to withdraw but were still uncertain of who they were to hand over these barracks to when the orders came. The situation in Limerick was becoming critical for the authority of the Provisional Government and Arthur Griffith was urging the Free State army to attack the IRA's positions and take control of the entire city no matter what the implications. However, the IRA in the city and throughout the country still held the military advantage and Richard Mulcahy ruled out any prospect of a Free State attack when he received Michael Brennan's report on the strength of the IRA in Limerick city. Mulcahy's only option was to open negotiations with the IRA and avoid open warfare until his troops were in a stronger military position and could mount an offensive at the time of the Free State army's choosing.

In Dublin, Liam Lynch, the commander of the 1st Southern division of the IRA, and Oscar Traynor, commander of the Dublin brigade, were called to a meeting at the Free State army's new headquarters at Beggars Bush barracks. As a result, Lynch and Traynor travelled to Limerick and negotiated a solution to the stand-off. The four RIC barracks in the city still occupied by RIC and Black and Tans and the evacuated military barracks were handed over to Limerick Corporation. The military barracks were to be garrisoned by a small IRA force under Liam Lynch's command while Michael Brennan's troops would withdraw back to East Clare and Galway. When it became clear that the majority of the IRA were opposed to the treaty Richard Mulcahy used the situation in Limerick city as an excuse to cancel the IRA's army convention. In response Liam Mellows and Rory O'Connor called their own army convention for 26 March attended by 233 IRA officers from all over Ireland representing fifty-two of the seventy-three brigades throughout the country, or about 75 per cent of the IRA's Volunteers. At this convention the IRA rejected the treaty and set up their own sixteen-man executive to control the organisation.

On 7 March the Free State government announced the formation of the civic guards, their new police force to replace the RIC. Patrick Brennan from Clare was appointed head of the new force. Some 129 former members of the RIC joined the civic guards, including a number of Black and Tans.

In February the former barracks at Broadford was taken over by Free State troops from Michael Brennan's 1st Western division. On Friday 21 April local Volunteers raided and captured the barracks. At 6 p.m. the following Sunday Free State troops surrounded the barracks and demanded that the IRA garrison inside surrender. When they refused, the Free State's soldiers attacked the barracks and re-captured it, except for one room still occupied by William O'Brien and other republicans. After a brief firefight the republicans realised that their situation was hopeless and agreed to end their resistance and leave the barracks after a ceasefire was arranged with the Free State troops who now held the rest of the barracks. As O'Brien led his men out of the room carrying his revolver the Free State soldiers attempted to disarm him by force and shot him dead during the struggle.

On 14 April, Rory O'Connor led a large force of Volunteers into the centre of Dublin where they commandeered the Four Courts and a number of other strategic buildings. This was a direct challenge to the authority of the provisional Free State government but Michael Collins and the other Free State leaders ignored the challenge. Collins still needed to prevent the outbreak of civil war while recruitment continued for the new Free State army which was mainly composed of raw recruits, former pro-treaty units of the IRA and ex-British army soldiers. Recruitment and training for the Free State army went ahead at a rapid pace and two months later it contained 8,000 well armed and well paid professional troops. Desmond Fitzgerald made a request that the Free State army would absorb the British regiments recruited in Ireland. This was refused by the British government but many members of these regiments joined the Free State army when their regiments were disbanded.

On 23 April ex-RIC Sergeant John Gunn was shot dead in Ennis. Initially the IRA were suspected of the shooting, but there were persistent rumours in the town that Gunn was shot by worried former British collaborators because he knew exactly who these people were and what information they had given during the war.

On the political front de Valera was in a difficult situation. In an attempt to unify the anti-treaty movement he formed a new political party called Cumann na Poblachta. Rory O'Connor declared that he was 'no more prepared to stand for de Valera than for the treaty'. In February de Valera made an agreement with Collins to postpone the elections to the Free State parliament in Dublin until June. This caused friction between Griffith and Collins, but Collins calmed his fears by claiming that he was attempting to win de Valera and Cumann na Poblachta over to their side. Collins planned to change the constitution of the Free State just enough to win over de Valera's anti-treaty supporters and instructed the lawyers who were drawing up the constitution to leave out all references to the king and the oath. To avoid deepening the split de Valera and Collins worked out a joint pact for the June elections under which both the pro-treaty and anti-treaty factions would fight the election jointly and form a coalition government afterwards.

Despite the signing of the treaty, sectarian violence continued to flare up in Northern Ireland. Tensions increased as the republican communities living in the six counties continued to protest their inclusion against their will in a unionist-dominated sectarian state. As economic depression took hold early in 1922 unemployment rose sharply and as competition for jobs increased unionist mobs supported by the RUC and B-Specials led sectarian raids on housing estates and workplaces in Belfast in an attempt to drive Catholics and so-called 'rotten Prods' – Protestant republicans and Protestants married to Catholics – from their jobs and homes. Craig's government strengthened the hand of the sectarian rioters attacking northern republicans by introducing the 'Special Powers Act' in April which was used to increase the number of B-Specials in the six counties by recruiting former UVF members. The number of British army soldiers in Northern Ireland was also rapidly increased and they were placed under the command of the rabidly sectarian ex-British army commander Sir Henry Wilson who used these forces and the Special Powers Act exclusively against northern republican and Catholic communities. Though angered by these developments Michael Collins was still eager to prevent the outbreak of civil war until the Free State army was ready to take action. He made an arrangement with the IRA to send arms to the six counties to protect republican areas from further sectarian attack.

In June, Griffith and Collins presented the new Free State constitution to the British government for approval. As it contained no oath or references to the king it was immediately rejected by Winston Churchill and Lloyd George who threatened to scrap the entire treaty and impose an economic blockade on Ireland unless these were included. The constitution was hurriedly rewritten to include these and Michael Collins returned to Ireland on 16 June only two days before the elections to announce that the election pact with de Valera and the anti-treaty candidates was off. Despite Michael Collins' promise that the final draft of the constitution would be published at least ten days before the election, this did not happen until election day itself. As a result the majority of voters outside Dublin had no chance to read and consider it before voting on its contents.

Cumann na mBan's unequivocal stand against the treaty and the fact that all six female TDs had voted against it meant that many women voters were likely to vote republican and could hold the balance of power in the election. Arthur Griffith and the pro-treaty TDs made every effort to prevent women getting an equal right to vote and breaking their hold on power, with the result that only men aged over twenty-one and women over thirty were allowed to vote. Sinn Féin TD Kate O'Callaghan raised the issue on 2 March calling for the rights of women as equal citizens enshrined in the 1916 Proclamation of the Irish Republic to be enacted, and proposed that all women over twenty-one should be allowed to vote in the upcoming election. Griffith and his pro-treaty supporters angrily dismissed O'Callaghan's arguments as 'a trick on the Irish people' and voted against her motion with the result that thousands of women were unable to vote and express their opinion on the treaty. At the same time the generation of young men under twenty-one who had been considered old enough to fight and die for their country were not considered old enough to vote in its elections. In addition, many of the veterans of the war against the British who were old enough to vote were not on the 1918 electoral register still in use in 1922, because to have registered to vote during the war would have been nearly impossible and certainly foolhardy for an IRA Volunteer or Sinn Féin member on the run, as it would have alerted the British forces to their whereabouts.

Less than 60 per cent of the electorate voted. The pro-treaty candidates won fifty-eight seats, Sinn Féin (and Cumann na Poblachta) won thirty-four, Labour seventeen, the unionists four and independents and farmers' candidates fourteen. Of the 620,283 people who voted, 239,192 gave first preference votes to Free State candidates while

133,864 voted for the republicans. Therefore no party had an overall majority to form a government but the oath of allegiance effectively barred the thirty-four republicans who were elected from attending, thus ensuring a pro-treaty majority.

Since April, Winston Churchill had been demanding that Collins use the Free State army to dislodge the IRA from the Four Courts. On 22 June Sir Henry Wilson was assassinated in London on the orders of Collins in retaliation for Wilson's role in encouraging sectarian violence in Belfast. The British government were outraged by Wilson's killing and automatically assumed that Rory O'Connor and the IRA command in the Four Courts were responsible. They immediately sent orders to General Macready, commander of the remaining British forces in Dublin, to mount an attack on the Four Courts, which was guaranteed to restart the war between the British forces and the IRA. However, the next day, before Macready could begin the attack, Churchill withdrew the order and instead publicly demanded that Collins and the Free State government take action against the IRA in the Four Courts. On 27 June an IRA unit from the republican garrison in the building began commandeering motor vehicles to transport weapons northwards for an attack on the British forces in the six counties to restart the war against the British. Leo Henderson, the IRA officer leading this unit, was arrested by Free State forces. In retaliation the IRA arrested J.J. O'Connell, the deputy chief of staff of the Free State army. O'Connell's arrest gave Collins the excuse he needed to attack the Four Courts and allow him to claim he was acting on his own initiative rather than following the British government's orders. On 28 June the Free State army, acting on Collins' orders and armed with field artillery guns borrowed from the British army, issued an ultimatum to O'Connor and the Volunteers inside the Four Courts to leave the building by four o'clock that morning and surrender to the Free State troops outside. The IRA ignored the order. Ernie O'Malley was inside the Four Courts with Rory O'Connor when the Free State army's deadline arrived:

'Time's up,' said Rory, and as he spoke a machine gun from outside echoed across the night, to be answered by a shout from each of our sections. A heavy boom came next, and we knew artillery was being used; the crash of an 18-pound shell announced that those who stood in arms for an independent Ireland were to be attacked by some of their former comrades.

After months of careful negotiations and efforts to avoid open conflict, the first shots in the inevitable civil war had finally been fired.

The very first casualty of the war was IRA Volunteer Joseph Considine, from Clooney in County Clare. He was stationed inside the Four Courts with other members of the Mid Clare brigade when he was badly injured by the Free State army's opening barrage of fire on the building and died a few hours later in Jervis Street hospital. The IRA's position inside the four courts quickly became untenable as they were constantly raked by rifle and machine gun fire and the barrages from British field guns used by the Free State army. Trapped by the spreading fires inside the collapsing shell of a building the IRA garrison's leaders, Rory O'Connor and Joe McKelvey, finally decided that they had no option but to surrender. Both Liam Mellows and Ernie O'Malley wanted to continue the fight but they were out-ranked by the others and reluctantly agreed to the surrender.

On 30 June Ernie O'Malley led the IRA garrison out of the crumbling ruins of the Four Courts to surrender to their Free State attackers. Among the Free State soldiers who had attacked the Four Courts were a number of Claremen who had previously been IRA Volunteers during the war against the British. O'Malley recognised one of them from his time in Clare four years earlier and approached him:

Among the officers was a Clareman. I walked over to him. He was in uniform and carried a captain's tabs. 'Hello. I did not expect to see you here.' He looked confused and ashamed. 'We were rushed into it. We did not realise what we were doing and we were into it before we knew. I'm sorry.'

O'Malley shook hands with him before rejoining his men as a prisoner of the Free State. The Free State captain O'Malley had recognised may have been Ignatius O'Neill, a former commandant with the IRA's Mid Clare brigade. If this is correct then tragically O'Neill had commanded the artillery crew that had opened the attack on the Four Courts that began the Civil War and killed his former comrade Joseph Considine.

The IRA in Dublin continued to fight on for another week, but bad communications, their overly defensive tactics and the superior Free State munitions and fire power supplied by the British government meant that a republican defeat in the city was inevitable. One of the last IRA units to surrender in Dublin was stationed at the organisation's headquarters at the Hammond hotel in O'Connell Street. Before the surrender de Valera and a number of other IRA officers escaped from the building and made their way to the Mount Street area. Cathal Brugha ordered the remaining IRA Volunteers under his command to surrender but refused to do so himself. Brugha drew his revolver and charged from the building; he was immediately shot down by the Free State soldiers and died of his wounds that night. With Brugha's death, the fighting in Dublin city centre effectively came to an end but the conflict was already spreading to the rest of the country.

During the fighting in the capital the Free State government was wary of how its acceptance of British military aid and munitions to crush the IRA would be seen by the public. By the time the fighting ended in Dublin a new song mocking the Free State was already growing in popularity on the streets of the city. It ran:

> England gave the orders
> And she gave the cannon too
> And Michael Collins sent the boys in green
> To murder Cathal Brugha.

The Free State government quickly took action to prevent any such criticism of their actions appearing in print. The night the Four Courts was attacked the Free State cabinet summoned all newspaper editors and their representatives to a meeting and informed them that all newspaper articles relating to the military and political situation were now subject to censorship, or complete withdrawal, by a Free State-appointed censor. On 7 July the Free State government decided that captured IRA Volunteers and republican activists would now be charged with criminal offences and denied prisoner-of-war status. The Free Staters who had previously suffered hunger strikes and prison protests with their former comrades in the IRA, during the fight against the British authorities' attempts to criminalise republicans, were now adopting the same British tactics.

Now that republican prisoners were to be automatically condemned as criminals by the Free State, all that remained was for the establishment newspapers to play their role by attempting to convince the Irish people that the IRA were criminals, murderers and thieves with no political principles or ideology. The *Irish Independent*, which had led a public campaign in 1916 to have James Connolly executed and had wholeheartedly supported the treaty in a complete abandonment of the principal of a fair and neutral press, now went far beyond the Free State's press guidelines and regulations, and denounced the IRA as murderers, looters, bank robbers and criminals. The day after the fighting ended in Dublin the *Free State Journal* editorialised:

> To save a Republic which never existed in fact, a number of young men, partly blustering bullies, partly fanatics honest with the terrible honesty of a monomania, partly boys with no mind but for an escapade, broke away from the army of the nation, set themselves up as a directing force of the country to plunder and destroy, threaten and lie, uniting all their diverse qualities of bravado, unreason and irresponsibility to render any government impossible but theirs.

Harsh words written by Free State men who only months earlier had pledged their lives for the Irish Republic and were now denouncing their comrades who refused to abandon their republican principals. What a difference six months of power had made, proof if ever it was needed that power corrupts.

As the Civil War began, the IRA held the military advantage over the Free State army, having the advantage of superior numbers outside Dublin with a total fighting strength throughout Ireland of approximately 12,900 Volunteers, mostly experienced veterans of the war against the British, motivated by their republican ideals and armed with 7,000 rifles. In addition, the republicans had almost complete control of Munster and the entire west coast, where each IRA unit was deeply connected with the local area and its people and having all the military advantages this entailed. By contrast, the Free State army consisted of 8,000 men confined largely to the Dublin area and the midlands, areas which were unfamiliar to many of its troops and commanders. The Free State army's only real advantage was in terms of weaponry and British support. By July 1922 the British government had supplied the Free State army with 11,900 rifles, seventy-nine Lewes machine guns, 4,200 revolvers, 3,500 hand grenades, armoured cars and artillery. If the war continued for any length of time the republicans would have to rely on weapons seizures for supplies while the Free State army would be supplied regularly with as much weaponry as they needed by the British; it was also likely that the longer the war continued the more unpopular the fighting would become. For these reasons the IRA needed to end the war with a quick and decisive victory over the Free State army.

The IRA made the fatal mistake of retreating from Dublin as the fighting ended; this left the capital under the control of the Free State government, allowing them to present themselves to the world as the lawful government in control of Ireland. The fighting started in a haphazard fashion throughout the country as former friends and comrades who had been living in the vain hope that civil war could be avoided now committed themselves to the battle. The IRA's military capacity was greatly disorganised and weakened by the Four Courts surrender, during which three of the organisation's most capable leaders – Rory O'Connor, Liam Mellows and Tom Barry – were captured. The IRA in the six counties were crushed between British, unionist and Free State forces and were unable to mount anything more than a token resistance to either the unionist or Free State governments in support of the Republic. In the

Free State-controlled areas of Dublin and Leinster the IRA were unable to operate and most IRA Volunteers fled to republican controlled areas. The remainder were reorganised by Ernie O'Malley, who had escaped after the Four Courts surrender on 30 June and began mounting small-scale sniping operations and ambushes in the Dublin area against the Free State army. Liam Lynch and Liam Deasy had managed to escape from the Dublin fighting and Lynch was appointed chief of staff of the IRA. Lynch ordered all IRA Volunteers to return to their command areas to prepare for all-out war. Acting on Lynch's orders the IRA began consolidating their positions in the rest of Ireland and formed a strongly defended frontier stretching from Limerick city in a south-easterly direction all the way to Waterford. The area south-west of this line became known as the 'Munster Republic'. The republican control of the rest of Munster and Connaught was interrupted by the presence of garrisons of Free State soldiers in some of the larger towns in parts of Clare, Galway, Roscommon and Leitrim.

As soon as word of the shelling of the Four Courts spread to the country, IRA units from Cork and Kerry began marching northwards through west Limerick towards Limerick city. By this time the 400 troops in the city from the 1st Western and 4th Southern divisions of the Free State army commanded by Michael Brennan and O'Hannigan were far outnumbered by the 700 IRA Volunteers under Liam Lynch's command. Brennan and O'Hannigan met frequently with Lynch and held talks to arrange another agreement to prevent the outbreak of fighting in Limerick city. Brennan's Free State troops in East Clare and south-west Galway were badly armed and it was obvious to him that if the IRA captured Limerick city they would be free to march northwards and capture these areas:

> The holding of Limerick was the holding of the whole south and west … My whole fright was that Lynch would attack me before the guns turned up, because we couldn't last. I had to keep him talking to keep him from attacking. We met and we met altogether about a dozen times. We used to meet in the presbytery of the Augustinian church where we argued and argued.

As soon as rumours reached O'Duffy at Free State army GHQ in Dublin that Brennan and O'Hannigan were negotiating a settlement with Lynch he despatched Diarmuid MacManus, a high-ranking Free State officer, to Limerick ordering him to prevent any further peace talks taking place and to report back immediately on the situation there. When he arrived, MacManus quickly realised why Brennan and O'Hannigan were trying to negotiate an agreement with Lynch. The day before the agreement was signed MacManus wrote to O'Duffy in Dublin warning: 'Unless rifles and armoured cars arrive within twenty-four hours of now, 10 a.m. 6/7/22 we will be in very grave danger of disaster.' MacManus ordered some limited offensive action against the IRA but did not prevent Brennan and O'Hannigan signing a truce agreement with Lynch on 7 July. The agreement called for a meeting of the leading military commanders from both armies 'in the interests of a united Ireland, and to save our country from utter destruction'. The agreement also set out which buildings the Free State army could occupy in the city and that the IRA would withdraw to their barracks.

Liam Lynch believed that the Limerick truce was a major success for the republicans, that it would lead to republican control of Munster and prevent the spread of the civil war he had fought so hard to avoid. According to Paddy Coughlin, an IRA Volunteer from Michelstown in Cork: 'Liam Lynch did not want a war'. Lynch also hoped that his actions would take the three Free State military commanders involved in the negotiations – Brennan, O'Hannigan and Seán Mac Eoin – out of the war.

Troops were already marching on Limerick, but they were Free State army soldiers sent from Dublin via Galway and East Clare to reinforce the Free State garrison for a planned offensive. They arrived in Limerick on 11 July, and Michael Brennan immediately sent word to Lynch that the agreement was off, claiming that the IRA had shot a Free State soldier and thereby broken the agreement. Brennan had given his solemn word to Lynch about the agreement and broke it again as soon as it was to his advantage. Low-intensity fighting broke out between the Free State army and the IRA as both sides continued to erect barricades and reinforce their makeshift barracks. As soon as Lynch realised what had happened he saw that the Free Staters had won a major victory, changing the whole nature of the war through their dishonesty. He wrote to Ernie O'Malley: 'The second agreement reached at Limerick has been broken by the enemy … I believe … we will eventually have to destroy all our posts and have to operate as of old in columns.'

With the military situation looking increasingly bleak for the IRA and with no political leadership coming from the scattered and disorganised Sinn Féin TDs in the Dáil, the republicans tried to show leadership and rally the people of Ireland by implementing new social policies in the areas under their control. Liam Lynch, the IRA chief of staff, was not particularly interested in radical politics, so two of the socialist republican IRA leaders – Liam Mellows and Ernie O'Malley – tried to implement the new campaign. O'Malley wrote to Lynch urging:

> The need for a Democratic Republican constitution is felt and I believe it would get the workers' [support] … Under the Republic all industry will be controlled by the state for the workers' and farmers' benefit; all transport, railways, canals etc. will be operated by the state – the Republican State – for the benefit of workers and farmers; all banks will be operated by the State for the benefit of industry and agriculture; all loans, mortgages etc. with the lands of the aristocracy will be seized and divided among those who can and will operate it for the owners' benefit.

O'Malley's despatch was based on his correspondence with Mellows, who was in Mountjoy prison. Mellows had written:

> We should certainly keep Irish Labour for the Republic; it will be possibly the biggest factor on our side. In our efforts now to win back support to the republic we are forced to recognise, whether we like it or not, that the commercial interests – the so-called money and the gombeen men – are on the side of the Treaty. Because the treaty means imperialism and England. We are back to Tone and it is just as well relying on that great body of 'men of no property'. The 'stake in the country people' [the wealthy] were never with the Republic. They are not with it now

– and they will always be against it – until it wins! ... The position must be defined. FREE STATE = Capitalism and Industrialism: Empire. REPUBLIC = Workers: Labour.

When details of Mellows' and O'Malley's social programme were captured in a raid, they were immediately published in an attempt to portray the programme as a conspiracy to set up a communist dictatorship. The Free State government and its newspapers followed this claim by again denouncing the IRA as disorganised bands of criminals and fanatics led by mafia-style godfathers who were intent on ruining Ireland from end to end. Connie Neenan, an IRA veteran from Cork, put it bluntly: 'In the days before December we were saints and heroes, now we're burglars and bank robbers.'

In Clare the IRA were taking advantage of the absence of Michael Brennan and his Free State troops by launching attacks against Free State positions in the county. The fighting began on 6 July when a convoy of Free State troops commanded by John Joe Neylon found a barricade at Droichead na Gabhar blocking their route to Ennis. The Free State soldiers jumped down from their lorries to clear the way when they were fired on by a group of Volunteers waiting in ambush. After a running battle the Free Staters succeeded in routing the republicans and captured two of them, Captain F. Butler and Volunteer T. McNamara. Both were taken to the Home barracks in Ennis as prisoners where they went on hunger strike. The next day two lorries carrying Free State soldiers were ambushed by the IRA as they travelled towards Gort. The first managed to force its way through the ambush position but the second turned back towards the temporary barracks at the courthouse in Ennis where the Free Staters came under attack again from republican snipers.

On 15 July Michael Brennan, Seán Mac Eoin and Eoin O'Duffy held a conference with the officers of the Free State army's 1st Western division at the Queen's hotel in Ennis. Two Free State officers travelling to the conference by car, Captain Lynch and Lieutenant Roche, were sniped at by Volunteers. The bullets shattered the car's windscreen and one even struck the steering wheel; both men escaped unharmed. That night the IRA launched an offensive against Free State-held barracks and positions in towns and villages throughout the West and Mid Clare brigade areas. The republicans began by destroying the bridges around Ennis to prevent Free State troops from Limerick rushing to the area. They had already destroyed bridges at Droichead na Gabhar and Claureen and were preparing to detonate a mine under Latoon Bridge on the main Ennis to Limerick road when they were surprised by a company of Free State soldiers and withdrew leaving the bridge intact.

After dark the IRA began attacks on Free State barracks in the west of the county. They succeeded in capturing the towns of Kilrush and Kilkee but not without losses. During the attack on Kilrush IRA Volunteer Patrick O'Dea was shot dead while fighting against the Free State army and two days afterwards on 17 July an IRA captain, Seán O'Halloran, was killed fighting against Free State troops at Bunahowe between Gort and Ennis. To hold this ground the IRA needed to make travel to the county difficult and keep Clare isolated from Free State forces in Limerick, Dublin and the midlands. The republicans began tearing up tracks and removing wooden sleepers on railway lines throughout Clare and a week later no trains were travelling to or from Ennis on either the West Clare or Great Southern Railways.

The Crusheen IRA company were desperately short of arms and explosives needed to attack the garrison of Free State soldiers stationed at the former local RIC barracks. The IRA in Galway had captured a small brass cannon, used by the British army during the Crimean War. The IRA had used cannon stolen from Ross Castle to attack the Rathmore RIC barracks in Kerry during July 1920. The Crusheen company decided to use the cannon from Galway for the same purpose. It was swiftly named 'Peggy' and after it arrived in Crusheen, Jim Guinnane, a gunsmith from Ennis, was called in to take charge of maintaining and firing the gun. 'Peggy' was mounted on an improvised gun carriage and brought to the top of a hill overlooking the barracks. But when primed for her first shot, the wheels on the gun carriage had not been properly secured, and the first shot sailed high over the barracks. The cannon was adjusted and the second shot hit its target, crashing through the roof of the building. However, the republicans were unable to get the cannon to fire a third shot despite repeated attempts, and the attack was called off. Years later the Volunteers involved heard from members of the Free State garrison who had been inside that the second shot that hit the barracks terrified them so much they were ready to surrender if a third shot had been fired.

Despite the IRA's activities in Clare, the Free State army's attention was still focused on Limerick, where they needed to strengthen their position before they could press home their attacks on IRA positions in the city with any confidence, or launch a counter-offensive against the IRA in Clare. Eoin O'Duffy led a large convoy of Free State troops, supported by one Rolls Royce armoured car, two Lancia cars, four military lorries and ten Lewes machine guns, which captured Killaloe. O'Duffy established his field headquarters at the Lakeside Hotel before sending the main force of his troops south to Limerick.

The Free State army's attack on the IRA positions in Limerick city was launched at 5.30 p.m. on 19 July using 18-pound artillery guns borrowed from the British army to shell the republican-held Strand barracks. After ten days of fighting in the city the IRA burned the barracks they still held and retreated to the Limerick countryside. Though O'Duffy failed in his objective of preventing the Volunteers from retreating from the city, their withdrawal meant that the Free State army now controlled the Shannon estuary and could patrol Clare's coastline and commandeer boats to be used for transporting men and munitions. Though the county's isolated geographical position had aided guerrilla warfare during the war against the British, it now meant that the IRA in Clare were firmly cut off from their comrades in the 'Munster Republic'. Once Limerick city was firmly under the control of the Free State army, Michael Brennan's 1st Western division turned their attention back to reversing the IRA's advances in Clare.

On 23 July Free State soldiers from Limerick arrived in Ennis to reinforce their troops stationed in the Home barracks and occupied the County Club, Ennis Club and Masonic Hall. They began a series of attacks on republican positions, quickly followed by wide-scale raids to arrest known Volunteers. Having established their barracks in the Ennis area, another group of Free State troops occupied Porterstown House, a former RIC barracks south of the bridge on the River Fergus. The Free Staters at Porterstown House immediately sent to Limerick for artillery to mount an attack on the IRA garrison in Corofin workhouse. Shortly before the artillery was due to arrive the republicans were warned about the imminent attack. Knowing they could not hold out against the larger force of Free State troops they burned the workhouse on 24 July and retreated into the countryside to prevent the Free State army from using it as a barracks. The East Clare brigade attacked a Free State army barracks at Meelick the same night but failed to capture it.

With the Free State army in almost complete control of the county, the IRA in Clare resorted to guerrilla tactics to fight against them. On 1 August Peadar O'Loughlin died of tuberculosis; the divisional adjutant of the First Western division of the IRA, he had been attempting to regroup Volunteers for a counter-attack on the Free State troops who had captured Corofin. Free State army raids in Miltown Malbay captured eighteen Volunteers who were imprisoned in Ennistymon barracks. Volunteer Thomas Guinnane was seriously wounded when he tried to escape from a Free State army patrol in Clarecastle. A Free State army officer, Sergeant Neville, was attacked by the IRA in the town, but escaped uninjured having fired fifteen shots in a running gun battle through the streets.

On 6 August the IRA's West Clare brigade attacked the Free State garrison in Kildysart barracks. The republicans crept towards the barracks to plant a mine against the end of the building, but it exploded prematurely throwing one Volunteer, Tom Howard, off the roof and seriously wounding Volunteer John O'Gorman and Lieutenant John McSweeney. The startled Free State soldiers inside the building immediately opened withering fire on the republicans, until Michael Falahee, vice-commandant of the 1st battalion of the West Clare brigade, set fire to several haystacks in the adjoining lawn, creating a thick blinding smokescreen that allowed the IRA to withdraw safely. O'Gorman and McSweeney were immediately taken to Ennis hospital for treatment. O'Gorman succumbed to his injuries and died on 11 August. McSweeney died of his wounds later that month.

On 19 August the Free State army barracks at Clarecastle was attacked by forty members of the IRA's Mid Clare brigade. Their attack continued, using hand grenades and rifle fire, for over two hours until the IRA withdrew as Free State troops arrived from Ennis and attempted to surround and capture them. Volunteers withdrawing from the attack at Clarecastle ran into a party of Free State soldiers near Ballynacally but managed to escape after a short engagement.

In the north of the county the IRA ambushed a car with three Free State soldiers in it who were travelling between Barefield and Crusheen. The driver was wounded in the attack and lost control of the car which careered into the ditch and overturned. The soldiers in the car survived with minor wounds but were relieved of their arms and ammunition by their attackers. Two cars of Free State troops were attacked by the IRA at Newmarket on Fergus on 21 August. The next day another Free State convoy travelling from Ennistymon to Moy was attacked and sniped at four times on its journey. That evening the IRA killed Patrick Kelly, a Free State soldier stationed at Kilrush.

By the end of the month the Free State army were still firmly in control of the county despite the IRA's attacks and the civic guards now occupied barracks in Ennis, Ennistymon, Lisdoonvarna, Sixmilebridge, Tulla, Kildysart, Kilkee and Killaloe.

On 22 September the body of Volunteer Michael Neville from Lisdoonvarna was found at Killester in Dublin. He had been a member of the Dublin city brigade and was murdered while held in custody in Oriel House by members of the Free State criminal investigation department of the civic guards, better known as the 'Oriel House Gang'.

On 12 August Arthur Griffith died of a brain haemorrhage; ten days later Michael Collins was shot dead during an IRA ambush in Cork. They were replaced by William Cosgrave as head of the Free State government and Richard Mulcahy as commander in chief of the Free State army. On 9 September the Free State Dáil or Provisional

Parliament of Southern Ireland was established. The Irish Labour Party's seventeen elected members offered token opposition to the Free State government inside the southern parliament. The so-called 'democrats' of the Free State government quickly passed Emergency Powers legislation which gave secret military courts the power of life and death over every civilian and republican prisoner in the country. When the leader of the Irish Labour Party, Thomas Johnson, realised the draconian powers that the Free State government were calling for, he protested that the parliament was being asked to vote for a military dictatorship. When Richard Mulcahy replied that only snipers, bombers and assassins had reason to fear the bill, Johnson asked him if the IRA prisoners would be treated as prisoners-of-war. Cosgrave replied: 'No, certainly not.' It was a war crime to execute prisoners-of-war, so the Emergency Powers legislation transformed the illegal into the legal. The legislation came into effect on 15 October 1922. The passing of this legislation was quickly followed by a 'last chance' amnesty in October and after this any IRA Volunteer who took up arms against the Free State could be sentenced to death and executed by a military court. The Free State army now held limitless powers of arrest and could imprison anyone within the Free State without any enquiry, accusation or trial.

A week after the Free State politicians passed the Emergency Powers legislation, Cardinal Logue and the Catholic archbishops and bishops issued a pastoral letter in support of the Free State, read at all masses on Sunday 22 October and published just as widely by the Free State authorities for propaganda value. It condemning republicans as criminals, thieves and murderers in exactly the same way the bishops had condemned republicans during the struggle for freedom waged against the British.

The pastoral, composed by a group that had repudiated the authority of Dáil Éireann elected by a majority of the Irish people in 1918, now asserted the moral authority of majority rule under the Free State government as a tenet of Christian morality. Republicans were put under general excommunication and refused Catholic sacraments for as long as the war continued. This pastoral from the bishops pressured some devout Catholics within the IRA to walk away from the fight but the majority of the republican forces resented the corrupt use of religious authority for political purposes and simply ignored the Catholic Church's ruling.

Meanwhile the republican resistance against the Free State continued in Clare. On 6 October the IRA ambushed a Free State army convoy at Tullycrine. The attack began as an ambush that afternoon but developed into a running battle which continued until darkness, during which time IRA Lieutenant Michael J. Keane from Gortglass was killed. On 7 November Volunteer John Sharry, who had been shot by the Black and Tans outside Moymore church during the war against the British forces, finally died of his wounds. Later that month two Volunteers, William Campbell and John Grady, both from Cooraclare, mounted a sniping attack on a Free State army patrol travelling by lorry through Dromelihy. The Free State soldiers hastily returned fire as they sped away from the scene of the attack. Apparently Campbell and Grady's rate of rifle fire was so rapid that the soldiers thought they were being ambushed by a much larger force and immediately rushed away to report the attack and the presence of an IRA flying column in the area. A short time later, Campbell and Volunteer Thomas Killeen from Miltown Malbay attacked a party of Free State troops travelling by train along the West Clare Railway. Campbell and Killeen escaped uninjured, but by now it was clear that the railway was being used extensively by the Free State forces to transport troops, prisoners and supplies. So the West Clare brigade of the IRA destroyed the railway bridge at Doonbeg, temporarily halting the Free State army's activities in the area. At the end of the month Frank Barrett reported to IRA headquarters: 'As a result of the capture by the enemy of nearly all the best officers in the area, the organisation showed very grave signs of collapse; consequently all our energies are directed towards reorganising.'

On 17 November Kevin O'Higgins, the Free State Minister for Home Affairs and Justice, announced that four IRA Volunteers, Peter Cassidy, John Gaffney, James Fisher and Richard Twohig, were executed by the Free State army for unlawful possession of revolvers. The first the men's relatives heard of the executions was when copies of the following standard form arrived at their homes with the names of the dead men and other details written into the blank spaces:

> I am to inform you that .... was tried by .... That he was found guilty of .... and was sentenced to death. This sentence was executed on the morning of .... Respectfully Yours, ...

O'Higgins explained that the Free State cabinet chose four ordinary Volunteers for the first of the executions because: 'If we took some man who was outstandingly active ... the unfortunate dupes throughout the country might say that he was killed because he was a leader, because he was an Englishman, or because he combined with others to commit raids.'

O'Higgins' reference to 'an Englishman' is particularly important because the court-martial of the man the Free State government really wanted to kill, Erskine Childers, began on the same day. Arthur Griffith held a deep personal hatred of Childers, a committed republican, English Protestant and IRA leader who had been a troublesome thorn in the Free State government's side for some time. During the treaty debate when Childers had cornered Griffith with a difficult question about the treaty, Griffith refused to answer him and instead flew into a rage, replying: 'I refuse to answer any Englishman, any damned Englishman.' Because Arthur Griffith had refused to use stenographers to keep an official record of the treaty negotiations in London, Childers – 'that damned Englishman' – as the secretary for the Irish delegation was the only republican with an in-depth knowledge of the backroom deals and private conferences which had led to the signing of the treaty. Armed with this knowledge, Childers was a very dangerous opponent of the Free State politicians and he needed to be kept silent. So the Free State executed the four unknown young men on 17 November to cover up their vendetta against Childers and to condition the public for his execution.

Erskine Childers was executed on 24 November 1922, while his case was still under appeal, for possession of a .22 pistol which had been given to him for his personal security by Michael Collins a year earlier. In a final vile act of indignity one member of the firing squad, Lieutenant Murtagh, approached Childers' body after it had been placed in a coffin and fired his revolver at point blank range into the face of the corpse.

On Sunday 7 December the IRA assassinated Seán Hales, a member of the Free State government. Outraged, Richard Mulcahy sought revenge and went to the members of the Free State cabinet seeking their consent to execute four leading republicans, Rory O'Connor, Liam Mellows, Richard Barrett and Joe McKelvey, as an official reprisal for Hales' death. The four men had been held for months without trial, long before the Free State amnesty and Emergency Powers legislation had come into effect, and therefore were not eligible for execution under its terms. Each member of the Free State cabinet gave their consent for the executions without any debate. The next morning the four men were woken early and told that they would be executed within a few hours. Like the republican leaders shot by the British after the Easter Rising, the four IRA leaders were executed without the sacraments of their religion because the Catholic Church still sided with the rich and powerful against those who fought for the freedom of the Irish people. Liam Mellows spent the last hours of his life arguing with the prison's Catholic chaplain, who refused to give him confession or absolution until Mellows accepted the content of the bishops' pastoral and that republican resistance to the Free State authorities was a sin. Mellows refused to abandon his republican principals and died without receiving the Catholic sacraments. It is reported that the first volley only wounded Mellows. A second volley completed the task. The Catholic hierarchy was perturbed, though not by the murders. Their complaint was that the executions had been carried out on a Catholic feast day.

In January 1923 independent parties were busy trying to arrange peace talks to end the war, but these came to nothing. The IRA were losing the war but refused to consider compromise, despite a lack of supplies, low ammunition, dwindling numbers and the loss of public support. At the same time the Free State government's policy of official executions gained momentum as they came under pressure to finish the war before the summer and before the tide of Irish public opinion hardened against the state killings.

The new phase of executions began on 20 January when two members of the IRA's Mid Clare brigade, Commandant Con McMahon and Volunteer Patrick Hennessy, both from Clooney, were executed at Limerick jail. On the same morning ten other republican prisoners were executed by the Free State. On 16 January the Free State army had arrested McMahon and Hennessy with Seán Darcy, a member of the Cooraclare company of the IRA, and charged them with the destruction of Ardsollus railway station, burned by the IRA two days earlier. They were court-martialled by military tribunal in Limerick and found guilty of having illegal arms and ammunition and taking part in the destruction of the station. McMahon and Hennessy were executed without appeal. On 10 February 1923 Albert O'Brien from Kilfenora was accidentally shot dead by Volunteers near Lemanagh Castle; they had mistaken O'Brien for a Free State officer they were waiting in ambush for.

Patrick Buckley, the former member of the RIC who had joined the East Clare brigade of the IRA during the war against the British, moved back to his native Kerry after his life was threatened by his former comrades in the RIC during the truce. Having arrived home in Castleisland he volunteered for duty with the 3rd battalion of the Kerry brigade. In August 1922 after the Dublin Guards unit of the Free State army landed at Fenit, Buckley was captured and interned in Tralee.

When a series of republican victories caused heavy casualties, Free State troops resorted to a campaign of terror as brutal and cold-blooded as any atrocities the British forces had ever committed to break the republican resistance. On Wednesday 6 March Patrick Buckley, Stephen Fuller and seven other republican prisoners were taken from Tralee to Ballyseedy Cross, tied to a landmine and blown up by Free State soldiers. When the soldiers detonated the mine the blast blinded and deafened Stephen Fuller. The power of the explosion, which killed the two men he was tied to, had severed the ropes holding him and thrown him across the road into a ditch. As he lay at the bottom of the ditch, bloodied in ragged and burned clothes, he heard the faint sounds of gunfire and at least five grenades exploding as his hearing returned. The Free State army was attempting to make sure that there were no survivors from the explosion. The blast made such a gruesome mess of the men's bodies that the soldiers had no way of counting them or knowing that Stephen Fuller had survived and was crawling to safety over the fields. The soldiers shovelled the gory remains of the eight dead men into nine coffins and returned to their barracks for breakfast.

But for the fact that Stephen Fuller survived the blast, the truth of what happened that night at Ballyseedy Cross would probably never have been known. The Free State soldiers had prepared nine coffins and were intent on murdering nine men that night. Undoubtedly John Shanahan, a local Volunteer captured with some of the others killed at Ballyseedy, was originally selected as one of the prisoners to be murdered but his serious medical condition and ·collapse after repeated beatings at the hands of the Free State soldiers saved his life. The Free Staters needed a substitute and Patrick Buckley, who had defected from the RIC to join the East Clare brigade during the War of Independence, became the ninth prisoner.

On Monday 9 April a party of Free State soldiers raided houses in Inagh to capture known republicans. They surrounded the home of Mortimer Moloney at Cloontismara and surprised his two sons Martin and Thomas, both members of the IRA's Mid Clare brigade, who were unarmed. After they surrendered Martin was fatally wounded by one of the Free State soldiers; his brother Thomas was arrested and taken to Ennistymon. According to their father, Mortimer, Martin was murdered after surrendering:

My son went away about forty or fifty yards. I saw him standing at Michael Clune's yard with his hands up, and a few seconds afterwards I saw him fall after a shot had been fired. I went towards him when I saw him fall, and I found him lying on his back, and he told me he was shot. I saw two soldiers in the yard. I knew one of them, Stephen Foody, but not the other. My son said: 'That man Collins shot me.' The man named by him as Collins said: 'I did not shoot him. It was Foody shot him.' Foody said: 'I fired no shot at him.' My son said again: 'It was Collins shot me.' Nothing more was said, and three or four of us carried my son home and put him to bed, and after a while undressed him. We then sent for the priest and doctor, and he was attended by Fr Grace, CC, Inagh and Dr Hillery of Miltown Malbay. He was removed by an ambulance to Ennistymon hospital.

Martin Moloney died of his wound the next day.

By spring 1923 it was clear to most republicans that the war was over and that the Free State had won. De Valera and a number of senior IRA commanders were calling for an end to the war but Liam Lynch, the commander in chief of the IRA, wanted to fight on. After the fighting in Dublin, de Valera was made adjutant to Seán Moylan, IRA director of operations. De Valera remained an important figure but had no decision-making power. Frank Barrett of the Mid Clare brigade and now a member of the IRA leadership was arrested by the Free State army in Waterford on 10 April.

Liam Lynch refused to admit defeat. The Free State army officers' betrayal of trust in breaking the Limerick agreement at the start of the war meant that Lynch refused to put his trust in them again long enough for peace negotiations to begin. According to his comrade Liam Deasy, Lynch was ready to see the civil war through to its bloody conclusion:

> Liam Lynch remained adamant and would not entertain any suggestion of seeking terms. He was to the very end an idealist with the highest principles as his guide and it was not in his nature to surrender or to compromise. He ultimately gave his life for his principles. I have always felt that his promise to support the Four Courts garrison if they were attacked remained a sacred trust and the two broken treaties which he had signed in Limerick with Donnchadh O'Hannigan and Michael Brennan confirmed his determination that this would be a fight to the finish.

Lynch was killed during a running battle with Free State soldiers in the Knockmealdown mountains in Tipperary on 10 April and the more moderate Frank Aiken replaced him as commander in chief of the IRA.

Éamon de Valera sent out peace feelers to the Free State government to try and negotiate an end to the fighting but William Cosgrave refused to discuss any settlement or terms with the republicans. On 25 April Aiken announced an IRA ceasefire. There would be a complete cessation of activities and all hostilities against the Free State forces from 30 April. For the republicans the ceasefire was not a surrender; it was a pause in the struggle for the republic and they planned to resume the fight again at another time in the future when they had a better chance of success. For the Free State it was a victory and a chance to consolidate their hold on power.

Despite the republican ceasefire it was business as usual for the Free State authorities, who were intent on seeing their campaign of executions through to the bitter end. The IRA's ceasefire came too late to save the life of Volunteer Patrick O'Mahony, who was executed by the Free State army at Ennis jail on 26 April, the morning after the IRA ceasefire was announced. O'Mahony had been arrested with another Volunteer, J. O'Leary, after a Free State patrol was ambushed by the IRA in Carmody Street in Ennis on 21 April. One member of the patrol, Private Stephen Canty, was shot dead by IRA Volunteer Miko Casey. The following Monday the jury at the inquest into Canty's killing ruled: 'That Stephen Canty, Private in the National army, was unlawfully shot in Carmody Street on the night of 21 April 1923 by some persons unknown. From the evidence we further find that neither the prisoners O'Mahony or O'Leary could have fired the fatal shot.' Despite this verdict O'Mahony and O'Leary were found guilty at their courts-martial of being involved in Private Canty's killing and the illegal possession of revolvers. Both men were sentenced to death, O'Leary's sentence was commuted to ten years' imprisonment but O'Mahony was executed.

The next day Cumann na nGaedheal, a new political party, was formed by the members of the Free State government who up until then had simply traded under the title of pro-treaty Sinn Féin. Eoin McNeill, TD for Clare, was elected leader; his son, Volunteer Brian McNeill, was killed fighting on the republican side during the Civil War. On 2 May 1923, two days after the war ended, Christopher Quinn and William O'Shaughnessy were executed at Ennis jail. They had been arrested in Ennis on the day of Private Canty's shooting and charged with his killing. These two Claremen were the last republicans executed by the Free State during the Civil War, bringing the total number of official executions by the Free State to seventy-seven. This grim record far outweighed the twenty-four Irish republicans executed by the British during the period 1920–1 yet the policy of executions was repeatedly defended by the Free State government. William Cosgrave defended the actions of his government by again condemning republicans as mindless thugs and criminals, saying: 'They were dealing with the dregs of society, people who had no regard for life or property, or all that the people held dear.' His colleague Kevin O'Higgins later said: 'I stand by these seventy-seven executions and 777 more if they become necessary.' Though the Free State's official executions had ended, the unofficial murders continued for months afterwards. One of the most brutal was the murder of Noel Lemass, who was arrested by the civic guard on 3 July and tortured. He was never seen alive again. His mutilated body was found in the Dublin mountains on 12 October.

In the region of 1,500 died in the Civil War, including 350 IRA Volunteers, 730 Free State soldiers and 400 civilians. Some £47 million worth of damage was done and the cost to the Irish people was even higher as they were left bitterly divided for decades afterwards. Seventy-seven Volunteers were executed by the Free State army and another 113 were 'unofficially executed' or murdered.

Even though the war had ended the Free States jails were still full of republican prisoners. With 15,000 of the country's leading republican activists still in jail unable to canvass or vote in elections, the Free State government called a snap election in August. The Free State had passed more emergency legislation which allowed them to hold these prisoners indefinitely and were able to conduct their election campaign in full confidence of victory while they held their main political opposition in prison.

Despite Free State intimidation and arrest of Sinn Féin candidates, de Valera was determined to get to Ennis to address his constituents.

On 15 August a large crowd of republicans gathered at O'Connell Square in the town to hear de Valera speak. As soon as he stood on the platform, a company of Free State soldiers rushed into the square followed by an armoured car and began firing over the heads of the assembled crowd. Panic ensued and the crowd scattered in all directions, some of them suffering gunshot wounds. When the firing began, the Barrett sisters, Peg and Dell, both members of Cumann na mBan, who were standing on the platform near de Valera threw him to the floor and lay on top of him as a human shield. De Valera rose to his feet as the Free State soldiers surrounding the platform were preparing to fire a second volley and surrendered to them. He was taken to Limerick prison and interned.

Those 15,000 republicans still in prison would undoubtedly have been the most active election workers for Sinn Féin. The Free State army and civic guards were used to disrupt Sinn Féin's campaign machine. Electoral offices were raided, literature was seized, republicans putting up posters were beaten and Sinn Féin speakers were arrested. By polling day, eighty-seven of Sinn Féin's candidates were interned by the Free State. Despite the conditions the elections were held under, the republicans scored a minor success, winning an extra eight seats to give them a total of forty-four, compared to Cumann na nGaedheal's sixty-three seats out of a total of 153. Sinn Féin topped the poll in East Clare with both de Valera and Brian O'Higgins elected. Eoin McNeill was elected for Cumann na nGaedheal, Patrick Hogan for Labour and C. Hogan for the Farmers' Party.

Though the war and executions had ended, the death and suffering had not. Late in 1922 the republican prisoners in Limerick prison organised an escape attempt by digging a tunnel from the compound under the prison walls towards Shaws' bacon factory where a number of republican sympathisers were working. With the IRA in the city in complete disarray, members of Cumann na mBan from Limerick and Clare coordinated the preparations for the escape attempt on the outside. However, the Free State authorities in Limerick prison were well aware or the tunnel's existence and its progress and decided to allow the escape attempt to continue in order to capture their supporters on the outside. The night of the planned escape, Free State soldiers arrested seven Cumann na mBan women waiting outside the prison to help the escaping republican prisoners, including twenty-four-year-old Annie Nan Hogan, the captain of the Cratloe unit of Cumann na mBan.

Annie Hogan was interned without trial in Kilmainham jail. Conditions in the women's wing of the prison were very overcrowded at the time and the female republican prisoners went on hunger strike in March 1923 for better conditions and prisoner-of-war status. At the time the cells were packed and some of the girls who were interned were as young as fourteen. Not only did the Free State censor ban press reports of the women's plight and hunger strike, but the women also met with outright condemnation from the Catholic Church. When the practising Catholics among the hunger striking prisoners attended mass they found that the ordinary criminal prisoners were allowed to receive communion while they were refused the sacrament and lambasted with political sermons from the prison chaplain.

If one of the republican women attempted to have her confession heard or receive communion, she first had to accept the content of the Catholic bishops' pastoral which declared that opposition to the Free State government was a crime and a sin. None of them would submit to this, though only a few refused to attend mass and stopped practising the Catholic faith. The rest debated the Church's blind support for the Free State with the priests who came to visit them but this was completely in vain. During one of these debates when Eithne Coyle challenged the bishops' political stance, the priest told her that the bishops were always right. She retorted by asking if the bishops were right when they burned Joan of Arc and the priest became so angry he almost hit her.

On Monday 30 April Mary MacSwiney and Kate O'Callaghan were on their twenty-fifth day of hunger strike when the female republican prisoners heard that eighty-one of them were to be transferred to the North Dublin Union. Normally the women would have welcomed the transfer out of the squalid conditions at Kilmainham but they were anxious about the health of these two women and refused to leave the prison until the hunger strikers were released. The republican women were locked in their cells until 10.20 p.m. that night when Kate O'Callaghan was released in an effort to end the women's protest.

At midnight Free State soldiers and members of the civic guards, supported by women from Cumann na Saoirse, the Free State women's organisation made up of former members of Cumann na mBan (better known to republicans afterwards as Cumann na Searchers) rushed onto the top landing of the prison where the republican women were being held. They began dragging the Cumann na mBan and Irish Citizen Army women down the stairs to ground level; some who put up a fight were actually thrown down the flights of stairs by the Free State soldiers. The women fought tooth and nail for over five hours, during which many of them were stripped, beaten and sexually assaulted before they finally lost the battle and seventy women including Annie Hogan were taken to the North Dublin Union.

Eventually the hunger strike was called off when it became obvious that the Free State authorities were prepared to see the republicans die rather than give in to their demands. Unfortunately this development was too late to save Annie Hogan. She was released in September 1923 but her health was broken after her term in prison and she died of the long-term effects of her hunger strike four months later.

In autumn 1923 there were still 15,000 republicans interned in filthy overcrowded conditions in jails, internment camps, courthouse cellars, army barracks, workhouses and prison ships. In September the new governor of Mountjoy prison attempted to revoke the few privileges given to the republican prisoners in his charge, sparking a fierce resistance from the IRA Volunteers inside the prison and a new battle between republicans and the Free State government. Following the suppression of a prisoner riot in Mountjoy by hundreds of Volunteers, they resorted to a mass hunger strike on 13 October for unconditional release. The previous protests for prisoner-of-war status or better conditions seemed an insufficient reason for so many Volunteers to risk their lives on hunger strike because the war had finished five months before. When the hunger strike began about 400 republicans refused food but the strike quickly spread to other prisons and internment camps until there were nearly 8,000 prisoners on hunger strike at the protest's height.

The Free State government refused to yield and the heavily censored press gave the hunger strike little or no coverage until its final stages. The huge number of men taking part in the strike practically ensured its failure because it made it more difficult to keep discipline among such a large group of men and only a few republican prisoners had the courage and ability to endure a prolonged hunger strike. With hundreds of prisoners abandoning the strike each day, the government was able to claim that it was a disastrous failure for the republicans. The strike's original leaders realised their situation was hopeless and ended their protest on 23 November after forty-one days without food and the deaths of three Volunteers. No concessions were won from the Free State.

The Catholic Church used the strike as another opportunity to show its support for the status quo. During the hunger strike Bishop Fogarty, while on a visit to Miltown Malbay, had stepped down from the altar at the beginning of mass and ordered out all the republicans present because he would not have anyone praying for republican prisoners in 'his' church. When the body of hunger striker Andy Sullivan was brought back to Cork for burial the local bishop refused to admit his funeral in any Catholic church in the diocese. During and immediately after the Civil War another four IRA Volunteers from Clare died of the effects of hunger strike. Captain Nicholas Hawes from Lisdoonvarna and Dan Killoury from Moymore, Ennistymon both died in 1922. Dan Crawford from Coore died after his release in October 1924 and Captain Patrick McNamara died in 1925 of broken health caused by his hunger strike and the harsh treatment he received in prison.

The Free State won the Civil War but it was a hollow and bloody victory; the IRA were finally defeated but as General 'Bloody' Maxwell, the man who had ordered the execution of the leaders of the 1916 Rising, observed, the Free State won 'by means far more drastic than any which the British government dared to impose during the worst period of the rebellion'.

Fifty-three republicans from Clare gave their lives in the fight for freedom during the War of Independence and Civil War for the impoverished downtrodden and oppressed. In the end what had it all been for?

Roll of Honour – Clare Republicans 1918–1925

IRA Volunteer John Ryan	Shot by RIC	1 Mar 1918
IRA Volunteer Thomas Russell	Murdered by British army	28 Mar 1918
IRA Volunteer Michael D'Arcy	Killed in action	19 Jan 1920
IRA Vice-Comdt Martin Devitt	Killed in action	24 Feb 1920
IRA Volunteer Michael Fahy	Accidental shooting	19 Mar 1920
IRA Volunteer John O'Loughlan	Shot by British army and RIC	14 Apr 1920
IRA Volunteer Seán Breen	Killed in action	18 Apr 1920
IRA Volunteer Michael Malone	Accidental shooting	20 May 1920
IRA Volunteer Michael Conway	Killed in action	22 July 1920
IRA Staff Captain Joe McMahon	Accidental explosion	15 Aug 1920
IRA Volunteer Matthew Lynch	Died on active service	15 Aug 1920
IRA Volunteer Patrick Lehane	Fire started by RIC and Black and Tans	22 Sep 1920
IRA Volunteer Michael McMahon	Murdered by RIC Auxiliaries	16 Nov 1920
IRA Volunteer Alfred Rodgers	Murdered by RIC Auxiliaries	16 Nov 1920
IRA Volunteer Martin Gildea	Murdered by RIC Auxiliaries	16 Nov 1920
IRA Vice-Brigadier Peadar Clancy	Murdered by RIC Auxiliaries	21 Nov 1920
IRA Volunteer Michael McNamara	Murdered by RIC and Black and Tans	22 Dec 1920
IRA Volunteer William Shanahan	Murdered by British army	22 Dec 1920
IRA Volunteer Patrick Hassett	Accidental shooting	21 Mar 1921
IRA Captain Patrick White	Shot dead by prison sentry, Spike Island	May 1921
IRA Captain Patrick Gleeson	Killed in action	15 Jun 1921
IRA Captain Christopher McCarthy	Murdered by British army	15 Jun 1921
IRA Volunteer Thomas Healy	Died on active service	29 Jun 1921

IRA Volunteer Patrick Bourke	Effects of imprisonment	Aug 1921
IRA Volunteer Michael McGreal	Accidental shooting	17 Apr 1922
IRA Volunteer William O'Brien	Killed in action	24 Apr 1922
IRA Volunteer Joseph Considine	Killed in action	28 Jun 1922
IRA Volunteer Patrick O'Dea	Killed in action	15 July 1922
IRA Captain Seán O'Halloran	Killed in action	17 July 1922
IRA Adjutant Peadar O'Loughlin	Died on active service	1 Aug 1922
IRA Volunteer John O'Gorman	Killed in action	11 Aug 1922
IRA Lieutenant John McSweeney	Died of wounds received in action	Sep 1922
IRA Volunteer Michael Neville	Murdered by Free State forces	22 Sep 1922
IRA Lieutenant Michael Keane	Died on active service	1922
IRA Volunteer John Sharry	Died of wounds received in action	7 Nov 1922
IRA Volunteer Patrick Keating	Killed in action	Nov 1922
IRA Captain Nicholas Hawes	Effects of earlier hunger strike	1922
IRA Volunteer Dan Killoury	Effects of earlier hunger strike	1922
IRA Volunteer Peadar McInerney	Died on active service	1922
IRA Captain John Hourigan	Died on active service	1922
IRA Volunteer Thomas McNamara	Died on active service	1922
IRA Commandant Con McMahon	Executed by Free State army	20 Jan 1923
IRA Volunteer Patrick Hennessy	Executed by Free State army	20 Jan 1923
IRA Captain Martin Moloney	Murdered by Free State army	9 Apr 1923
IRA Volunteer Patrick O'Mahony	Executed by Free State army	26 Apr 1923
IRA Volunteer Christopher Quinn	Executed by Free State army	2 May 1923
IRA Volunteer William O'Shaughnessy	Executed by Free State army	2 May 1923
Cumann na mBan Annie Hogan	Effects of earlier hunger strike	Sep 1923

IRA Volunteer Dan Crawford	Effects of earlier hunger strike	Oct 1924
IRA Captain Patrick McNamara	Effects of earlier hunger strike	1925
IRA Volunteer J. Glynn	Died on active service	
IRA Volunteer Andrew Rynne	Killed in action	

Clare Civilians killed during the War of Independence

01 - 07 - 1919	Patrick Studdert	Shot by British army
14 - 02 - 1920	Michael Ensko	Struck by British army lorry
14 - 04 - 1920	Thomas Leary	Shot by British army and RIC
14 - 04 - 1920	Patrick Hennessy	Shot by British army and RIC
22 - 09 - 1920	Capt. Alan Lendrum	Shot by IRA
22 - 09 - 1920	P. J. Linnane	Murdered by RIC and Black and Tans
22 - 09 - 1920	Joseph Samon	Murdered by RIC and Black and Tans
22 - 09 - 1920	Tom Connole	Murdered by RIC and Black and Tans.
23 - 09 - 1920	Dan Lehane	Murdered by RIC and Black and Tans
01 - 10 - 1920	Seán Keane	Murdered by British army
21 - 10 - 1920	Charles Lynch	Murdered by British army
16 - 11 - 1920	Mike Egan	Murdered by RIC Auxiliaries
21 - 11 - 1920	Conor Clune	Murdered by RIC Auxiliaries
29 - 11 - 1920	Martin Walsh	
06 - 12 - 1920	Thomas Curtin	Murdered by RIC & Black and Tans
23 - 12 - 1920	Michael Considine	
09 - 01 - 1921	Joe Greene	Shot dead in land dispute.
07 - 02 - 1921	Patrick Falsey	Accidentally shot by the IRA
20 - 02 - 1921	Cecil O'Donovan	Shot by British army and RIC
20 - 02 - 1921	Aidan O'Donovan	Shot by British army and RIC
27 - 02 - 1921	Patrick Conlon	Shot by British army
13 - 03 - 1921	Thomas Shanahan	Shot by British army
22 - 04 - 1921	Patrick O'Rourke	Shot by British army
25 - 04 - 1921	Thomas McGrath	Shot by British army
24 - 06 - 1921	Patrick Morrissey	Killed by crossfire during IRA attack on British forces
29 - 07 - 1921	James Grogan	Shot by British army
	S. McGrath	

	R. Russell	
	M. McCarthy	
	S. Boylan	

Free State army casualties in Clare 1922–1923

22 - 08 - 1922	Private Patrick Kelly
04 - 04 -1923	Corporal Martin O'Loughlin
21 - 04 - 1923	Private Stephen Canty

British casualties in Clare during the War of Independence 1919–1921

Date	Name
04 - 8 - 1919	RIC Sergeant John Riordan
05 - 8 - 1919	RIC Constable Michael Murphy
21 - 4 - 1920	Private Thomas Sibthorpe, Royal Highland Light Infantry, British army*
19 - 8 - 1920	RIC Constable Jason Duffy*
21 - 8 - 1920	RIC Detective Constable John Hanlon
22 - 8 - 1920	RIC Constable Reginald Hardiman (Black and Tan)
22 - 8 - 1920	RIC Constable Michael Harte
22 - 8 - 1920	RIC Constable John Hodnett
22 - 8 - 1920	RIC Constable Michael Kelly
22 - 8 - 1920	RIC Constable John McGuire
24 - 8 - 1920	RIC Sergeant Michael Hynes
25 - 9 - 1920	RIC Constable Michael Brogan
29 - 9 - 1920	RIC Constable John Downey
29 - 9 - 1920	RIC Constable John Keeffe
07 -10 - 1920	RIC Sergeant Francis Doherty
07 - 10 - 1920	RIC Constable Stanley
18 - 10 - 1920	RIC Constable John Lougheed
14 - 11 - 1920	RIC Constable Driscoll*
14 - 11 - 1920	RIC Constable Fleming (Auxiliary)*
14 - 11 - 1920	RIC Constable Roper (Auxiliary)*
15 - 11 - 1920	Private Dailey, Royal Scots, British army*
18 - 11 - 1920	Private Spackman, Oxfordshire Regiment, British army
? - ? - 1920	Unknown private, Royal Highland Light Infantry, British army
13 - 01 - 1921	RIC Sergeant Stephen Carthy
20 - 01- 1921	RIC Constable Michael Moran (Black and Tan)
20 - 01- 1921	RIC Constable Frank Morris (Black and Tan)
20 - 01- 1921	RIC Constable William Smith (Black and Tan)
20 - 01- 1921	RIC Sergeant Mulloy
20 - 01- 1921	RIC Constable John Doogue
20 - 01- 1921	RIC District Inspector William Clarke

02 - 02 - 1921	Private Robins Oxford Regiment, British Army
19 - 02 - 1921	Private D.J. Williams, Oxford Regiment, British Army
19 - 02 - 1921	Private W.S. Walker, Oxford Regiment, British Army
19 - 02 - 1921	Private H. Morgan, Oxford Regiment, British Army
?? - 02 - 1921	Private G. Robinson, Royal Highland Light Infantry, British army
12 - 03 -1921	RIC Constable Daniel Murphy (Black and Tan)
31 - 03 - 1921	RIC Constable Stanley Moore (Black and Tan)
16 - 04 - 1921	Sergeant Rue, Royal Scots British army
21 - 04 - 1921	Unknown private, Royal Highland Light Infantry, British army*
21 - 04 - 1921	Corporal Bolton, Royal Marines
21 - 04 - 1921	Private Chandler, Royal Marines
23 - 04 - 1921	RIC Sergeant John McFadden
26 - 05 - 1921	RIC Constable Edgar Budd (Black and Tan)
12 - 06 - 1921	Lance Corporal M. Hudson, Oxfordshire Regiment
28 - 06 - 1921	First Lieutenant Richard Warren, Oxford Regiment, British army
?? - 06 - 1921	RIC Constable Stackdale (Black and Tan)*
07 - 07 - 1921	RIC Constable James Hewitt (Black and Tan)
10 - 07 - 1921	RIC Constable Alfred Needham (Black and Tan)
10 - 07 - 1921	Private R. W. Williams, Royal Welch Fusiliers, British army
28 - 10 - 1920	Martin Counihan (suspected British spy), executed by the IRA
22 - 04 - 1921	John Reilly (suspected British spy), executed by the IRA
21 - 06 - 1921	Patrick Darcy (suspected British spy), executed by the IRA

* indicates troops who died by suicide or accident

Claremen who joined the Auxiliaries

Name	RIC Number	Religion	Previous Employment
Thomas Gore-Hickman	69943	Protestant	Ex-army officer
Thomas W. Conlin	72970	Catholic	Ex-army officer
Patrick Cullinan	79137	Catholic	Ex-army officer
Maurice Burke	79171	Catholic	Ex-army officer
Patrick Keshan	79635	Catholic	Ex-soldier
Joseph Malone	79636	Catholic	Ex-soldier
Francis Noonan	79637	Catholic	Ex-soldier
William Malone	79638	Catholic	Ex-soldier
Michael Greene	80030	Catholic	Ex-army officer
John Considine	80834	Catholic	Ex-soldier
Jason McCormack	81305	Catholic	Ex-soldier
Cyril J. G. Convery	81698	Protestant	Ex-army officer
Edward Elward	81836	Catholic	Ex-army officer
Daniel McKenna	82760	Catholic	Ex-army officer
Charles Shaw	82959	Catholic	Ex-soldier

Claremen who joined the Black and Tans

Name	RIC Number	Religion	Previous Employment
William McGregor	70008	Catholic	Shop assistant
Adam Albert Jones	70103	Protestant	Ex-soldier
George Hunter	70104	Protestant	Ex-soldier
Patrick Scales	70105	Protestant	Farmer
William Hayes	70140	Catholic	Ex-soldier
Maurice Meehan	70355	Catholic	Labourer
Herbert Porter	70358	Catholic	Ex-soldier
John T. Glennon	70360	Catholic	None
Edward Cooke	70380	Catholic	Ex-soldier
Thomas O'Connell	70430	Catholic	Fitter
Jason Harold	70431	Catholic	Shop assistant
Charles Reynor	70510	Presbyterian	Dentist
John Murphy	70539	Catholic	Ex-soldier
Michael McNamara	70684	Catholic	Farmer
William J. Somers	70959	Catholic	None
George R. McMillan	70960	Protestant	Ex-soldier
William E. Coffey	71091	Catholic	Ex-soldier
Michael Forde	71135	Catholic	Ex-soldier
Martin M. Keane	71144	Catholic	Ex-soldier
Martin J. Hayes	71146	Catholic	Ex-soldier
Edward Bruen	71309	Catholic	Royal Air Force
Edward T. Sullivan	71331	Protestant	Gamekeeper
John J. Fitzpatrick	71937	Catholic	None
Thomas McNamara	72510	Catholic	Ex-soldier
John Reidy	72610	Catholic	Ex-soldier
Joseph George Weeks	73113	Catholic	Sailor
Richard O'Higgins	74272	Catholic	Ex-soldier
Alfred O'Neill	74328	Catholic	Ex-soldier
John Kearney	74501	Catholic	Sailor

Vincent Maguire	75038	Catholic	None
Robert Mitchell	75512	Protestant	Student
Patrick Dolan	76261	Catholic	None
Michael Hanlon	78315	Catholic	None
Michael J. Fitzgerald	78328	Catholic	Ex-soldier
Francis O'Brien	78405	Catholic	Ex-soldier
Patrick Walsh	78775	Catholic	Ex-soldier
John Mahon	79382	Catholic	Motor driver
John Walsh	79596	Catholic	Ex-soldier
Peter Joseph Dolan	80011	Catholic	General Engineer
Charles O'Connor	80347	Catholic	Motor driver
Patrick O'Reilly	80385	Catholic	Ex-soldier
Martin F. O'Connell	81050	Catholic	Ex-soldier
Michael Joseph Regan	81103	Catholic	Ex-soldier
John King	81153	Catholic	Farmer
Daniel J. O'Leary	82204	Catholic	Shop assistant
John Valentine Dolan	83700	Catholic	Shop assistant

Bibliography

Archive Sources

Bureau Of Military History, Witness statements, National Archives, Dublin:

Seán Moylan, Liam Haugh, Michael Brennan, Art O'Donnell, Seán Moroney, Joseph Honan, William McNamara, Thomas McNamara, Andrew O'Donoghue, Thomas Tuohy, Peter O'Loughlin, John Joe Neylon, Thomas Shalloo, Seán MacConmara, Henry O'Mara, Seán Murnane, Anthony Malone, Seán McNamara, Edward Lynch, Joseph Barrett, Eamon Fennell, Michael O'Dea, Michael Russell, Patrick Kerin, Joseph Daly, John Jones, John Quinn, Martin Chambers, Michael McMahon, Patrick Mulcahy, Michael Gleeson, J.J. McConnell, Seamus Connely, T.S. McDonough, James Quinn, Patrick Devitt, Patrick Reidy, John Flanagan, Eugene Bratton, Diarmuid Coffey, Ernest Blythe, Colonel J.M. McCarthy, Corporal George Roberts.

Sir Hugh Jeudwine Papers, Imperial War Museum, London

Newspapers

The Clare Champion
The Clare Chronicle
The Limerick Leader
The Irish Times
The Cork Examiner

Books and Journals

Abbot, Richard, *Police Casualties in Ireland 1919–1922* (Dublin & Cork, Mercier Press, 2000)
Andrews, C.S., *Dublin Made Me* (Dublin & Cork, Mercier Press, 1979)
Barry, Tom, *Guerrilla Days in Ireland,* (Dublin, The Irish Press Ltd, 1949)
Berresford Ellis, Peter, *A History of the Irish Working Class* (London and Chicago Pluto Press, 1996)
Blake, Francis M., *The Civil War and What it Means for Irish People* (London, Information on Ireland, 1988)
Brennan, John, *The Years Flew By. Recollections of Madame Sidney Gifford Czira* (Dublin, Gifford and Craven 1974)
Brennan, Michael, *The War in Clare* (1980)

Browne, Kevin J., *Eamon de Valera & The Banner County* (Dun Laoighre, Glendale Press, 1982)

Coffey, Thomas M., *Agony at Easter. The 1916 Irish Uprising* (Middlesex, Penguin Books, 1969)

Collins, M.E., *Ireland 1869-1966* (The Educational Company, 1993)

Coogan, Tim Pat, *Michael Collins* (London, Arrow Books 1991)

Coogan, Tim Pat, *The I.R.A.* (London, Harper Collins 1995)

Crozier, Frederick P., *Ireland Forever* (Bath, Cedric Chivers Ltd., 1971)

Deasy, Liam, *Towards Ireland Free* (Dublin & Cork, Mercier Press, 1972)

Deasy, Liam, *Brother against Brother* (Dublin & Cork, Mercier Press, 1998)

Duff, Douglas V., *Sword for Hire* (London, 1936)

Durney, James, *On the One Road. Political Unrest in Kildare 1913-1994* (Naas, Leinster Leader Ltd, 2001)

Dwyer, Ryle T., *Tans, Terror and Troubles* (Dublin & Cork, Mercier Press, 2001)

Dwyer, Ryle T., *The Squad* (Dublin & Cork, Mercier Press, 2005)

Fitzpatrick, David, *Politics and Irish Life 1913-1921. Provincial Experience of War and Revolution* (Cork, Cork University Press, 1998)

Foy, Michael T., *Michael Collins's Intelligence War. The struggle between the British and the IRA 1919-1921* (Gloucestershire, Sutton Publishing, 2006)

Greaves, C. Desmond, *Liam Mellows and the Irish Revolution* (Belfast, An Ghlór Gafa Press, 2004)

Hopkinson, Michael *Green against Green. The Irish Civil War* (Dublin, Gill and Macmillan, 1988)

Kee, Robert, *The Green Flag* (London, Penguin Books, 1989)

MacEoin, Uinseann, *Survivors* (Dublin, Argenta Publications, 1980)

Malone, Tom, *Alias Seán Forde* (Dublin, Elo Press, 2000)

McCarthy, Daniel, *Ireland's Banner County. Clare from the fall of Parnell to the Great War 1890-1918* (Ennis, Saipan Press, 2002)

McCarthy, J.M. (ed.), *Limerick's fighting Story* (Dublin & Tralee, Anvil Books, n.d.)

McCoole, Sinead, *No Ordinary Women. Irish female activists in the revolutionary years 1900-1923* (Dublin, The O'Brien Press, 2003)

McMahon, Tim G., *Pádraig Ó Fathaigh's War of Independence. Recollections of a Galway Gaelic Leaguer* (Cork, Cork University Press, 2000)

Murphy, Jeremiah, *When Youth Was Mine. A Memoir of Kerry 1902-1925* (Dublin, Mentor Press, 1998)

Neligan, David, *The Spy in the Castle* (London, Prenderville Publishing, 1999)

O'Dwyer, Martin, *Tipperary's Sons & Daughters 1916-1923* (Cashel, Cashel Folk Village, 2001)

O'Dwyer, Martin, *Seventy-Seven of Mine said Ireland* (Cashel Folk Village, Deshaoirse Press, 2006)

Ó Gadhra, Nollaig, *The Civil War in Connaught 1922-1923* (Dublin & Cork, Mercier Press 1999)

Ó Luing, Seán, *I Die in a Good Cause* (Dublin & Tralee, Anvil, 1970)

O'Malley, Ernie, *On Another Mans Wound* (Dublin & Tralee, Anvil Books, 1979)

O'Malley, Ernie, *Raids and Rallies* (Dublin, Anvil Books, 1982)

Ringrose, Des, 'Hurling Cost Him His Life. The Death of Captain Patrick White on Spike Island, June 1, 1921', *Sliabh Aughty Journal*, 1998

Ryan, Annie, *Witnesses. Inside the Easter Rising* (Dublin, Liberties Press, 2005)

Ryan, Annie, *Comrades. Inside the War of Independence* (Dublin, Liberties Press, 2007)

Ryan, Meda, *The Real Chief – Liam Lynch* (Dublin & Cork, Mercier Press, 2005)

Share, Bernard, *In Time of Civil War. The conflict on the Irish railways 1922–23* (Cork, The Collins Press, 2006)

Sheedy, Kieran, *The United Irishmen of County Clare* (Ennis, 1997)

Sheehan, William, *British Voices from the Irish War of Independence 1918–1921* (Cork, The Collins Press, 2005)   .

Twohig, Patrick J., *Green tears for Hecuba* (Cork, Tower Books, 1994)

Walsh, Pat, *Irish Republicanism and Socialism. The Politics of the Republican Movement 1905 to 1994* (Belfast, Athol Books, 1994)

Ward, Margaret, *Unmanagable revolutionaries. Women and Irish Nationalism* (Brandon Press, 1983)

Wilkinson, Burke, *The Zeal of the Convert. The Life of Erskine Childers* (New York, Second Chance Press, 1985)

Various, *With the IRA in the Fight for Freedom 1919 to the Truce. The Red Path of Glory* (Tralee, The Kerryman Ltd., n.d.)

Younger, Calton, *Ireland's Civil War* (London, Fontana Books, 1970)

Index